1967

THE RHETORICAL WORLD
OF AUGUSTAN HUMANISM

Oxford University Press, Amen House, London, E.C.4

GLASGOW NEW YORK TORONTO MELBOURNE WELLINGTON
BOMBAY CALCUTTA MADRAS KARACHI LAHORE DACCA
CAPE TOWN SALISBURY NAIROBI IBADAN ACCRA
KUALA LUMPUR HONG KONG

Canaletto, *The Ruins of the Forum looking towards the Capitol*. See Chapters 8 and 12. (The Royal Collection: Reproduced by gracious permission of Her Majesty the Queen)

THE RHETORICAL WORLD OF AUGUSTAN HUMANISM

Ethics and Imagery from Swift to Burke

By

PAUL FUSSELL

CLARENDON PRESS · OXFORD

1965

SPOTTISWOODE, BALLANTYNE AND CO. LTD.,
COLCHESTER AND LONDON

TO BETTY

Felices ter et amplius,
  quos inrupta tenet copula nec malis
divolsus querimoniis
  suprema citius solvet amor die.

PREFACE

THIS book is about both the ethical convictions and the related rhetorical techniques—especially the polemic imagery—of six eighteenth-century writers who, because they exhibit a marvellous concurrence of imagination, design, and method, can be said to postulate a self-contained rhetorical world. The writers are Swift, Pope, Johnson, Reynolds, Gibbon, and Burke. In my view, this group resembles a sort of central nervous system running through the whole eighteenth century, from the first decade to the last; and the writings of this group largely redeem the period from its occasional but highly publicized faults of grandiosity, sentimentality, self-satisfaction, and archness. Of these six writers whom I have termed 'humanists', I consider Samuel Johnson the richest and the most central, and I have thus devoted more attention to him than to the others. The appearance of Gibbon in this company may cause surprise, until we recall his delightful contempt for innovation and for abstract and subjective theories of man, and thus perceive his interesting kinship with Swift at the beginning of the century, and with Burke at the end.

Because my purpose is to point to the common elements in the imagination and expression of these six, I have not emphasized their important differences. I can plead only that the differences between them seem to me more obvious and appear to have received their due; it is now time, I believe, to attempt something like a synthesis. I shall assume that the reader's awareness of significant distinctions between these six writers will serve as a sufficient corrective if one is needed.

Although the term 'Augustan' is used by most people to refer to the characteristics of the Age of Swift and Pope only, I have here given it a wider meaning. In my title and throughout, I have used the term to suggest the 'orthodox' ethical and rhetorical tradition wherever found in the eighteenth century.

Indeed, the lively persistence of Augustan habits in ethics and expression—especially in the hands of Burke—clear into the last, revolutionary decade of the century is precisely my point.

The chief critical assumption on which this book is based is that, the mind being a thing that must work by means of metaphors and symbols, imagery is the live constituent in that transmission of shaped illumination from one intelligence to another which is literature. Another assumption is that habitual recourse to certain image-systems and a preference—however unconscious—for them over others seems almost to shape the mind itself, or at least to predispose it towards certain equally habitual objects of concern. While there may be many meaningful interpretations of a given image-system, I believe that analysis reveals—and this is what I have tried to do in Part II— that some interpretations are more likely than others to discover the kind of fully-rounded meaning that is the inseparable property of poetry or any other kind of highly controlled or self-conscious rhetoric.

I have tried to write a work less of literary or historical scholarship than of interpretation, suggestion, and recommendation. My task has been to define a quality of mind, a quality at best elusive and paradoxical, and a quality which—or so it is easy to imagine—has drifted largely beyond the awareness of the modern sensibility. It is out of a conviction of the beauty of this quality that the following pages are written. It is hard to speak either precisely or objectively about what one takes to be moral beauty, and I suspect that here and there I have been led by passion into simplification, imprecise interpretation, and perhaps needless insult. I am confident that both friends and enemies will bring such faults to my attention. When tempted towards immoderate objectivity, I have tried to be mindful of the late Arthur O. Lovejoy's eminently humanistic warning: 'The student of the history of ideas must approach his historical sources certainly with an open but not with a passive mind'.

I am happy to acknowledge the generous and patient support of the Rutgers Research Council. I must thank the Rutgers University Press for permission to reprint materials which first appeared in *Essays in Literary History Presented to J. Milton French* (1960); the New York Public Library for materials from the *Bulletin of the New York Public Library* (1962); the editors of

Philological Quarterly for materials that appeared in their journal in 1958; and the editors of *Studies in English Literature: 1500–1900* for materials that appeared there in 1962.

I am delighted to have a chance once again to pay tribute to Professor W. J. Bate and to the memory of Professor George Sherburn. Each in his way has contributed greatly to this book. I also want to thank Professors Charles S. Holmes and Joseph W. Angell, of Pomona College, for their encouragement many years ago. Among my graduate students who have been kind enough to react to these materials I remember Mr. Frederick Kiley, Mrs. Faith Patten, and Mrs. Barbara Streeter with special pleasure. Without the friendship and interest of R. W. B. Lewis this book would probably not be finished yet. I hope that I have imbibed a degree of caution from my brother Edwin Fussell's salutary observations on some of my notions. To the encouragement and criticism of my friend and colleague C. F. Main I owe, as always, much. Richard Poirier's help with the proof has been the least of his kindnesses, and Daniel F. Howard has given valuable help. But my greatest debt is such that to suggest it in my dedication I have had to deviate into the decent obscurity of a learned language.

P. F.

Rutgers University
October 1964

CONTENTS

KEY TO THE REFERENCES

The following abbreviations are used for references in the text:

BD: Boswell for the Defence, ed. William K. Wimsatt, Jr., and Frederick A. Pottle (New York, 1959).

BLJ: Boswell's Life of Johnson, ed. George Birkbeck Hill, rev. L. F. Powell (Oxford, 1934–50, 6 vols).

BSW: Boswell in Search of a Wife: 1766–1769, ed. Frank Brady and Frederick A. Pottle (New York, 1956).

CAP: The Correspondence of Alexander Pope, ed. George Sherburn (Oxford, 1956, 5 vols).

GT: Boswell on the Grand Tour: Italy, Corsica, and France: 1765–1766, ed. Frank Brady and Frederick A. Pottle (New York, 1955).

H: Boswell in Holland: 1763–1764, ed. Frederick A. Pottle (New York, 1952).

JM: Johnsonian Miscellanies, ed. George Birkbeck Hill (New York, 1897, 2 vols).

JTH: Boswell's Journal of a Tour to the Hebrides, ed. Frederick A. Pottle and Charles H. Bennett (New York, 1936).

LJ: Boswell's London Journal: 1762–1763, ed. Frederick A. Pottle (New York, 1950).

LSJ: The Letters of Samuel Johnson, ed. R. W. Chapman (Oxford, 1952, 3 vols).

OY: Boswell, The Ominous Years: 1774–1776, ed. Charles Ryskamp and Frederick A. Pottle (New York, 1963).

P: Portraits by Sir Joshua Reynolds, ed. Frederick W. Hilles (New York, 1952).

PJB: Private Papers of James Boswell from Malahide Castle, ed. Geoffrey Scott (Mt. Vernon, N.Y., 1928–34, 18 vols).

PART I

THE HUMANIST CONCEPTION OF MAN

'*L'homme n'est qu'un roseau, le plus faible de la nature, mais c'est un roseau pensant.*'—PASCAL

I

WHAT IS 'HUMANISM'?

NEXT to terms like 'classic' and 'romantic', there is apparently no word invoked in interpretations of English thought and expression more barren of precise meaning at the present time than 'humanism'. Its use in our day by the literary old-fashioned is a common occasion of either smiles or yawns. During its vogue of over three hundred years the term has been employed as an emotive sign for practically anything valued by the speaker, from piety to scepticism, from aristocracy to egalitarianism, and from indifferentism to humanitarianism. Those people in universities who profess something that is neither science nor social science are today often called 'humanists', although, alas, very few of them are in the sense in which the word means something when applied to a group of major eighteenth-century authors. Used as it often is to describe emotional and intellectual phenomena of the sixteenth and seventeenth centuries, 'humanism' suggests a sort of wise and broad piety, a rich, civilized amalgam of Christian devotion and pagan wisdom—or even worldly wisdom; in our century the term, as used at least by the British Humanist Association, denotes something entirely different: it suggests what the eighteenth century was fond of calling 'freethinking', that is, religious scepticism founded on purely anthropocentric premises. This latter meaning comes close to Coleridge's sense of the term: he defines it as 'Belief in the mere humanity of Christ'. Matthew Arnold's conception of the meaning of 'humanism' brings us nearer to the meaning I have in mind. 'Milton was born a humanist', writes Arnold, 'but the Puritan temper mastered him.'

In Johnson's *Dictionary* (1755) the word had not yet assumed its late-nineteenth-century suggestions of broad wisdom. Johnson defines a humanist as 'A philologer; a grammarian: a term

B

used in the schools of Scotland'. And yet, as even this definition reminds us, the term once suggested a devotion to the texts of the ancients and, hopefully, an acquaintance as well with the conception of man embodied in Greek and Roman literature. The term thus tends to suggest the opposition of the 'humanist' to anything narrowly individualist, subjective, exclusive, relativistic, Puritan, or parochial. As Santayana has said, the humanist seeks out everywhere 'the normalities of human nature'.

Perhaps the best way to suggest how the term is descriptive of what can be called the 'orthodox' ethical tradition in the eighteenth century is simply to list certain postulates and characteristics generally shared by conservative writers of the period:

(1) The humanist either possesses or affects such broad and historical awareness of actual human nature as to justify grave doubts about the probability of any moral or qualitative 'progress'. This is not to say that a humanist like Johnson denies the reality of experiential or material progress; as he remarks in his *Life of Butler*, where he puzzles over the motive of Butler's satire on the Royal Society, 'The most zealous enemy of innovation must admit the gradual progress of experience, however he may oppose [as Johnson does] hypothetical temerity'. Any humanist, Johnson included, knows that a sedan-chair beats walking and that the world is the 'better' for the extirpation of the bubonic plague. What makes the humanist suspicious is facile analogizing between material and moral 'improvements'. The humanist tends to believe that, in all the essentials, human nature is permanent and uniform, quite unchanged by time or place. It is this idea in the eighteenth century that sanctions the orthodox conception of the permanence of the literary genres, each of which is thought to address itself to one unchanging element of the human consciousness. And because the fundamental nature of man is uniform, both historically and geographically, the impulse towards 'innovation' in important matters becomes naturally ludicrous:

BOSWELL. So, Sir, you laugh at schemes of political improvement.
JOHNSON. Why, Sir, most schemes of political improvement are very laughable things.

(*BLJ*, ii, 102)

And as Gibbon puts it, in the first chapter of his *Autobiography*, 'The satirist may laugh, the philosopher may preach, but Reason herself will respect the prejudices and habits which have been consecrated by the experience of mankind'. These 'habits' express a fundamental, permanent human nature to Gibbon, and this conviction informs his satire on the early Christians in Chapters XV and XVI of *The History of the Decline and Fall of the Roman Empire*. As he observes of the Roman Christians in Chapter XVI: 'They dissolved the sacred ties of custom and education, violated the religious institutions of their country, and presumptuously despised whatever their fathers had believed as true or had reverenced as sacred.' Gibbon's quasi-religious awareness of the dignity and value of long-practised, 'consecrated' human habits is re-experienced at the very end of the century by Burke in the *Reflections on the Revolution in France*. All this is to say that the humanist is necessarily a historian and that he derives his values always from the study of human history.

(2) The humanist believes that most human 'problems' cannot be solved, 'failures and defects', as Johnson says in *Rambler* 43, 'being inseparable from humanity'. And yet at the same time the humanist will argue passionately on behalf of the nobility of human nature, for he finds that man's paradoxical 'dignity' is in part the result of his being the only creature whose consciousness apprehends—or contrives—problems too complicated for solution.

(3) The humanist assumes, as Burke does, that it is both the index and the privilege of the human consciousness to be largely a construction of man's own imaginative making, and that, therefore, the mind and the imagination—what perhaps can be called the symbol-making power—are the quintessential human attributes. This is to insist that man becomes fully human, or properly realized, only when he uses his mind in a uniquely human way. Sir Joshua Reynolds thus establishes his aesthetics on man's observed capacity to 'raise' his nature by contemplating heroic images; like other humanists, Reynolds begins with and returns constantly to 'human nature, whence arts derive the materials upon which they are to produce their effects' (*Thirteenth Discourse*). The humanist emphasis on the symbol-making power as the focus of man's uniqueness is reflec-

ted in the humanist veneration for the practice of literature, for in literature as in no other human experience the mind is exercised—to the humanist, 'ennobled'—by a constant oscillation between things and symbols, between actualities and metaphors of actualities. One sign of the humanist, whether of the Middle Ages, the Renaissance, or the eighteenth century, is an apparently immoderate love of 'humane learning' (that is, literature). To Johnson's Imlac, in Chapter XXX of *Rasselas*, 'learning and ignorance . . . are the light and darkness of thinking beings'. The humanist, as Herschel Baker has observed, is likely to be 'a schoolmarm at heart'.[1]

(4) The humanist betrays so habitual and profound a concern with the act of evaluation that it often grows into what can be described as 'the evaluative obsession'. This 'vertical' cast of mind seems impelled to order everything in rank, whether the elements of animated nature which it delights to contemplate as a vertical scale of being, or the social stations in a society, or the various studies in a curriculum. This *libido aestimandi* is naturally accompanied by hierarchical rather than egalitarian expectations about society and politics; about literary genres and techniques, some of which are conceived to be in the nature of things 'better' than others; about periods of history, some of which are assumed to be more 'noble' than others; and even about the assumed elements of the human psyche, which is still imaged by the eighteenth-century humanist in a very seventeenth-century way—with 'will' in a position of almost military 'command' at the top, 'reason' or 'judgment' in the middle, and the senses or 'passions' as servants at the bottom. Pope exemplifies this evaluative habit of mind while subjecting it to irony at the same time:

> Tho' the same Sun with all-diffusive rays
> Blush in the Rose, and in the Diamond blaze,
> We prize the stronger effort of his pow'r,
> And justly set the gem above the Flow'r.
>
> (*Epistle to Cobham*, 97–100)

(5) The humanist is pleased to experience a veneration, which often approaches the elegiac, for the past, a feeling

---

[1] *The Dignity of Man: Studies in the Persistence of an Idea* (Cambridge, Mass., 1947), p. 270.

accompanied by a deep instinct for the tested and the proven in the history of human experience. This reverence for the experience of the past is inseparable from the humanist belief in the historical uniformity of human nature. Burke is characteristic in the way he looks with satisfaction, in the *Reflections*, on 'the powerful prepossession towards antiquity, with which the minds of all our [British] lawyers and legislators, and of all the people whom they wish to influence, have always been filled'.

(6) The humanist assumes that ethics and expression are closely allied. It is this assumption that makes possible Johnson's unique fusion of biographical, ethical, and aesthetic criticism in *The Lives of the Poets*. Like Swift exhibiting the 'modern' moral squalor of his Grub-Street *persona* in *A Tale of a Tub* by a corresponding structural and stylistic incoherence, the humanist finds it easy to believe that when a man has himself in order, when he has become a proficient at what Adam Smith calls 'self-command', the man's writing will naturally reflect his internal clarity and coherence. Good writing becomes thus, as it does to the Pope of the *Epistle to Dr. Arbuthnot* or *The Dunciad*, an index of moral virtue.

(7) The humanist is convinced that man's primary obligation is the strenuous determination of moral questions; he thus believes that inquiries into the technical operation of the external world ('science') constitute not only distinctly secondary but even irrelevant and perhaps dangerous activities. Johnson stresses the primacy of man's moral nature by insisting, in the *Life of Milton*, that 'We are perpetually moralists, but we are geometricians only by chance'. That is, our nature in itself does not oblige us to function as geometricians—or patriots, or Tories, or consumers, or other kinds of exclusive specialists—but it does oblige us to function as moral adjudicators. The English humanist is thus obsessed by ethical questions. He sees man not primarily as a maker or even as a knower, but rather as a moral actor. Prescription rather than description is the humanist's business. We may almost define a humanist as one who finds it impossible to leave serious moral subjects alone. This is why Thomas Gray, although a conservative, is not really a humanist; this is why Horace Walpole, for all his interest in human nature, is not a humanist. The humanist takes an almost sensual pleasure in the image of moral virtue, especially the image of self-

restraint triumphing over temptation, and his pleasure in this spectacle is similar to the pleasure taken by the Epicurean in images of erotic or gustatory delights. Only occasionally does the humanist's moral impulse decline into the moralistic, as it does in Swift's *A Project for the Advancement of Religion and the Reformation of Manners* (1709), which anticipates the tone of the mere Victorian 'moralist' in its exhortation to the Queen to put down drunkenness, deep play, and vice.

(8) The humanist is convinced that human nature, for all its potential dignity, is irremediably flawed and corrupt at the core. If the eighteenth-century humanist is oriented towards the Christian tradition, he will often conceive of this flaw by means of the myth of the Fall of Man. If the humanist's Christian impulse is weak or non-existent, he will often conceive of this flaw by means of the myth of the Decay of Nature. But whatever mythology or imagery he invokes, he will generally assume that man's dignity arises in part from his very perception of the human flaw. Self-distrust thus becomes a central humanist experience, and satire becomes a central literary action. The awareness which prompts Swift to satirize the self-sufficient spider in *The Battle of the Books* is identical with that which moves Johnson to assert that 'Man's chief merit consists in resisting the impulses of his nature'. Frances Reynolds, who records this remark of Johnson's, is careful to explain just what he means: 'Not what may be call'd his second Nature, evil habits, &c., but his Nature originally corrupted from the fall' (*JM*, ii, 285).

(9) The humanist tends to assume that the world of physical nature is morally neutral and thus largely irrelevant to man's actual—that is, his moral—existence. Whether 'scenery' is conceived of as static or as organic, the humanist images man as positioned against it rather than inside it. In some ways, indeed, as can be seen in the tenth and eleventh books of *Paradise Lost*, physical nature participates in man's corruption. To the humanist, therefore, physical nature can 'teach' man little that is morally useful; if it ever does speak to man, it speaks not to his moral centre. When Bolingbroke in a primitivist mood asserted that nature is man's nature, Burke rejoined vigorously with 'Art is man's nature'. The moral world of man and the natural world of plants and trees and oceans are perpetually sundered

by the unblinkable fact that man possesses an imagination which, willy nilly, persists in functioning by means of moral images.

(10) The humanist tends to be suspicious of theories of government or human nature which appear to scant the experienced facts of man's mysterious complexity. To the humanist, man's most dangerous temptation is his lust to conceive of his nature as simpler than it is. And this temptation often prompts man to conceive of his nature, erroneously, as entirely 'rational'. Perhaps the Gulliver of the end of the Fourth Voyage can serve as a case study of this anti-humanist syndrome. The humanist insists on the element of the unpredictable in man. Thus Johnson on 'social science' and conceptions of history based on simplistic cause-and-effect premises:

It seems to be almost the universal errour of historians to suppose it politically, as it is physically true, that every effect has a proportionate cause. In the inanimate action of matter upon matter, the motion produced can be but equal to the force of the moving power; but the operations of life, whether private or publick, admit no such laws. The caprices of voluntary agents laugh at calculation.

(*Thoughts on the Late Transactions respecting Falkland's Islands*)

(11) The humanist assumes that, because of man's flaw and his consequent need of redemptive assistance, man's relation to literature and art is primarily moral and only secondarily aesthetic. The eighteenth-century humanist is given to uttering and re-uttering the classical commonplace that the office of literature is to teach, but to teach through the agency of aesthetic delight. Johnson on pastoral poetry is typical: a man will not, he asserts, 'after the perusal of thousands [of pastorals], find his knowledge enlarged with a single view of nature not produced before, or his imagination amused with any new application of those views to moral purposes' (*Rambler* 35). Only if man were not flawed could the humanist justify a literary aesthetic of pure pleasure.

(12) Finally, the humanist believes that man is absolutely unique as a species. This is the belief from which all the others seem to depend. The humanist scorns analogies between men and dogs, even though both salivate similarly; between men and lower animals, even though both breed similarly; and between

men and insects, even though both tend to organize societies
similarly. The humanist suspicion of analogies between men and
other creatures assumes that there is no help for man but within
himself, within his own moral universe imaginatively conceived,
in which unremitting self-conscious volition is the active principle. Despite his devotion, as we shall see, to received modes of
metaphor as a technique of expression, the humanist tends to
distrust analogy as a mode of thought. As Thomas R. Edwards
observes in connexion with Pope's *Essay on Man*, 'Analogy is not
a solution; to know something by analogy is painfully unlike
knowing it by experience'.[2] To the humanist, analogy may be
conceived of as imposing a 'system' on the will, which, in the
humanist view of things, must be regarded as entirely free.
Swift's mockery throughout *A Tale of a Tub* of the intellectual
technique of ready and complacent analogy is suggestive of one
major thrust of the whole eighteenth-century humanist enterprise. Man's dignity depends on his belief that he has a free
power of choice sufficient to overcome the apparent determinisms of environment and physical nature, for, as Joseph
Wood Krutch and other humanistic revivalists have argued in
our own time, human nature is an 'independent reality, not
merely a product'.[3] If man cannot attain an improved physical
circumstance through the operation of his will, he does always
have it in his power to will a different attitude toward his circumstance. 'Acceptance', and thus 'happiness'—that primary
eighteenth-century objective—is always within his own power.
This is the eighteenth-century humanistic version of the conclusion of Socrates in the *Apology* that 'no evil can happen to a
good man, either in life or after death'.

    This, then, is the general humanist code. As Krutch sums up
the definition:

    . . . a humanist is anyone who rejects the attempt to describe or
account for man wholly on the basis of physics, chemistry, and
animal behavior. He is anyone who believes that will, reason, and
purpose are real and significant; that value and justice are aspects
of a reality called good and evil and rest upon some foundation
other than custom; that consciousness is so far from being a mere

    [2] *This Dark Estate: A Reading of Pope* (Berkeley and Los Angeles, 1963),
p. 34.
    [3] *Human Nature and the Human Condition* (New York, 1959), p. 170.

epiphenomenon that it is the most tremendous of actualities; that the unmeasurable may be significant; or, to sum it all up, that those human realities which sometimes seem to exist only in the human mind are the perceptions, rather than merely the creations, of that mind.[4]

It seems clear that the humanist code constitutes a more or less diminished and secularized version of the Christian humanism of the English Renaissance, although the Christian element in eighteenth-century humanism is very hard to measure. Swift, for example, in his sermon on *The Excellency of Christianity*, directed to unsophisticated listeners, rejects pagan wisdom as gravely inferior to Christian revelation. And yet, in his *Letter to a Young Gentleman Lately Entered into Holy Orders*, where, playing the role of a wise and experienced person of quality, he is at pains to warn his addressee against a stylish contempt of classical learning, he appears to value ancient ethics very highly indeed. He says 'nothing can justly be laid to the Charge of the [ancient] Philosophers further, than that they were ignorant of certain Facts which happened long after their Death. But I am deceived, if a better Comment could be any where collected upon the moral Part of the Gospel, than from the Writings of those excellent Men'.

Except in Johnson and perhaps in Swift, the proportion of Christianity to classical wisdom in eighteenth-century humanism is roughly what it is in the following account in the *Gentleman's Magazine* for 1733 of the funeral of Mr. John Underwood, of Whittlesea, in Cambridgeshire:

the six gentlemen who followed [the coffin] to the grave sang the last stanza of the 20th Ode of the second book of Horace. No bell was tolled, no one invited but the six gentlemen, and no relation followed his corpse; the coffin was painted green, and he laid in it with all his clothes on. Under his head was placed Sanadon's Horace, at his feet Bentley's Milton; in his right hand a small Greek Testament . . .; in his left hand a little edition of Horace . . . and Bentley's Horace, *sub podice*. After the ceremony was over, they went back to his house, where his sister had provided a cold supper; the cloth being taken away, the gentlemen sang the 31st Ode of the first book of Horace, drank a chearful glass, and went home about eight.

[4] *Human Nature and the Human Condition*, p. 197.

One interesting thing about Augustan humanism is that it may make as little use of a religious dimension as John Underwood and his friends, and yet still locate its absolutes as readily as the Christian humanism of the Renaissance. And what Herschel Baker has said of Erasmus and the Northern humanists is true of the Augustan humanists as well: 'they were not original thinkers . . . Erasmus and his friends hankered for what was safe and settled: . . . the Faustus-mood of radical individualism passed them by'.[5] An entry made by the eight-year-old Samuel Johnson in his diary seems to symbolize the persistence of this strain of Renaissance humanism into a new age: proudly recording the accession of a new book, the boy Johnson writes, 'I got an English Erasmus'. The illustrative citations in Johnson's *Dictionary* attest abundantly to Johnson's devotion to the Renaissance English humanists, especially Richard Hooker, whose *Laws of Ecclesiastical Polity* Johnson knew intimately. When the eighteenth-century humanist looked back to the preceding century, he was likely to be more impressed by the judiciousness of a Hooker or the seriousness of a Milton than by the passion of a Marlowe or even a Donne. The Renaissance admired by the eighteenth-century humanist was likely to be a serious world of intellectual order and 'correspondences' rather than a gay theatre of exuberant individualism or neo-pagan hedonism.

Because it is characteristic of humanism to look at the central rather than the peripheral, it will not surprise us that the main seventeenth-century literary 'sources' of Augustan humanism appear to be *Hamlet, King Lear*, and *Paradise Lost*. And what seems to excite the Augustan humanist in these works is the tenderness and penetration of their version of man's condition as a unique creation in a largely foreign world of mere organic vitality. It is passages like those in *Hamlet* which stress man's obligations as man that the humanist recalls most vividly: Hamlet's observation on the haste of Gertrude's second marriage, for example,

> O God! a beast that wants discourse of reason
> Would have mourn'd longer;
>
> (I, ii, 150–1)

[5] *Dignity of Man*, p. 272.

or his recollection of his father:

> *Horatio.* I saw him once. He was a goodly King.
> *Hamlet.* He was a man, take him for all in all.
>   I shall not look upon his like again.
>
> (I, ii, 186–8)

or his scheme of the ideal internal psychic hierarchy in which man's will is liberated from mechanism and released for its glorious work of choice and command; as Hamlet tells Horatio,

>   blest are those
> Whose blood and judgment are so well commingled
> That they are not a pipe for Fortune's finger
> To sound what stop she please. Give me that man
> That is not passion's slave, and I will wear
> Him in my heart's core, ay, in my heart of heart
> As I do thee.
>
> (III, ii, 73–79)

To see Johnson in 1775 playing an aging Hamlet to Boswell's recidivist Horatio is to appreciate the power of such scenes to persist deep in the conservative consciousness throughout the eighteenth century. Johnson writes to Boswell, 'Never, my dear Sir, do you take it into your head that I do not love you; you may settle yourself in full confidence of my love and my esteem; I love you as a kind man, I value you as a worthy man, and hope in time to reverence you as a man of exemplary piety. I hold you as Hamlet has it, "in my heart of heart" . . .' (*LSJ*, ii, 83). The allusion here just sufficiently hints Boswell's obligations to liberate himself from his slavery to passion and 'Fortune'. If we know Boswell, we are fully aware that too often he was unable to follow Johnson's moral injunctions. But even in the midst of his backslidings Boswell himself recovers *Hamlet* for his own purposes. As readers of his *London Journal* (1763) will recall, the actress Louisa Lewis finally consents to grant Boswell the ultimate favour. But Boswell is destined for an ironic fall from felicity. Eight days after the triumphal night which has brought him his happiness he perceives that he has been severely poxed. 'Too, too plain was Signor Gonorrhea', he laments in his journal. Since he is convinced that Louisa has been aware of her condition all along, he conceives that a manly confrontation is in order, but he is momentarily perplexed about the way it

should be conducted. What if he should appear ridiculous
before Louisa? One way of appearing ridiculous, he imagines,
would be to upbraid her with an hysterical severity: 'Enraged
at the perfidy of Louisa', he writes, 'I resolved to go and upbraid her most severely; but this I thought was not acting with
dignity enough.' Momentarily baffled in his search for a literary
model for the forthcoming 'scene', he consults his memory and
takes a hint from his recollection of Hamlet's 'I will speak
daggers to her, but use none'. Now firm in his sense of role, Boswell proceeds: 'So I would talk to her coolly and make her feel
her own unworthiness'.

> I then went to Louisa. With excellent address did I carry on this
> interview, as the following scene, I trust, will make appear. . . .
> BOSWELL. Do you know that I have been very unhappy since I last
> saw you?
> LOUISA. How so, Sir?
> BOSWELL. Why, I am afraid that you don't love me so well, nor
> have such a regard for me, as I thought you had.
> LOUISA. Nay, dear Sir! (Seeming unconcerned.)
> BOSWELL. Pray, Madam, have I no reason?
> LOUISA. No, indeed, Sir, you have not.
> BOSWELL. Have I no reason, Madam? Pray think.
> LOUISA. Sir!

The dramatic situation here, that of the abused and deceived
youth reproaching the guilty older woman in her closet; the
formal tone; the youth's archness in posing his questions; the
rapid, almost stichomythic repetitions in lines of similar length
near the end of the interchange—these particulars all suggest
Hamlet iv, iii, where, at the beginning of the closet scene,
Hamlet confronts Gertrude and proceeds to 'set . . . up a glass /
Where you shall see the inmost part of you'. Boswell's pleasure
in playing Hamlet here must have been enhanced by knowing
that Louisa herself had played Gertrude in a production of
Hamlet at Covent Garden the year before (*LJ*, 84–85. n. 4).

If *Hamlet* permeates the Augustan humanist consciousness
because of its dramatization of man's offices as man, *King Lear* is
laid under contribution, especially by Burke, because of its
continuous definition of man as non-animal and non-mechani-
cal, a definition conducted through imagery as often as through
literal precept or dramatic situation. The principle of hierarchy

as natural to the human imagination is insisted upon in *King Lear*. As the fool tells the King,

> When thou clovest thy crown i' the middle and gav'st away both parts, thou bor'st thine ass on thy back o'er the dirt.
>
> (I, iv, 174–6)

The imagery of *King Lear* asserts likewise that, as Swift seems to recollect in *A Tale of a Tub*, a man is not to be made by his tailor; and it insists throughout that a man is not in his nature analogous with a rat, a vulture, a dog, a goose, a wolf, an owl, a bear, a lion, a hog, a fox, a pelican, a worm, a horse, or a fly. Surrounded and attacked, as he imagines, by the savage brutes of Jacobinism, and abandoned now by his colleagues of the Foxite persuasion, Burke astonishes the House of Commons in the spring of 1791 by quoting Lear's puzzled observation on his own altered condition:

> The little dogs and all,
> Tray, Blanch, and Sweetheart, see, they bark at me.
>
> (III, vi, 65–66)

And as we shall see, the heart of Burke's impassioned argument against the oversimplified version of man embraced by the Jacobins derives both substance and figure from Lear's.

> Allow not nature more than nature needs,
> Man's life is cheap as beasts'.
>
> (II, iv, 269–70)

Augustan memories of *Hamlet* and *King Lear* thus provide a multitude of general humanist motifs and images which are recovered and exploited by conservatives throughout the eighteenth century. But of *Paradise Lost* the main Augustan use can be more precisely located. Although the Augustan humanist values highly the Miltonic myths of human frailty and of both external and psychological hierarchy, his moral imagination luxuriates especially in recalling one particular scene. The humanist mind in the eighteenth century returns again and again to Book VIII of *Paradise Lost* and to the dialogue between Raphael and Adam about what we would call 'science'. As the 'Argument' to Book VIII sums it up: 'Adam inquires concerning celestial Motions, is doubtfully answer'd, and exhorted to

search rather things more worthy of knowledge'. In the preceding book, Raphael, narrating to Adam the events of Creation, has concluded by inviting Adam to inquire further about
his condition:

> if else thou seek'st
> Aught, not surpassing human measure, say.
>
> (639–40)

As Book VIII opens, Adam humbly accepts Raphael's invitation and ventures to wonder why God has contrived so many
visible planets and stars, many of them apparently more impressive than Earth. Raphael first replies—humanistically—that

> Great
> Or Bright infers not Excellence,
>
> (90–91)

and goes on to suggest that the pursuit of virtue and wisdom,
rather than the quest for astronomical knowledge, is the primary
duty incumbent upon such a creature as man:

> be lowly wise:
> Think only what concerns thee and thy being;
> Dream not of other Worlds. . . .
>
> (173–5)

Adam, apparently 'clear'd of doubt', now becomes the spokesman of Milton's point:

> not to know at large of things remote
> From use, obscure and subtle, but to know
> That which before us lies in daily life,
> Is the prime Wisdom.
>
> (191–4)

Adam's use of the term 'remote' here reminds us of the Swiftian
exploitation of this motif in the Third Voyage of *Gulliver's
Travels*, where the Laputians, like creatures who have chosen
not to hear Raphael's warning, have elected the quantitative
life of stargazing and mathematics and as a result have lost the
use of both their memories and their senses. Pope, in the *Essay
on Man*, treats the same Miltonic point, speaking like a kind of
sardonic Raphael, skilled in sarcasm, to the reader's naïve
Adam:

Go, wond'rous creature! mount where Science guides,
Go, measure earth, weigh air, and state the tides;
Instruct the planets in what orbs to run,
Correct old Time, and regulate the Sun; . . .
Go, teach Eternal Wisdom how to rule—
Then drop into thyself, and be a fool!

(II, 19–22; 29–30)

And we think also of the astronomer in *Rasselas*, whose researches have served only to disorder his intellect to the point where *post hoc* and *propter hoc* have become hopelessly confused.

Modern readers of Johnson's *Life of Milton* easily remember Johnson's interesting hostility to Milton's politics and his curious pietistic reaction to *Lycidas*. But they remember less readily something which is probably more important, Johnson's extraordinary admiration for the wisdom embodied in the anti-scientific colloquy between Raphael and Adam. It would be hard to find an occasion where Johnson, who often rebuked Mrs. Thrale for her bad habit of loose and irresponsible commendation, paid higher praise to anything merely human; he writes, 'Raphael's reproof to Adam's curiosity after the planetary motions, with the answer returned by Adam, may be confidently opposed to any rule of life which any poet has delivered'. Johnson's rare hyperboles and absolutes here—'any rule of life which any poet has delivered'—are almost shocking. And they become the more startling when we recall Johnson's final estimate of *Paradise Lost*, which he pronounces 'not the greatest of heroic poems, only because it is not the first'. It is, in short, second only to the *Iliad*, and superior to the *Odyssey*, the *Aeneid*, and the epics of the Italian Renaissance.

This Johnsonian low assessment of scientific knowledge would seem to indicate more accurately his real feelings on the subject than any inferences drawn from his trivial interest in home-made chemical experiments, the condition of dried orange peelings, or the rate of growth of his own fingernails. Commenting on Milton's ideal scheme of education, Johnson further observes:

the truth is, that the knowledge of external nature, and the sciences which that knowledge requires or includes, are not the great or the frequent business of the human mind. Whether we provide for action or conversation, whether we wish to be useful or pleasing, the first requisite is the religious and moral knowledge of right and wrong; the next is an acquaintance with the history of mankind, and with those examples which may be said to embody truth, and prove by events the reasonableness of opinions. Prudence and justice are virtues and excellencies of all times and of all places.

What all this is leading up to is the famous next sentence about our being moralists essentially but geometricians only adventitiously. And he proceeds, reminding us of the humanist prayer of Erasmus, '*Sancte Socrates, ora pro nobis*': 'I have Socrates on my side. It was his labour to turn philosophy from the study of nature to speculations upon life; but the innovators whom I oppose are turning off attention from life to nature. They seem to think, that we are placed here to watch the growth of plants, or the motions of the stars. Socrates was rather of opinion, that what we had to learn was, how to do good, and avoid evil.'

Johnson seems never to lose contact with the Raphael-Adam conversation; he treats it in *Rambler* 180 and returns to it in *Adventurer* 107. And in his admiration for the wisdom of Milton's Book VIII he is in distinguished company. John Locke himself, in his *Essay Concerning Human Understanding* (1690), that book which attained an authority almost scriptural during the eighteenth century, puts it this way: 'Our business here is not to know all things, but those which concern our conduct' (i, i, 6). And later in the *Essay* Locke reveals the way his empiricism lends support quite naturally to the humanist tradition in learning:

since our faculties are not fitted to penetrate into the internal fabric and real essence of bodies . . ., it will become us . . . to employ those faculties we have about what they are most adapted to, and follow the direction of nature, where it seems to point us out the way. For it is rational to conclude that our proper employment lies in those inquiries, and in that sort of knowledge which is most suited to our natural capacities, and carries in it our greatest interest, i.e. the condition of our eternal estate. Hence I think I may conclude, that *morality* is *the proper science and business of mankind in general*.

(IV, xii, 11)

Milton's and Locke's point is echoed frequently by Burke, who scorns the chemists and mathematicians who constitute the revolutionary National Assembly because, as he says, '*Hominem non sapiunt'*; the contrivers of the new French system of parliamentary representation, he writes,

> have much, but bad, metaphysics; much, but bad, geometry; much, but false, proportionate arithmetic. . . . It is remarkable, that in a great arrangement of mankind [i.e. a rearrangement into new, geometrically shaped departments, communes, and cantons], not one reference whatsoever is to be found to any thing moral or any thing politic; nothing that relates to the concerns, the passions, the interests of men.

And Gibbon reacts similarly to the implications of the new science. In his *Autobiography* he recalls his youthful experience with the study of mathematics and remembers the delight with which he turned away from it; 'nor can I lament', he says, 'that I desisted before my mind was hardened by the habit of rigid demonstration, so destructive of the finer feelings of moral evidence, which must, however, determine the actions and opinions of our lives'. Gibbon's emphasis here on the 'finer feelings' and on 'moral evidence' resembles Burke's later stress on the moral incapacity of the mere scientist. He writes in his *Letter to a Noble Lord*: 'The geometricians and the chemists bring, the one from the dry bones of their diagrams, and the other from the soot of their furnaces, dispositions that make them worse than indifferent about those feelings and habitudes which are the supports of the moral world'.

The insistence that man is made not for inquiry into 'celestial motions' but for moral decision is thus a central literary action of the Augustan humanists, who, brought up as they were on *Paradise Lost* and *An Essay Concerning Human Understanding*, would be wholly astonished by something like C. P. Snow's recent suggestion in *The Two Cultures and the Scientific Revolution* that not to know the second law of thermodynamics is as grave an intellectual want as not to be steeped in a given work of traditional—that is, moral—literature. The distance we have drifted from the world of the Augustan humanists can be gauged by the fervour with which Snow's formulation has been embraced by many 'humanists' in American and British universities. Perhaps we catch an echo of Samuel Johnson's conversational tone of voice in F. R. Leavis's vigorous characterization of Snow: 'he is intellectually as undistinguished as it is possible to be'.[6]

[6] *Two Cultures? The Significance of C. P. Snow* (New York, 1963), p. 28.

C

The dependence of the Augustan humanists on Shakespearian and Miltonic figures and motifs bespeaks their close alliance with a conservative literary past, a literary past which is perhaps as justly termed 'Renaissance' as 'classical'. Their cause was beginning to look thoroughly old-fashioned even by the early years of the eighteenth century, and by Johnson's time the English humanist found it quite natural to conceive of himself as a small fortified city besieged by Goths.

Modern scholars and critics are perceiving increasingly that the Augustan humanists, far from being 'representative' of the general tendencies of their time, constitute actually an intensely anachronistic and reactionary response to the eighteenth century. Their rhetorical careers conduct a more or less constant warfare with the 'official' assumptions of their age, assumptions held by most of their contemporaries. It is certainly true that Samuel Johnson enjoyed arguing for the fun of it, but it is also true that he had plenty to argue about; his recorded conversation indicates how frequently he found it necessary to oppose the progressivist or sentimental truisms of his own time: 'The woman's a whore, and there's an end on't!' Joseph Wood Krutch is one who has perceived the reliance of Augustan humanism on seventeenth-century habits of thought and feeling. Commenting on Johnson's contrast between man's roles as moralist and geometrician, he observes that 'When Johnson wrote that passage he was defending what was already beginning to look like a lost cause'.[7] Earl R. Wasserman likewise has perceived that 'Pope's mind, like Swift's, was the product of a body of learning that was fading, or had already faded, by the end of the seventeenth century. To this degree, Pope and Swift, like Milton earlier, were anachronisms . . .'.[8] And Thomas R. Edwards, explicating Pope's moral and economic notions in the *Epistle to Bathurst*, reminds us that in his own time Pope's position was 'ultraconservative, appealing to an aristocratic ethic, firmly rooted in classical and medieval traditions of conduct, which by the 1730's had become obsolete except as a literary ideal'.[9] Ezra Pound, perhaps pre-eminent among twentieth-century readers of literature, is another who has apprehended

[7] *Human Nature*, p. 200.
[8] *Philological Quarterly*, xli (July 1962), 617.
[9] *This Dark Estate*, p. 52.

Johnson's profound dislocation from his own times; Pound says of Johnson that he is ' "fuori del mondo", living in the seventeenth century, so far as Europe is concerned'.[10]

The vigour of the assertion and embodiment of seventeenth-century ideas by the eighteenth-century humanists is a measure of their severe moral discomfort in a world rapidly turning 'modern' all about them. Indeed, the power and, in Burke especially, the fury of Augustan humanist expression suggests ideas of actual wartime conditions. And the enemies are fairly clear: they are the mechanism, relativism, and 'Rationalism' ascribed to the influence of Hobbes and Descartes; the new system of finance capitalism, whose 'bubbles' can be observed bursting through the eighteenth century; the 'new science', especially in its role as midwife to the new industrialism; the new sentimentality attributed to Shaftesbury and Hutcheson; the newly sanctified commercial and acquisitive ethic, visible not merely in Grub Street and the City, but, to Pope's and Swift's horror, in Westminster and the West End as well; the new conception of art as an end-product of self-expression, a conception issuing from the pleasing premise—among others— that man is by instinct virtuous and that he comes equipped with an inborn 'moral sense'; the new lower-middle-class prudential religious 'enthusiasm', with its built-in threat to authority and traditional usages; and what can be called the new utopian flippancy about man and his mortal state, a flippancy apparent in works like Soame Jenyns's *A Free Inquiry into the Nature and Origin of Evil* (1757). The continued resuscitation of Renaissance moral ideas is the Augustan humanists' response to what Edwards has seen as 'the breakdown of the public images of heroism and piety in the politics of the seventeenth century'.[11]

It is characteristic of the humanist attitude, wherever in history we encounter it, that it relishes the opportunity to make large and clear choices. The humanist attitude, indeed, is as easily defined by its rejections as by its acceptances. Geoffrey Scott, discoursing on classical architecture, sees a similar sort of 'great rejections' at the heart of the humanist architectural enterprise: 'Great architecture, like great character, has been

[10] *ABC of Reading* (Norfolk, Conn., 1951), p. 186.
[11] *This Dark Estate*, p. 17.

achieved not by a too inclusive grasp at all values, but by a supreme realisation of a few. In art, as in life, the chief problem is a right choice in sacrifices. In life, and in the arts, civilisation blends a group of compatible values into some kind of sustained and satisfying pattern, for the sake of which it requires great rejections'.[12]

Once we perceive the fundamental unity of the ethical tradition articulated by Swift and Pope and transmitted to Johnson and Reynolds, to Gibbon, and finally to Burke, we are in a position to measure its 'great rejection' of what is sometimes thought of as 'the eighteenth century'. Against the humanist tradition running from Swift to Burke we must place the optimistic tradition bounded on one end by Defoe and on the other by Burns and Blake, and including writers like Addison and Steele, James Thomson, Samuel Richardson, Edward Young, Robert Blair, Mark Akenside, William Shenstone, Oliver Goldsmith, Thomas Chatterton, and William Cowper. This other tradition, although it may draw some strength from classical literature, tends to operate as if the classics are largely irrelevant to the modern experience; regardless of its occasional quarrels with industrialism, it tends to draw its real strength from the new industrial and commercial evidence of the validity of the idea of progress. It is notable that the very few writers of the century whose infant minds escaped subjection to a severe course in classical literature are to be found in this group: it is here that we find Defoe, Chatterton, Burns, and Blake. The replacement of the classics by the new evangelical materials is happily expressed by Blake in his Preface to *Milton*: 'We do not want either Greek or Roman models if we are but just and true to our own Imaginations, those Worlds of Eternity in which we shall live forever, in Jesus our Lord'. This other tradition is generally friendly to religious evangelicism and often looks on the mercantile revolution with a feeling very like satisfaction. It feels delight rather than horror at the prospect of innovation and change. It takes pleasure in conceiving of man as a creature who, far from being flawed by some sort of original defect, exhibits an almost unwavering 'goodness of heart'. Where the humanists are devoted to prescribing and proscribing, the

[12] *The Architecture of Humanism* (2nd ed.: London, 1924), p. 163.

spokesmen for the newer morality tend towards an amiable mitigation of the orthodox moral rigour. The difference between human life conceived as 'action' (as it is by Johnson) and human life conceived as 'behaviour' (as it is by Sterne) is one important point at issue between these two ethical and expressive traditions. When the non-humanist writer does aspire to the moral, he often deviates, like Edward Young or William Cowper, into the merely moralistic. We can see the opposition between humanist and 'modern' in the eighteenth century re-enacted in later literature if we juxtapose the tradition passed from Conrad and James to Fitzgerald and Faulkner against the tradition represented by, say, Steinbeck, Thornton Wilder, and the self-parodic Hemingway of *The Old Man and the Sea*.

One hallmark of the non-humanist tradition is the decay of satire in its hands. In Addison, for example, satire turns gentle and optimistic; frequently it softens to a sort of mild kidding, suggesting that human corruption is only skin-deep within a fundamentally benign and almost automatically redemptive new world of trade, compromise, and general benevolence. By contrast, the satire in Pope and Swift, even in works so apparently cheerful as *The Rape of the Lock* or the *Compleat Collection of Genteel and Ingenious Conversation*, suggests always the presence just off-stage of dark threats and of immitigable primeval dangers. But in works like Cowper's *Task* satire becomes increasingly conceived of as at best a waste of time and at worst an indication of bad taste:

> Disgust concealed
> Is oft-times proof of wisdom, when the fault
> Is obstinate, and cure beyond our reach.
>
> (III, 38–40)

One of Cowper's more significant transitions in *The Task*, a work in which transitions can be said to be the primary subject-matter, is: 'But truce with censure'. This injunction can stand almost as the motto of the new tradition as it proceeds systematically to abdicate ethical rigour and seriousness. We are already light-years away from the moral universe of 'great rejections': we have only to recall the conception of satire held in common by Swift, Pope, and Johnson—'O sacred Weapon! left for

Truth's defence'—to perceive the extremity of the collapse of satire under the soft assaults of sentimentalism, mercantilism, and egalitarianism.

Johnson's inability to take seriously benign characters from Fielding's fictions like Squire Allworthy in *Tom Jones* and Thomas Heartfree in *Jonathan Wild* suggests why we should place a writer like Fielding just outside the humanist tradition. Characters like these—and we can include as well the Reverend Dr. Primrose, the saintly vicar of Wakefield—belong, as Johnson perceives, in romances rather than in novels: their appearance in novels, where they are surrounded by all the seductively lifelike empirical data of actual contemporary experience, constitutes an ethically dangerous, sentimentalist falsification of the conditions of life and choice. And William Blake's similar distance from the humanist centre can be measured by the degree of his impulse towards philosophic monism. The humanistic tradition happily accepts a dualistic conception of man, of which Pope's related oppositions 'Wit' and 'Judgment', 'Passion' and 'Reason', help define the terms. The boundaries between unequal entities, insisted upon by the humanists, it is Blake's ambition to obliterate for the sake of energetic totality. We end with witty, novel injunctions—Proverbs, it is true, of Hell—like this:

Exuberance is Beauty.

Blake's interesting quarrel with Reynolds in the margins of the first eight of the *Discourses on Art* also reveals his distance from the humanist position. Reynolds's sober, Lockean account of the real as the humanist 'norm' of external objects Blake confronts with this quasi-evangelistic remark suggestive of the utterance of one of Swift's comical Puritans: 'Knowledge of Ideal Beauty is not to be Acquired. It is Born with us. . . . The Man who says that we have No Innate Ideas must be a Fool & Knave, having No Con-Science or Innate Science.'

Although Blake's quarrel with Reynolds seems to be about the validity of Locke's account of the mind, it is actually as much about the humanist premise of the natural depravity of human impulse. Here is an example of the sort of perpetual re-enactment of seventeenth-century oppositions which we see throughout the century. Here Blake takes the unwitting role of

Swift's hysteric spider in the *Battle of the Books* and plays out the traditional quarrel with Reynolds's serene bee.

Douglas Bush has written of the Renaissance, 'The complex literary and philosophic tendencies of the Renaissance can be best understood if we regard the humanistic tradition as the central road and the other more or less antagonistic movements as departures from that road'.[13]

Although this view stacks the cards perhaps needlessly, there is a sense in which it is applicable to eighteenth-century literary history. Without necessarily insisting that the humanist tradition constitutes the pristine highway and the heterodox tradition the dirty divagations, we can suggest that the contrast between humanist orthodoxy and its opposition offers perhaps a more meaningful way of sensing the shape of literary history than the customary chronological opposition of one 'period' to another. This kind of contrast offers for contemplation perhaps more important distinctions—moral rather than predominantly technical—than the more traditional way of regarding the relation between the eighteenth century and its chronologically neighbouring complexes. This kind of contrast throws into relief the important opposition between the 'aristocratic orthodoxy'—the phrase is Bush's—of the line Hooker–Milton–Johnson–Coleridge–Arnold–Eliot and the progressivist heterodoxy of the line Bacon–Defoe–Benjamin Franklin–Darwin–John Dewey. Seen in this way, the confrontation of these two traditions in the eighteenth century becomes less an opposition between 'classicism' and 'romanticism' than a continuation clear through the century of the old Renaissance battle of the Ancients and the Moderns. Swift's quarrel with conventicle and Grub Street, his satiric attack on innovators in the allied worlds of devotion and discourse, is re-enacted eighty-six years later in Burke's assaults on Dr. Richard Price's tabernacle sedition and on the National Assembly's mechanical clichés about the Rights of Man. Both Swift's and Burke's battles are against the same enemy, a simple-minded Puritan utopianism which has seized the arguments of the seventeenth-century party of the Moderns and applied them, with a superficially persuasive admixture of the new sentimentalism, to the same old reality, a reality as complex and unmanageable as ever.

[13] *The Renaissance and English Humanism* (Toronto, 1939), p. 39.

The case of James Boswell is instructive here. In his interesting psychic career we find projected with almost unique
poignancy this confrontation of Ancient and Modern in the
eighteenth century. Boswell is urged both backwards and forwards: he can be considered a highly representative man
standing ill-at-ease between the two worlds, the world of
medieval and Renaissance faith and heroism, on the one hand,
and, on the other, the modern 'industrial' world of prudence,
materialism, 'consumption', simple hedonism, and pragma-
tism. By his lust for a ripe and gaudy religious faith, and by his
desire to conceive of himself as a feudal hero and to engage,
thus, in meaningful symbolic actions, he betrays his loyalty to
what he images as the old world. And by his frequent painful
awareness of his own triviality and worthlessness, his desire to
become less eccentric and better 'adjusted', he reveals his
identification with the new. It is a very Renaissance Boswell
who, upon taking his leave of Edinburgh for the infinitely more
'modern' and stylish London, writes in 1763: 'As I passed the
Cross, the Ladies and chairmen bowed and seemed to say, "GOD
prosper long our noble Boswell".' The poignancy of Boswell's
whole experience is suggested by the phrase *'seemed to say'*.
What he is imitating in this action is, of course, the first line of
the ballad of 'Chevy Chase', a poem which had been recommended to him as an instance of the noble by Addison in
Spectator 70 and 74. The interesting thing is that the world of
'Chevy Chase'—a world in which one could croon 'GOD prosper long our noble King' without any consciousness of the
character and person of George III—is the world of the fifteenth, not the eighteenth century. In this way Boswell is like
one of our contemporaries, who, while caught up in the
premises of the twentieth century, hungers to chat with Christopher Marlowe—imaged perhaps as Dylan Thomas—or to
tote canteens across a decorative battlefield to Sir Philip Sidney.
Boswell's consciousness of the conflict between his two worlds,
the confrontation of these two implicit views of man's nature
and possibility, is one of the causes not only of his neurosis but
also of his unremitting—and highly productive—curiosity about
the nature of Boswell as man. Underneath his lust for drink,
popularity, and escape, underneath his quest for moments of
crude sexual forgetfulness, his obsession is with the question,

'What is Boswell, and art Thou mindful of him?' To see him saying merely hours apart 'I have indeed a noble soul' and 'I am a miserable, sarcastical Scots dog' is to sense his tentative awareness of his plight. Much of what he was eternally searching for, in his grotesque attachments to Hume, Paoli, Burke, Reynolds, Rousseau, Voltaire, and Johnson, is a kind of large, rare Renaissance wisdom which, transmitted in the form of 'sincere' homilies and letters, could help him anchor himself in values other than the prudential and utilitarian official values of his time. In fact, it may not be entirely wrong to say that what he really wanted was to live in the age of Shakespeare and Hooker and Milton, for everything that he genuinely admires is there. His perpetual anxiety about the threat of determinism, his pathetic impulse to believe that his dignity—and that of his teachers—reposes squarely upon the absolute freedom of the will, indicates something of the force with which the humanist invitation extended itself to him. And although his approaches to a confirmed humanist position were erratic, we are touched and perhaps instructed to see that, for all his hopeless comedy and even farce, when he was most the humanist, even the humanist-*manqué*, he was the most admirable.

2

THE HUMAN ATTRIBUTES

MAN is significantly distinguished from other creatures, according to Aristotle, by his impulse to know and learn. To Cicero, he is distinguished by his awareness of causality. To the Christian, man is differentiated from animal by 'soul', conceived as a capacity for imaging the distance between the actual and the ideal, the capacity which makes possible the figure of redemption. One constant activity of the humanist of any stamp, ancient or modern, religious or secular, is the contemplation and expression of his sense of the uniqueness of man in a world of apparently meaningless organism and purposeless impulse. The humanist's primary motive in asserting man's uniqueness is to locate and articulate arguments sanctioning man's unique moral obligations as man. This motive is especially powerful in an age like the eighteenth century when traditional sanctions—revelation and the church—are appearing to lose authority. The humanist assumes two general opponents with whom he conducts a ceaseless debate. One is the naturalist, who, finding that man is in many ways almost identical with other living creatures, assumes that man, like them, ought to act as impulse and his own 'nature' move him. The other humanist opponent is the mechanist, who argues that man is so like a machine in his actions—or better, 'behaviour'—that he performs most in accord with his nature when he adjusts himself to the assumed determinisms of his external environment. Since the seventeenth century the naturalist opposition to humanism has found its spokesman in the physical and natural scientist; since the late eighteenth century, the mechanist opposition has found its spokesman in the social scientist. It is apparently both opponents that William Golding, performing like a sort of latter-day redactor of the comedy of the Houyhnhnms, is addressing ironically in *Free Fall*

(1959): 'Do not tell us that we are highest animals and then expect from us only the fierce animal devotion to the young, the herd instinct and not the high, warring hooves of the stallion. As for that light round the brow, the radiance of the unending morning of paradise—that is an illusion, a side effect. Pay no attention to it.'

Faced in our own time by disconcerting suggestions from the sciences, natural and social, that man is probably not unique among living creatures, modern humanists have insisted on certain human attributes as the index of man's singularity. Arthur O. Lovejoy, for example, finds man unique in his possession of an 'other-consciousness which is deeply interwoven with his self-consciousness'. Man is thus 'an animal aware of the fact that there are others "having insides *of* their own", though like *his* own'. And Lovejoy concludes: 'this, so far as we have any means of judging, is not true of any other animal'.[1] Because man is uniquely aware of the responses of others to his own actions, he develops a singular characteristic which Lovejoy, appropriating a nineteenth-century phrenological term, calls 'approbativeness', which, as he says, 'consists in a *susceptibility to pleasure in, or a desire for, the thought of oneself as an object of thoughts or feelings, of certain kinds, on the part of other persons*'.[2] To Lovejoy, a corollary of 'approbativeness' as the distinctive human attribute is the human habit 'of passing judgments of approval, admiration, &c., and their opposites, upon the qualities or acts of other individuals'.[3] That is, man is unique in his exercise of a critical capacity.

Joseph Wood Krutch is another who has laboured to locate some characteristics in man which will distinguish him from animals. One of Krutch's findings is that man is the only creature whose nature leads him to dispose of the cadavers of his species 'in *some* traditional and ritual fashion'.[4] Indeed, 'some sort of respect for his dead may have been a part of the nature of man for as long as there has been man to have a nature'.[5] Again, Krutch holds that 'moral judgment itself has been a constantly continuing activity of the human mind', as has been the exercise of 'prejudices'.[6] Norman O. Brown, in his turn,

---

[1] *Reflections on Human Nature* (Baltimore, 1961), p. 87.   [2] *ibid.*, p. 88.
[3] *ibid.*, p. 93.   [4] *Human Nature*, p. 177.
[5] *ibid.*, p. 178.   [6] *ibid.*, pp. 179, 180.

finds that 'repression (and consequently neurosis) distinguishes man from the other animals'.[7] Other humanist contemporaries, like their older counterparts, have focused on the physical in their search for the human attributes. Man, they point out, is the only creature who laughs, who spits, and who blushes. He is the only creature who stands upright. He is the only creature who feels disinclined to perform sexual intercourse in public. Others, pointing to qualities of mind and imagination, have emphasized that man is the only creature who contrives rituals for the important stages of his life, rituals like christenings, namings, puberty and initiation rites, marriage ceremonies, testimonial banquets, *Festschriften*, and funerals. As Johnson says in *Rambler* 110, 'Incorporated minds will always feel some inclination towards exterior acts and ritual observances'. Johnson's phrase 'incorporated minds' beautifully suggests man's 'middle state' between the extremes of pure mind (angels) and pure corporeal matter (brutes), his paradoxical location in a larger scheme of value which obliges him unremittingly to define his own nature. Other humanists, both ancient and modern, have stressed the human attribute of memory, pointing out that man is the only creature who knows who his grandparents are and who thinks it worth his while both to inquire into history and to keep annals of the present for the use of the future. Others focus on man as maker and argue that man is the only creature who contrives complex tools and works of art, who utters narratives, and who indulges in stylized miming by means of theatre and games. And still others, occupying a more gloomy vantage point, find that man is the only creature who worries and the only creature whose consciousness of internal division moves him, on occasion, to destroy himself after some appalling vision of unworthiness.

One preoccupation common to humanists of all times and places is thus a concern with a definition of the uniquely human. This act of definition is central to the careers of the Augustan humanists, and it is this act which unites writers so apparently far apart as the pious Johnson and 'Infidel' Gibbon. It comes as no surprise that in defining man the eighteenth-century humanist discovers that man is uniquely the 'social' creature.

---

[7] *Life Against Death: The Psychoanalytical Meaning of History* (New York, 1959), p. 28.

Johnson is the main humanist spokesman here. 'We were born for the help of one another', he insists in *Idler* 80, and thus 'to know the world is necessary.' From the proposition that man is the only social creature follow certain important Johnsonian conclusions. For example, the importance of truth in human intercourse and in literature and art: says Johnson in *Idler* 20, 'There is no crime more infamous than the violation of truth. It is apparent that men can be social beings no longer than they believe each other.' Johnson's last sentence is equivalent to saying that man can be man only so long as he lives in a climate of strict veracity. It is clear that a humanist of the Johnsonian stamp will feel uneasy in a world in which commerce, acquisitiveness, 'politics', and advertising constitute the apparent centre of action. It follows naturally in Johnson's literary theory that pastorals, romances, incredible anecdotes of the superhuman virtue of famous persons, and the perpetual white lies ('cant') of normal middle-class social intercourse are all reprehensible in the same way, for they end by turning man away from his nature as a social being. And because man is the only social creature, for him to prefer solitude to society constitutes another perversion of his nature. Hence Johnson's contempt for Thomas Gray's cloistered life at Cambridge; hence Johnson's suspicion of monasteries and convents and his ready satire of hermits and solitaries. Because man is not only the social animal but the sole creature who can imagine himself as issuing from a depraved original, 'stillness and solitude', says Johnson in *Adventurer* 34, 'can afford satisfaction only to innocence'. They can afford satisfaction, that is, to no one. Johnson's reaction to the primitivist ideal of solitude is exhibited with characteristic irony in Chapter XXI of *Rasselas*. Here a hermit tells his story to the Johnsonian travellers, and one of the main causes of the hermit's ultimate disillusion with his decision to retire from a naughty world proves to be his sense of shame at what he has done: 'I am sometimes ashamed', he confesses, 'to think that I could not secure myself from vice but by retiring from the exercise of virtue.' We are reminded of the spirit both of Milton's *Areopagitica* and of Gibbon's satire of the early monastic Christians. The hermit continues: 'I have been long comparing the evils with the advantages of society, and resolved to return into the world tomorrow. The life of a solitary man will be cer-

tainly miserable, but not certainly devout.' Young Rasselas and
Nakayah are surely jolted by the ironic coincidence between the
hermit's decision and the moment of their visit; and what
follows the hermit's decision is even more illuminating: 'He dug
up a considerable treasure which he had hid among the rocks,
and accompanied them to the city [of Cairo], on which, as he
approached it, he gazed with rapture.' The hermit's having
carefully provided himself with ample means for re-entering
society in style is Johnson's way of saying that man by his very
nature knows that the life of solitude is ultimately anti-human,
cant as man will about its primitivist and pastoral attractions.
James Thomson's 'Hymn on Solitude' (1729) provides a useful
contrast to Johnson's humanistic response to the subject. Thomson's poem ends with the following silly performance which
exactly reverses the action of Johnson's enlightened hermit:

> Perhaps from Norwood's oak-clad hill,
> When Meditation has her fill,
> I just may cast my careless eyes
> Where London's spiry turrets rise,
> Think of its crimes, its cares, its pain.
> Then shield me in the woods again.
>
> (43–48)

William Cowper, the 'self-sequestered man', likewise exhibits
the 'modern' conception of solitude with which Johnson's orthodox idea is at war. As Cowper writes in *The Task*, Book III:

> Retreat
> . . . has peace, and much secures the mind
> From all assaults of evil; proving still
> A faithful barrier, not o'erleaped with ease
> By vicious custom, raging uncontrolled
> Abroad, and desolating public life.
> When fierce temptation, seconded within
> By traitor appetite, and armed with darts
> Tempered in hell, invades the throbbing breast,
> To combat may be glorious and success
> Perhaps may crown us; but to fly is safe.
>
> (676, 679–88)

The expression of effeminate, prudential cautions here in a
rhetoric and prosody full of Miltonic associations demonstrates

the kind of ultimate aesthetic incoherence which makes most of Cowper's work so entirely unrewarding. To Johnson, one of the dangers of Thomson's and Cowper's position would lie in its abdication of social responsibility. As Johnson says in *Adventurer* 67, 'To receive and communicate assistance, constitutes the happiness of human life: man may, indeed, preserve his existence in solitude, but can enjoy it only in society'. The actions of 'receiving' and 'communicating' assistance assume a necessary distinction of capacity, and we see thus that Johnson's basic definition of man as the social creature implies his commitment to the idea of 'subordination' of social ranks and orders within the community: without recognized principles of subordination there may be attempts to 'communicate assistance', but there can hardly be any open and frank 'receiving', that is, acceptance of charity in a spirit which does not debase the recipient's conception of his own ultimate worth.

One of Johnson's favourite dicta in his letters of advice to friends is the avoidance of solitude. Boswell is exhorted many times to 'Be not idle; be not solitary'. Richard Congreve is told: 'Solitude is certainly one of the greatest obstacles to pleasure and improvement' (*LSJ*, i, 6). And Elizabeth Aston of Lichfield is reminded that 'Solitude excludes pleasure, and does not always secure peace' (*LSJ*, i, 203-4). The distance between the humanistic and the Thomsonian–Cowperian attitudes towards solitude can be gauged from a letter of Johnson's to Mrs. Thrale. Travelling on the Hebridean tour in 1773, Johnson writes:

> I sat down to take notes on a green bank, with a small stream running at my feet, in the midst of savage solitude, with Mountains before me, and on either hand covered with heath. I looked around me, and wondered that I was not more affected, but the mind is not at all times equally ready to be put in motion. If my Mistress, and Master, and Queeny [the Thrale's nine-year-old daughter] had been there we should have produced some reflections among us either poetical or philosophical, for though [as Thomas Parnell puts it in his 'Hymn to Contentment'] *Solitude* be *the nurse of woe*, conversation is often the parent of remarks and discoveries.
>
> (*LSJ*, i, 355)

Everyone is aware of Johnson's lust for social conversation, and perhaps we have been told often enough that his neurotic fear of loneliness is his main motive for keeping companies up to all hours with talk. On the other hand, it is important to notice that Johnson's suspicion of solitude is as much an expression of a clear, public, and orthodox body of humanistic philosophical thought as it is a manifestation of a mere personal idiosyncrasy.

Indeed, the deeper one penetrates into the heart of Samuel Johnson, the more one perceives that what at first looks like personal singularity is actually often some manifestation of Renaissance humanism slightly disguised.

To Johnson, a number of moral vices are readily identified because of their inconsistency with man's nature as a social creature. Envy, for example, is known to be a vice less because it is found to be prohibited by the Commandments than because experience demonstrates that it depraves man's social nature. To Johnson, 'envy is mere unmixed and genuine evil; it pursues a hateful end by despicable means, and desires not so much its own happiness as another's misery. To avoid depravity like this, it is not necessary that any one should aspire to heroism or sanctity, but only that he should resolve not to quit that rank which nature assigns him, and wish to maintain the dignity of a human being' (*Rambler* 183).

Like envy, fraud constitutes another perversion of man's social nature. Society coheres only by means of the general assumption that men are truthful in their dealings with each other. As Johnson says in *Rambler* 79, 'Whoever commits a fraud is guilty not only of the particular injury to him whom he deceives, but of the diminution of that confidence which constitutes not only the ease but the existence of society'. Fraud, in being an anti-social crime, is a direct assault on man's nature and dignity. We may recall here Swift's ironic observations on the 'peculiarity' of some Lilliputian notions. Gulliver writes: 'They look upon Fraud as a greater Crime than Theft, and therefore seldom fail to punish it with Death; For they alledge, that Care and Vigilance, with a very common Understanding, may preserve a Man's Goods from Thieves; but Honesty hath no Fence against superior Cunning.' That is, fraud is worse than theft because it necessarily entails a specific violation of an individual human agreement. Every unpunished fraud diminishes the victim's ability to believe in the general human capacity for honest dealing. A nation in which fraud is not considered the worst of crimes becomes inexorably a nation of cynics. Even Rasselas the naïve learns enough during his wanderings to perceive this point. Objecting to Nekayah's and Pekuah's proposal to introduce themselves in disguise to the mad astronomer, Rasselas says: 'I have always considered it as treason against the great republick of human nature, to make any man's virtues the means of deceiving him. . . . All imposture weakens confidence, and chills benevolence.'

Reynolds and Burke are at one with Johnson in their stress on man's social nature. To the Reynolds of the *Twelfth Discourse* the intercourse between contemporary art students and the ancient and Renaissance masters should be an open, amiable social dependence emanating from a feeling for individual human frailty: 'Such conduct in the commerce of life has never been considered as disgraceful, or in any respect to imply intellectual imbecility; it is a sign rather of that true wisdom, which feels individual imperfection; and is conscious to itself how much collective observation is necessary to fill the immense extent, and to comprehend the infinite variety, of nature.'

And in a sense Burke's whole 'organic' awareness of political change issues from his humanist conviction that man is best defined as that creature who requires society, in Burke the society of the past as well as of the present and the future. As he reminds the Rights-of-Man doctrinaires in *Letters on a Regicide Peace*: 'As to the right of men to act anywhere according to their pleasure, without any moral tie, no such right exists. Men are never in a state of *total* independence of each other. It is not the condition of our nature. . . .' And even James Boswell, no philosopher himself and only occasionally an aspirant humanist, suggests his cheerful agreement with the definition of man as social creature. 'How pleasant it is', he ruminates, 'to live well with our fellow creatures, and interchange civilities' (*BSW*, 266).

In Bertolt Brecht's Marxist-oriented *Aufstieg und Fall der Stadt Mahagonny* (1930) there is a passage which in shape as well as in substance curiously recalls another eighteenth-century humanist theme. A chorus consisting of Jakob, Heinrich, and Joe seeks to persuade Paul that life in Mahagonny is satisfactory. After each of their portentous, pseudo-Biblical announce-

D

ments of the delights of Mahagonny, Paul answers abruptly that something is still wanting:

JAKOB, HEINRICH, JOE

Wunderbar ist das Heraufkommen des Abends
Und schön sind die Gespräche der Männer unter sich!

PAUL

Aber etwas fehlt.

JAKOB, HEINRICH, JOE

Schön ist die Ruhe und der Frieden
Und beglückend ist die Eintracht.

PAUL

Aber etwas fehlt.

JAKOB, HEINRICH, JOE

Herrlich ist das einfache Leben
Und ohnegleichen ist die Gröse der Natur.

PAUL

Aber etwas fehlt.

To the chorus's harmonious and official praise of the beauty of evening, the beauty of peace and quiet, and the beauty of the simple life in the midst of nature, Paul can answer only, 'But something's missing'. This sense of human incompleteness Brecht enlists on behalf of a scathing critique of the economic basis of contemporary society. The same sense of human incompleteness as an important attribute of man the Augustan humanists enlist on behalf of a critique of man himself.

Johnson is again the main spokesman for the humanist sense of man's incompleteness. As Rasselas puts it: 'What makes the difference between man and all the rest of the animal creation? . . . I am hungry and thirsty like [the beast], but when thirst and hunger cease I am not at rest; I am, like him, pained with want, but am not, like him, satisfied with fulness. . . . Man surely has some latent sense for which [the Happy Valley] affords no gratification, or he has some desires distinct from sense, which must be satisfied before he can be happy.' Ironically, Rasselas, despite his prolonged tour of inquiry, never does discover what the desires are that must be satisfied for man to be happy. All he discovers is that, in every choice of life, '*etwas fehlt*', or, as Johnson says in *Rambler* 196, 'something is always wanting to happiness'. It is man's fate, as Johnson writes in his *Life of Sir Thomas Browne*, that 'in all sublunary things there is something to be wished which we must wish in vain'. When we are full and satisfied, we have become something less than man.

To Johnson, there is a portion of the human imagination, considered, in Lockean terms, as a sort of vessel or container, which can never be 'filled', although it is man's constant employ—at once his curse and his glory—to attempt to fill it. An analogy is usually implied between the mind and the stomach, as when Imlac, trying to find some explanation for the existence of the Egyptian pyramids in Chap. xxxii of *Rasselas*, speculates that the pyramids seem 'to have been erected only in compliance with that hunger of imagination which preys incessantly upon life, and must be always appeased by some employment'. Anything, no matter how trivial or silly or shameful, will serve the imagination as nourishment in its incessant search outside itself for something to 'fill' it. Johnson's basic critical criterion, a literary work's being interesting, rests squarely upon this sense of the natural incompleteness of the mind. Johnson's irreducible critical value, the degree to which a work persuades the reader not to hurl the book from him in a fury of boredom, assumes this lust of the mind to be completely, if only momentarily, filled. With all its obvious faults, *The Merry Wives of Windsor*, Johnson finds in *General Observations on Shakespeare's Plays*, is partly redeemed by possessing 'that power by which all works of genius shall finally be tried': 'it never yet had reader or spectator, who did not think it too soon at an end'. In the same way, the parodic dimension of Shenstone's *The Schoolmistress* staves off boredom momentarily and partially redeems another second-rate work; according to Johnson, *The Schoolmistress* 'is surely the most pleasing of Shenstone's performances. The adoption of a particular style, in light and short compositions, contributes much to the increase of pleasure: we are entertained at once with two imitations, of nature in the sentiments, of the original author in the style, and between them the mind is kept in perpetual employment' (*Life of Shenstone*). Which is to say that even so tepid a performance as Shenstone's poem has the merit of momentarily filling the mind and preventing it from turning inward to torment itself with visions of depravity. And by contrast with these two works of the second rank, a work like *Paradise Lost*, even though it 'never fails to fill the imagination', apparently does not succeed, for all its splendour, in satisfying the 'hunger of imagination', for no reader 'ever wished it longer than it is'. In short, 'All the attainments possible in our present state are evidently inadequate to our capacities of enjoyment: . . . and after all our labours, studies, and enquiries, we are continually at the same distance from the completion of our schemes, have still some wish importunate to be satisfied, and some faculty restless and turbulent for want of its employment' (*Rambler* 103). Just as we have seen that Johnson's attraction to social life represents less a singular neurotic fear of solitude than an enactment of generally received humanist doctrine, so here too we should avoid assuming that Johnson's sense of man's incompleteness is entirely singular rather than partly traditional. When we find Johnson saying, as he does in *Adventurer* 111, that 'such is the state of this world, that we find in it absolute misery, but happiness only comparative', or, as he puts it in the anonymous dedication he wrote for *The Evangelical History of Jesus Christ* (1758), 'such is the condition of our nature, that we are always attempting what it is difficult to perform', we should not leap to the assumption that what he is articulating is a sense of his own personal frustration: he is rather re-expressing a traditional and objective view of the incompleteness, not of Samuel Johnson, but of man. Writing to Mrs. Thrale in 1767, he laments his own failures and the frustration of many of his own hopes; and then, assuming the premise of the uniformity of human nature, he turns from his own situation and rises to an observation on the general condition of mankind. He writes: 'I suppose it is the condition of humanity to design what will never be done, and to hope what never will be obtained' (*LSJ*, i, 198).

The other great eighteenth-century humanists, despite their minor differences over exactly what it is that defines man, have in common an irresistible impulse to define him and to distinguish him from other living creatures. The whole of *Gulliver's Travels*, but especially 'A Voyage to the Country of the Houyhnhnms', is, like *Hamlet* or *King Lear* or *Paradise Lost*, a dramatized definition of man in his proper harmonious state

and in addition a series of rowdy warnings against the tendencies of the human mind which, improperly indulged, are most
likely to transform man into either brute or machine. To Swift,
man is unique in being the only creature *capax rationis*—capable,
with great effort, of reason; but man visits disasters upon himself when he makes the mistake of considering himself *animal
rationale*—a creature already reasonable and requiring, thus, no
redemption through the device of self-distrust. In his examination into the nature of man Pope focuses on a less profound
attribute. To Pope, man is unique because he is the only
creature aware of his mortality:

> To each unthinking being, Heav'n a friend,
> Gives not the useless knowledge of its end:
> To Man imparts it.
>
> *(Essay on Man,* iii, 71–73)

To the arch-humanist Reynolds, man's foremost attribute is his
capacity for entertaining ideas and images of the heroic. Because
the history-painter must 'represent in every one of his figures
the character of its species', all the figures in any painting
executed in the grand style must bespeak the human attributes
of 'intellectual grandeur' and 'philosophick wisdom, or heroick
virtue' (*Third Discourse*). And Burke, in a central passage in the
Reflections, expresses in his own way and for his own purposes
Reynolds's definition of man as the creature whose imagination
enables him to conceive ideas of himself as potentially noble:
'Every sort of moral, every sort of civil, every sort of politic
institution, aiding the rational and natural ties that connect the
human understanding and affections to the divine, are not
more than necessary, in order to build up that wonderful structure, Man; whose prerogative it is, to be in a great degree a
creature of his own making; and who, when made as he ought
to be made, is destined to hold no trivial place in the creation.'
Burke is implying here that a rare man may be able to perform
this imaginative transmutation of himself unaided, but that the
job becomes easier for most men the more they surround themselves with traditional institutions devoted to the interpretation
of man as potentially dignified, or *capax rationis*. Such institutions are established churches, hereditary aristocracies, houses
of lords and parliaments, and even galleries of history-paintings,

which can remind man that he is, although not always heroic, at least, in Swift's sense, *capable* of heroism. And perhaps established churches are the fittest means 'to build up that wonderful structure, Man', since, as Burke says elsewhere in the *Reflections*, 'We know, and it is our praise to know, that man is by his constitution a religious animal . . .'.

As Burke conceives, man possesses a sort of built-in gauge of his humanity if only he will recognize it: it is the degree to which he is capable of experiencing sympathetic horror, imaged in terms of Aristotelian fear and pity, at the spectacle, both theatric and actual, of the downfall of kings and noble persons. This gauge is notably different from that of the mere benevolist, who would want to measure instead the copiousness and extravagance of a man's 'moral weeping' in the face of the merely pathetic. Condemning the revolutionists' confiscation of the Archbishop of Rouen's property, Burke writes: 'Can one hear of the proscription of such persons, and the confiscation of their effects, without indignation and horror? He is not a man who does not feel such emotions on such occasions.' And Burke complicates this argument in one of the most brilliant passages of the *Reflections*, where he asserts that an important attribute of man is exactly the one which has moved him, as a humanist, to protest the outrages of the Revolution, namely, the capacity for the kind of tragic feeling defined and illustrated in Aristotle's *Poetics*. Discussing the downfall of kings, Burke begins by posing the question, 'Why do I feel so differently from the Reverend Dr. Price . . .?' He prepares the reader for the answer with the words 'For this plain reason', which perhaps reminded the eighteenth-century reader of Pope's similar question and answer—suggestive of the imagery of *King Lear*—in the *Essay on Man*:

> Why has not Man a microscopic eye?
> For this plain reason, Man is not a Fly.
>
> (i, 193–4)

Both Pope and Burke are here busy at their humanist work of discovering man's essence in his natural limitations. Just as man is not a fly to Pope—nor a horse to Swift—so to Burke he is not a self-sufficient director of his own fate. Burke proceeds:

For this plain reason—because it is *natural* I should; because we are so made as to be affected at such spectacles [as the downfall of kings] with melancholy sentiments upon the unstable condition of mortal prosperity, and the tremendous uncertainty of human greatness; because in those natural feelings we learn great lessons; because in events like these our passions instruct our reason; because when kings are hurl'd from their thrones by the Supreme Director of this great drama, and become the objects of insult to the base, and of pity to the good, we behold such disasters in the moral, as we should behold a miracle in the physical order of things.

Burke's reference to 'the Supreme Director of this great drama' serves to introduce the imagery of classical tragedy by means of which he will conduct the latter stage of his argument. Because the effect of this 'miracle in the physical order of things' is, as we learn next, to 'alarm' us 'into reflexion', it is probably no cheerful miracle—like that at Cana—which Burke has in mind, but rather the miraculous darkening of the universe which attended the downfall of another King. Burke continues: 'We are alarmed into reflexion; our minds (as it has long since been observed) are purified by terror and pity. . . .' And now he proceeds to the heart of his argument: 'Some tears might be drawn from me, if such a spectacle were exhibited on the stage. I should be truly ashamed of finding in myself that superficial, theatric sense of painted distress, whilst I could exult over it in real life. With such a perverted mind, I could never venture to shew my face at a tragedy'. Thus 'the [tragic] theatre is a better school of moral sentiments than [Dissenters'] churches [like Dr. Price's], where the feelings of humanity are thus outraged'. Burke goes on to point out that the tragic poets, who must be learned in human nature in order to contrive the kind of effects that will generate fear and pity in the beholder, would not, like Dr. Price, expect the action of a king's downfall to cause feelings of satisfaction—indeed, as Dr. Price has it, 'exultation'—in the spectator. In a sense, Burke's argument here is equivalent to breaking a butterfly upon a wheel, for who would dispute that Sophocles and Aristotle are wiser in their reading of human nature than Dr. Richard Price? But the interesting thing for our purposes in Burke's argument is the way it re-enacts a century too late the Battle of the Ancients and Moderns by managing to imply that Dr. Price, like Swift's Puritans or Gibbon's Christians, is fatally ignorant of classical literature and wisdom. Notable also is the way the passage exploits the paradox of the theatre as 'reality' opposed to the perversions of actual life, at least as life is interpreted by non-men like Dr. Price and his followers. What Burke is saying is analogous to his assertion in *A Letter to a Noble Lord* that 'under the direction of reason, instinct is always in the right'. By denying pity to greatness in distress, Dr. Price has denied his own humanity. He is thus worse than a man who has made a mere mistake about politics: like Pope's Lord Hervey, he is a thorough moral pervert. For it is the 'passions' which constitute man; without them, man becomes an image of Satan himself: 'Nothing can be conceived', says Burke elsewhere in the *Reflections*, 'more hard than the heart of a thoroughbred metaphysician. It comes nearer to the cold malignity of a wicked spirit than to the frailty and passion of a man. It is like that of the principle of evil himself, incorporeal, pure, unmixed, dephlegmated, defecated evil'. So much for both Satan and his earthly vicegerent, Dr. Richard Price. It is hard not to be reminded again of Lord Hervey:

> *Eve's* Tempter thus the Rabbins have exprest,
> A Cherub's face, a Reptile all the rest.
> (*Epistle to Dr. Arbuthnot*, 330–1)

Thus Pope finds an echo as Burke returns again and again in the *Reflections* to his humanist inquiry into the nature of man's attributes. To say with Thomas Paine that Burke 'pities the plumage, but forgets the dying bird' is to miss the centre of Burke's argument, for the polemic that is the *Reflections* is less an attempt to do justice to the politics of revolution than a profoundly excited inquiry into the very foundations of the imaginative, symbolic activity that maintains man in his distinctively human position. The ultimate analogue to Burke is not Lord North or George III or any other 'political conservative' either ancient or modern, but the Coleridge of the *Biographia Literaria*.

We have seen the way the Augustan humanist distinguishes man as the social creature, the incomplete creature, and finally —whether regarded as actor or audience—the tragic creature. But overriding all these attributes of man is one even more consequential: man's pathetic capacities for both memory and hope, for looking before and after and pining for what is not.

Indeed, to Johnson, 'It is ... the faculty of remembrance, which may be said to place us in the class of moral agents'. The faculty of remembrance in man—analogous to the sense of history in society—is indispensable to his sense of causality and thus to his conception of the freedom of his will. To the humanist, man can be defined as the only sentient creature whose consciousness is so constructed that he experiences no present time—he can be aware of a past and of a future, but by the time he has focused his frail and wandering awareness on the 'present' it has become the 'past'. Snap your fingers and contemplate the *timbre* of the snap: the actual snap takes place, we imagine, in the 'present', but by the time the sound registers on ear and 'brain', it belongs to the irrecoverable past. Thus for man the present is entirely unknowable. It is an illusion fabricated from the desperate human need to seize and stabilize the future as it rushes past. The Augustan humanists seem intensely aware of this quality in the human experience: hence their obsessions with memory and hope, and hence also both their tender instinct for the elegiac and—as the names of Robertson, Hume, and Gibbon remind us—their flair for the writing of serious history on the grand scale.

In considering the Augustan theory of memory and hope, we can hardly do better than to take a close look at one of the key documents, Johnson's *Rambler* 41 (1750). Here we can see the way Johnson's conception of past and future is indissolubly allied with other elements of his humanism. He begins by grounding his view of past and future on the theory of man's incompleteness: 'So few of the hours of life are filled up with objects adequate to the mind of man, and so frequently are we in want of present pleasure or employment, that we are forced to have recourse every moment to the past and future for supplemental satisfactions, and relieve the vacuities of our being, by recollection of former passages, or anticipation of events to come'. It is thus the 'hunger of imagination', the natural curse of those belonging to 'the class of moral agents', that seeks for something other than the mere present to devour. And we should not miss the force of the phrase 'every moment': as we shall see, it means just what it says, that the real life of man takes place outside the 'present'.

Johnson proceeds to suggest that 'this necessity of searching

on every side for matter on which the attention may be employed' is 'a strong proof of the superiour and celestial nature of
the soul of man'; and he goes on to assert that this capacity for
looking before and after is a major mark of distinction between
men and animals. Here he is practically paraphrasing Cicero,
who writes in *De Officiis*: 'the beast . . . adapts itself to that
alone which is present at the moment; while man—because he
is endowed with reason, by which he comprehends the chain of
consequence, perceives the causes of things, understands the
relation of cause to effect and of effect to cause, draws analogies,
and connects and associates the present and the future—easily
surveys the course of his whole life and makes the necessary
preparations for its conduct' (i, iv; trans. Walter Miller).
Johnson's version of this Ciceronian observation takes an
expectedly empirical turn: he illustrates the absence of memory
in the animal world by pointing to the ease with which 'dams'
apparently forget their offspring. But this direction of thought
leads him into the sticky matter of distinguishing human
'reason' from animal 'instinct', and he extricates himself by a
combination of abuse, obscurantism, and good, empirical
sense:

It has been asked by men who love to perplex any thing that is
plain to common understandings, how reason differs from instinct;
. . . To give an accurate answer to a question, of which the terms are
not completely understood, is impossible; . . . but surely he that contemplates a ship and a bird's nest, will not be long without finding
out, that the idea of the one was impressed at once . . . and that the
other is the result of experiments, compared with experiments, has
grown . . . from less to greater excellence, and exhibits the collective
knowledge of different ages and various professions.

Notable here is the way Johnson implies a definition of 'reason'
based on 'the collective knowledge of different ages' and
suggests thereby the indispensability of the practice of history to
human conduct.

He moves next, by means of the humble image of a caterer or
perhaps even a military quartermaster, to exhibit the relation
of memory to 'will': 'Memory is the purveyor of reason, the
power which places those images before the mind upon which
the judgment is to be exercised, and which treasures up the

determinations that are once passed, as the rules of future action, or grounds of subsequent conclusions.' Here as elsewhere in the humanist tradition we are struck by the easy alliance between Cicero and Locke which the humanist cast of mind seems to invite.

Memory, he continues, is that which provides man with free will, for 'If we were to act only in consequence of some immediate impulse, and receive no direction from internal motives of choice, we should be pushed forward by an invincible fatality . . .'. And in addition to providing man with the free choice denied other sentient creatures, memory also is responsible for most of the 'intellectual pleasures', for 'almost all that we can be said to enjoy is past or future; the present is in perpetual motion, leaves us as soon as it arrives, ceases to be present before its presence is well perceived, and is only known to have existed by the effects which it leaves behind. The greatest part of our ideas arises, therefore, from the view before or behind us, and we are happy or miserable, according as we are affected by the survey of our life, or our prospect of future existence.'

Turning distinctly moral now as he moves on to examine the matter of hope and the future, Johnson begins to exercise his irony on the delusions which seem inseparable from hope. 'The solitary and thoughtful' love more to anticipate than to recollect, 'For the future is pliant and ductile, and will be easily moulded by a strong fancy into any form'. Such a one is the scholarly 'young enthusiast' of *The Vanity of Human Wishes*, whose hopes are destined by their extravagance to conclude in disappointment:

> O'er Bodley's dome his future labours spread,
> And Bacon's mansion trembles o'er his head.
>
> (139–40)

But the meditator more responsible than the budding young scholar will avoid the temptation to luxuriate in images of a gay futurity: 'the satisfactions . . . arising from memory are less arbitrary . . .'; 'they are more solid, and are, indeed, the only joys that we can call our own'. That is, they are finally exempt from chance. The frailty of both man and of his future is invoked as Johnson illustrates: 'Whatever we have once reposited, as Dryden expresses it, *in the sacred treasure of the past*, is out of the reach of accident, or violence, nor can be lost either by our own weakness, or another's malice.'

The conclusion of the essay Johnson devotes to a consideration of the moral pleasures of meditating on acts of past virtue. Here we encounter an instance of Johnson's perpetual emphasis on moral decision and action, as well as an appearance of one of his favourite moral motifs, that of the Parable of the Talents, as found in Matthew xxv. 14–30: 'Life, in which nothing has been done or suffered to distinguish one day from another, is to him that has passed it, as if it had never been, except that he is conscious how ill he has husbanded the great deposit of his Creator.' After the merest glance at the Christian conception of hope as preparation for eternal felicity, Johnson hurries on. He concludes by suggesting that the elderly, who have little more as materials for contemplation than their long past, may make themselves happy only by providing ahead of time and laying up 'such a treasure of pleasing [i.e. morally satisfying] ideas, as shall support the expences of that time [old age], which is to depend wholly upon the fund already acquired'. The final sentence embodies with some irony Johnson's gentle scepticism about the likelihood of the future's fulfilling its promises: 'In youth, however happy, we solace ourselves with the hope of better fortune, and however vicious, appease our consciences with intentions of repentance; but the time comes at last, in which life has no more to promise, in which happiness can be drawn only from recollection, and virtue will be all that we can recollect with pleasure.'

Thus moving easily from one great humanistic premise to another—from man's incompleteness to man's uniqueness to the indispensability of the sense of history to the freedom of the will —Johnson conducts himself finally to a logical exclusion of all but remembered virtue as a basis for happiness. Johnson's amateur epistomological theory of the non-existence of the present becomes the ultimate foundation for the implicit moral injunction with which the argument ends. Something very like physiology is carefully and almost imperceptibly transmuted into ethics. The action of *Rambler* 41 stands as supremely representative of the great Augustan humanist enterprise of deducing a stable ethics from the actual nature of man tenderly but no less rigorously considered.

Addressing in 1773 his friend William Samuel Johnson in far away Connecticut, Johnson writes: '[you] will be glad that I do not forget you. Merely to be remembered is indeed a barren pleasure, but it is one of the pleasures which is more sensibly felt, as human Nature is more exalted' (*LSJ*, i, 307). The implication is that it is an element of the dignity of human nature not merely to exercise memory but to conceive of oneself as the focus of approbative remembrance. Hamlet, the Renaissance paradigm of the noble surrounded and overcome by the corrupt, enjoins Horatio:

> If thou didst ever hold me in thy heart,
> Absent thee from felicity awhile,
> And in this harsh world draw thy breath in pain,
> To tell my story.
>
> (v, ii, 357–60)

Conversely, an inattention to posthumous reputation is one sure sign of the brutal. It is this conviction that informs one of Burke's passionate indictments of British policy in India. In his *Speech on Fox's East India Bill* (1783) Burke argues that the British relation to India has been such that

no pride erects stately monuments which repair the mischiefs which pride has produced, and which adorn a country out of its own spoils. England has erected no churches, no hospitals, no palaces, no schools; England has built no bridges, made no high-roads, cut no navigations, dug out no reservoirs. Every other conqueror of every other description has left some monument, either of state or beneficence, behind him. Were we to be driven out of India this day, nothing would remain to tell that it has been possessed, during the inglorious period of our dominion, by anything better than the orangoutang or the tiger.

Burke's final figure here reminds us of an eloquent image in *A Letter to a Noble Lord*, where we are told that the Jacobins have so far degenerated from the human condition that no genuine human being is safe from them: 'They have tigers to fall upon animated strength.' It would be hard to find a more succinct expression of the humanist sense of the paradox of man than Burke's phrase 'animated strength', whose force depends almost entirely upon the original suggestions—available only to 'Ancients'—of *anima*, just as Johnson's 'incorporated minds' fully exploits the Ancient sense of *corpus*. The use of memory and the sense of organic history Burke embodies over and over again in the *Reflections*, but nowhere more clearly, perhaps, than here: 'By this unprincipled facility of changing the state as often, and as much, and in as many ways, as there are floating fancies or fashions, the whole chain and continuity of the commonwealth would be broken. No one generation could link with the other. Men would become little better than the flies of a summer.' Although man differs from fly in not having a microscopic eye, a more ennobling because not merely physical difference is his use of memory by which he can earn both personal coherence and a meaningful connexion with the stream of history.

The past, accessible to memory, is the dimension where the virtuous should choose to live; but since so few are virtuous, it is rather the future, constructed by the operations of hope—'the radical principle of happiness', as Nekayah puts it—which is the dimension where most men actually do live. The paradox of hope, the support of Christianity and one of the springs of man's dignity as well as the primary source of his fatuity, is a recurrent topic to the Augustan humanist. And the topic is generally developed with all the subtle complexity of tone which we find in Pope's treatment of it in the *Essay on Man*. Here Pope is both satiric and sympathetic at once:

> Hope springs eternal in the human breast:
> Man never Is, but always To be blest:
>
> (i, 95–96)

How fortunate and how preposterous, the tone implies. Naturally Johnson was drawn to Pope's conception of the unsatisfactoriness of the present. Boswell reports:

He . . . enlarged upon Pope's melancholy remark,

> Man never *is*, but always *to be* blest.

He asserted, that *the present* was never a happy state to any human being; but that, as every part of life, of which we are conscious, was at some point of time a period yet to come, in which felicity was expected, there was some happiness produced by hope.

(*BLJ*, ii, 350–1)

It is characteristic of Boswell to imagine that Johnson's remark is more comforting than it is: it is obvious that the 'happiness produced by hope' is proved by experience to be fraudulent, since each uninspired present moment is one from which delight was, at one time, naïvely anticipated. 'Hope' is thus an externally willing party to a bitter swindle, and the sad thing about man's condition is that this swindle is about all he has as a technique for happiness. For Johnson to be fully aware that human 'happiness' is thus a philosophic delusion and yet to respond to this perception in a serio-comic way is one of his great feats of control. He will not despair; instead he will analyse and criticize. Writing to Mrs. Thrale in 1773 about a newly married couple, he comments: 'What a life do they image in futurity, how unlike to what they are to find it. But tomorrow is an old deceiver, and his cheat never grows stale' (*LSJ*, i, 329–30). But even though it is his reliance on hope that places man in the position of comical dupe, at the same time the capacity for hope is a humanizing and dignifying attribute; as Pope points out in the *Essay on Man*,

> Nature plants in Man alone
> Hope of known bliss, and Faith in bliss unknown:
> (iv, 345–6)

Hope is thus paradoxically both a psychological swindle, an index of human dignity, and the analogue and avenue to the Christian virtue of faith.

Johnson never tires of expatiating on the paradoxical delusions of hope, which he calls 'the universal conspiracy of mankind against themselves'. As he goes on to say in *Adventurer* 69, 'so scanty is our present allowance of happiness, that in many situations life could scarcely be supported, if hope were not allowed to relieve the present hour by pleasures borrowed from futurity'. And yet the wise observer is always aware of the fraud: 'the day is always coming to the servile in which they shall be powerful, to the obscure in which they shall be eminent, and to the deformed in which they shall be beautiful.' For all their doctrinal differences, Johnson would have applauded both the substance and the tone of this self-critical utterance with which Gibbon concludes his *Autobiography*: 'In old age the consolation of hope is reserved for the tenderness of parents, who commence a new life in their children; the faith of enthusiasts, who sing hallelujahs above the clouds; and the vanity of authors who presume the immortality of their name and writings.' But everyone—not just authors—is afflicted with the capacity for hope. And it is the universality of this affliction in humanity that makes literature itself possible, for to Johnson the universal capacity for hope provides the basis for the very literary process itself. As he explains in the *Life of Butler*: 'The great source of [literary] pleasure is variety. Uniformity must tire at last, though it be uniformity of excellence. We love to expect; and, when expectation is disappointed or gratified, we want to be again expecting. For this impatience of the present, whoever would please [in literature] must make provision.' Johnson's theory of literary pleasure can be called humanistic because, like Reynolds's theory of artistic pleasure, it starts from an empirical examination of the nature of man, the creature distinguished by an 'impatience of the present' which stimulates his perpetual 'hunger of imagination'.

As a practising writer making his own way independently Johnson had abundant opportunities for experiencing himself the delusions of hope. It is a man learned in disappointment who begins his anonymous preface to Richard Rolt's *Dictionary of Trade and Commerce* this way: 'No expectation is more fallacious than that which authors form of the reception which their labours will find among mankind. Scarcely any man publishes a book, whatever it be, without believing that he has caught the moment when the publick attention is vacant to his call, and the world is disposed in a particular manner to learn the art which he undertakes to teach.' And we remember the 'manly' ending of Johnson's letter to Chesterfield: 'I have been long wakened from that Dream of hope, in which I once boasted myself with so much exultation, My lord Your Lordship's Most humble Most Obedient Servant, Sam: Johnson' (*LSJ*, i, 65). Similar in its fusion of pathos, pride, and wit is the final sentence of the Preface to the *Dictionary*: 'I have protracted my work till most of those whom I wished to please have sunk into the grave, and success and miscarriage are empty sounds: I therefore dismiss it with frigid tranquillity, having little to fear or hope from censure or from praise.'

It is not surprising that a man so skilled as Johnson in the experience of disappointment comes to conceive of disappointment itself as a central moral exercise, an ethical tonic like contemplating the downfall of greatness or the limitations of mankind. As Johnson perceives, one seldom experiences disappointment without experiencing illumination at the same time: thus disappointment can function—as it does in *Rasselas*—as a moral workout: it can gradually strengthen a man's command over life and stimulate the exercise of the will by liberating him from the total tyranny of external event. These ethical ends the forty-nine-year-old Johnson seems to have in mind as he writes his young friend Bennet Langton, a 'young enthusiast' newly arrived at Trinity College, Oxford:

> I know not any thing more pleasant or more instructive than to compare experience with expectation, or to register from time to time the difference between Idea and Reality. It is by this kind of observation that we grow daily less liable to be disappointed. You, who are very capable of anticipating futurity, and raising phantoms before your own eyes must often have imaged to yourself an academical life, and have conceived what would be the manners, the views, and the conversation of men devoted to letters, how they would chuse their companions, how they would direct their studies, and how they would regulate their lives. Let me know what you expected and what you have found. At least record it to yourself before custom has reconciled you to the scene before you, and the disparity of your discoveries to your hopes has vanished from your mind.
>
> *(LSJ,* i, 110)

Perhaps a full measure of Johnson's character can be found in his knowing nothing more *pleasant*, as he tells Langton, than this exercise. This kind of disappointment of hope by experience is a motif which makes sly appearances even when Johnson is focusing on something quite different; for example, in the *Journey to the Western Islands* he writes: 'There was perhaps never any change of national manners so quick, so great, and so general, as that which has operated in the Highlands, by the last conquest [1746], and the subsequent laws [e.g. those forbidding the wearing of tartans, &c.]. We came thither too late to see what we expected, a people of peculiar appearance, and a system of antiquated life.'

The frailty of man is one humanist theme which is often implicit in Johnson's observations on hope. Writing to Joseph Warton in 1754, Johnson observes of the insane William Collins:

E

'how little can we venture to exult in any intellectual powers or literary attainments, when we consider the condition of poor Collins. I knew him a few years ago full of hopes and full of projects, versed in many languages, high in fancy, and strong in retention. This busy and forcible mind is now under the government of those who lately would not have been able to comprehend the least and most narrow of its designs' (*LSJ*, i, 53).

And running like a sardonic *Leitmotif* through *The Lives of the Poets* is the theme of the self-swindle of humanity by its pathetic propensity to hope. Sometimes these collapses from felicity to reality skirt the openly comic. In the *Life of Ambrose Philips* Johnson writes: 'Having purchased an annuity of four hundred pounds, he now certainly hoped to pass some years of his life in plenty and tranquillity; but his hope deceived him; he was struck with a palsy, and died June 18, 1749, in his seventy-eighth year.' The irony is akin to that in Johnson's account of the death of Pope, which appears to be designed with distinct mock-heroic overtones: 'The death of great men is not always proportioned to the lustre of their lives. Hannibal, says Juvenal, did not perish by a javelin or a sword; the slaughters of Cannæ were revenged by a [poisoned] ring. The death of Pope was imputed by some of his friends to a silver saucepan, in which it was his delight to heat potted lampreys.' We find another little *exemplum* in the *Life of Thomson*, where we are told of the two years which Thomson expended in the composition of his poem *Liberty*; when it was finally finished in over 2,000 lines of blank verse, 'the author congratulated himself upon it as his noblest work', but he woke from his dream of hope to find the poem a ghastly failure, 'condemned to harbour spiders, and to gather dust'; indeed, 'none of Thomson's performances were so little regarded'. Poor Sir John Denham is another whose experience proves instructive. Just after the Restoration, Johnson tells us, 'It might be hoped that the favour of [Charles II] and esteem of the publick would now make him happy. But . . . a second marriage brought upon him so much disquiet, as for a time disordered his understanding; and Butler lampooned him for his lunacy.' Even members of the animal kingdom occasionally give the appearance of aping their betters: thus Johnson on the plight of the flying-fish, which 'is not only pursued by fishes in his natural element, but attacked in the air, where he hopes for security, by the don, or sparkite, a great bird that preys upon fish' (*Life of Drake*).

It is a sense of human unsatisfactoriness which seems to underlie all this humanist inquiry into the attributes of man. The human being is essentially a failure. Transcendence and ecstasy, fawn's flesh and the saint's vision, are not for him. He must operate as a social and public creature only because he is too frail and incomplete to exist by himself; he is material for tragedy because he is ultimately ignorant of his own character and its relation to his destiny; incapable of sensing the present, he either takes refuge in the past or mocks himself by entertaining delusive images of the future. It is all too clear that, as Johnson observes in the *Life of Collins*, 'man is not born for happiness'. And no individual is exempted or ever will be from the 'general doom', for human nature is uniform and unchanging, and Johnson speaks for the whole humanist tradition when he asserts, in *Adventurer* 84, that 'in life . . . there appears an even uniformity'.

3

THE UNIFORMITY OF
HUMAN NATURE

ONE condition essential to the coherence and vigour of the humanist ethical world is that human nature be conceived as both historically and empirically uniform. To the humanist it is fixed, stable, and objectively knowable; and it always has been. Naturally, it promises few surprises. Looking about him at a Lockean phantasmagoria of human movement and colour, the humanist does not reject the evidence of his senses and report that all men look or appear to act the same; but he does maintain that down underneath their infinitely varied surfaces—Johnson calls them 'disguises'—they are the same: variations and even the smaller eccentricities of the surface are to be expected, but they are not to be allowed to obscure the more important uniformity of the centre.

Any suggestion of 'evolution' is sufficient to dissolve the whole humanist world, for evolution or 'development'—whether accidental and relativistic or purposive and absolutist—would imply not only that the past had been superseded and rendered unreal but also that man can escape the fixed and revealed paradigm of his nature, a paradigm partly expressed, as we shall see, in the long existence and acceptance of the standard literary genres. In the same way, this moral world has little tolerance for suggestions of anthropological relativism derived from broad descriptive surveys of contemporary 'foreign practices', surveys which in the humanist view almost always mistake the peripheral for the central. Inquiring back into the whole of history as well as viewing his contemporary environment from China to Peru, the humanist concludes, as Johnson affirms in his *Letter on Du Halde's History of China*, that 'virtue is in every place the same'. This premise of the uniformity of human nature is indispensable to the Augustan humanist conception of man as well as to the humanist sense of literature and art.

One of the assumptions of Locke's *Essay* is that every human mind works the same way in receiving, storing, and recalling the materials that 'fill' it. Since minds work alike and since the natural limitations of man imply that human experience is not infinitely variable, it will follow that minds contain roughly the same materials. Thus when Blake, quarrelling with Reynolds, asserts in his marginalia that 'Every Eye sees differently', he is striking directly at the vulnerable heart of the orthodox ethical and aesthetic system. And his further observation, 'As the Eye, Such the object', calls seriously into question the humanist premise that reality is 'out there' in the world of sensuously verifiable phenomena rather than 'in here' in a subjective world apprehensible only by the unique person. Because to the humanist minds contain roughly the same materials, and always have, it is in the nature of art to present the same kinds of experiences over and over again, just as it is the nature of artists to imitate each other in their efforts to domesticate for each age the large, general, received patterns of artistic experience. But here again Blake, in objecting to this premise as Reynolds advances it in his *Sixth Discourse*, takes up a novel, heterodox position; he writes, 'How ridiculous it would be to see the Sheep Endeavouring to walk like the Dog, or the Ox striving to trot like the Horse; just as Ridiculous it is to see One Man Striving to Imitate Another'. And he concludes with an observation that the Augustan would find morally and aesthetically catastrophic: 'Man varies from Man more than Animal from Animal of different Species.' In this statement the humanist would find—as Blake intended that he should—a direct challenge to existing codes of law, schemes of public symbolism, received and traditional artistic genres, the practice of literary 'imitation' of successful works of the past, and indeed the validity of the whole objective world of General Nature sanctioned by the implications of Locke's *Essay*.

But in the age of Swift and Pope there was happily no William Blake around to impugn so vigorously the idea of the uniformity of human nature, and innovations in the theory of man could easily be regarded as whimsies begotten by vanity upon boredom. Massive mockery is Johnson's response to Lord Monboddo's proto-evolutionary theories of man, and this kind of mockery is a sacrosanct humanist tradition. The whole fundamental assumption of Swiftian and Popian satire is that man has a uniform, knowable general nature from which it is criminal to deviate. And because human nature is uniform, affectations of personal singularity are, if not criminal, at least funny. One reason why the Puritans receive Swift's satiric onslaught in *A Tale of a Tub* is their very singularity, which seems to ask the rest of mankind to regard them as a unique species. Puritan logic is satirized in the following passage, but so is mere Puritan singularity: 'In Winter [Jack] went always loose and unbuttoned, and clad as thin as possible, to let *in* the ambient Heat; and in Summer, lapt himself close and thick to keep it *out*.' Johnson confirms the point in *Adventurer* 131: 'Singularity is, I think, in its own nature universally and invariably displeasing.' The kind of vanity which prompts the Puritans to assume that they are special also generates the more common but no less reprehensible impulse towards professional jargon and local terminology, which is a standard target of humanist contempt from Swift's mockery of sailors' jargon in the *Mariner's Magazine* (in the first chapter of Gulliver's Second Voyage) to Johnson's reproval of Dryden's arch and knowing use in *Annus Mirabilis* of specialized nautical terms like *oakum*, *marling*, and *tarpawling*. Similarly, local and untranslatable jokes—a sort of 'false wit' of the kind rejected by Addison in *Spectator* 58—are pernicious ethically as well as aesthetically, for they tend to stimulate self-satisfaction and feelings of specialness and exclusivism. Hence Swift's ardent satire of them in the *Complete Collection of Genteel and Ingenious Conversation* as well as in the Preface to *A Tale of a Tub*, where the preposterous 'author' complacently tells us that 'Such a Jest there is, that will not pass out of *Covent-Garden*; and such a one, that is no where intelligible but at *Hide-Park* Corner'.

One argument dear to the Augustan humanists is that the general similarity of men's bodies and physiognomies bespeaks a like similarity of their minds: just as we see no men with three arms or two noses, and just as 'mutations' in man's general form seem unlikely, so, the argument goes, it is equally unlikely that one man's mind differs significantly from another's. Thus it is that a man's claims to special inspiration or to singular intellectual or spiritual capacity are probably fraudulent. Pope enlists this argument on behalf of the practice of literary 'imitation', that is, the redaction of existing classical works with variations to fit them to the altered circumstances of a different time and place. In the preface to the 1717 edition of his *Works*, answering the heterodox objection that the practice of literary imitation betrays a want of 'originality' in the redactor, Pope says: 'whatever is very good sense must have been common sense in all times; and what we call Learning, is but the knowledge of the sense of our predecessors. Therefore they who say our thoughts are not our own because they resemble the Ancients', may as well say our faces are not our own, because they are like our Fathers'.' Johnson picks up the argument and gives it a highly naturalistic shape in *Rambler* 151: 'as every mind, however vigorous or abstracted, is necessitated, in its present state of union, to receive its informations, and execute its purposes, by the intervention of the body, the uniformity of our corporeal nature communicates itself to our intellectual operations; and those whose abilities or knowledge incline them most to deviate from the general round of life, are recalled from eccentricity by the laws of their existence'.

The implications are clear: 'the laws of . . . existence', that is, the requirements of the body, are so uniform in men that real— as distinguished from affected—eccentricity is all but impossible. Applying these findings to literature in *Adventurer* 95, Johnson argues that because 'there are many occasions in which all reasonable men will think nearly alike', and because 'the interests and passions, the virtues and vices of mankind, have been diversified in different times, only by unessential and casual varieties', we must not be surprised or disappointed to find writers returning to the same themes almost as if they were constantly plagiarizing: 'We must expect', he says, 'in the works of all those who attempt to describe [the human passions], such a likeness as we find in the pictures of the same person drawn in different periods of his life.' Johnson's exploitation of the portraiture image here is notably humanistic: to the humanist, the highest genres of painting are history and portrait, largely because both focus on 'the human face divine'. What Johnson is saying is that the themes and techniques of literature are not infinite: they are limited by the general uniformity of human emotion. As he says of 'the passions': 'their influence is uniform, and their effects nearly the same in every human breast: a man loves and hates, desires and avoids, exactly like his neighbour; resentment and ambition, avarice and indolence, discover themselves by the same symptoms, in minds distant a thousand years from one another'. And supporting these ideas of a general thematic uniformity is always the root equation between body and mind: 'the anatomy of the mind,' Johnson affirms, 'as that of the body, must perpetually exhibit the same appearances. . . .' The argument from the uniformity of men's bodies also helps buttress Reynolds's objective theory of taste and art. In the *Seventh Discourse* he finds 'a general uniformity and agreement in the minds of men', and he goes on to give his empirical reasons: 'We have no reason to suspect there is a greater difference between our minds than between our forms; of which, though there are no two alike, yet there is a general similitude that goes through the whole race of mankind.' On the basis of this perception, Reynolds ultimately erects his whole theory of the objective reality of taste and the objective hierarchy of the genres in painting.

It is amazing likewise how much of Johnson's theory of ethics and literature seems to be prompted by this one central idea of the uniformity of human nature. We find it lurking just below the surface in the most unlikely places. Consider, for example, this Boswellian anecdote: 'Johnson, whose robust frame was not in the least affected by the cold, scolded me, as if my shivering had been a paltry effeminacy, saying, "Why do you shiver?" Sir William Scott . . . told me, that when he complained of a head-ach in the post-chaise, as they were travelling together to Scotland, Johnson treated him in the same manner: "At your age, Sir, I had no head-ach" ' (*BLJ*. i, 462).

The general Johnsonian disinclination to believe in interesting wonders seems also due to the assumption that, as *Idler* 80 informs us, 'The uniform necessities of human nature produce in a great measure uniformity of life. . .'. Hence we find Johnson telling Boswell: 'Never believe extraordinary characters which you hear of people. Depend upon it, Sir, they are exaggerated. You do not see one man shoot a great deal higher than another' (*BLJ*, ii, 450). Johnson is always sceptical of claims to singularity and uniqueness, as he is in his *Life of Sir Thomas Browne*, where he expresses annoyance at what he sees as Browne's affectation—especially in *Religio Medici*—of something unique in his life and experience. To Johnson, 'what most awakens curiosity [in this book] is his solemn assertion, that "his life has been a miracle of thirty years; which to relate were not history, but a piece of poetry, and would sound like a fable" '. Johnson confronts this rhapsody with the weapon of cool analysis: 'There is, undoubtedly, a sense in which all life is miraculous; as it is an union of powers of which we can imagine no connection, a succession of motions of which the first cause must be supernatural; but life, thus explained, whatever it may have of miracle, will have nothing of fable; and, therefore, the author undoubtedly had regard to something, by which he imagined himself distinguished from the rest of mankind.' But when we scrutinize Browne's life we find there nothing, except perhaps an excess of egotism, that can distinguish him from any other mortal:

> Of these wonders, however, the view that can be now taken of his life offers no appearance . . . surely a man may [like Browne] visit France and Italy, reside at Montpellier and Padua, and at last take his degree at Leyden, without any thing miraculous. What it was that would, if it was related, sound so poetical and fabulous, we are left to guess; I believe without hope of guessing rightly. The wonders probably were transacted in his own mind; self-love, co-operating with an imagination vigorous and fertile as that of Browne, will find or make objects of astonishment in every man's life.

And Johnson goes on to elevate his ethical findings about Browne into a general principle and to express the principle with a characteristically tactful blend of satire and pathos: 'perhaps there is no human being, however hid in the crowd from the observation of his fellow-mortals, who, if he has leisure and disposition to recollect his own thoughts and actions, will not conclude his life in some sort a miracle, and imagine himself distinguished from all the rest of his species by many discriminations of nature or of fortune.' What is pleasant in this remark is Johnson's seizing on what, in his time, was a standard motif of pure comedy and farce in the Goldsmith way and sensing in it the materials for a generalized pathos which is all but inexpressible. Ironically, then, Browne, who sets out to establish his own uniqueness, succeeds only in thoroughly exposing his pathetic similarity to the rest of his 'fellow-mortals'. Such are the embarrassments and pitfalls which always attend the impulse to escape from the general human paradigm. And the uniformity of human nature throughout history suggests that 'innovations' constitute merely another delusive exhibition of collective vanity. Six years before the storming of the Bastille, Johnson bursts out in this strikingly prophetic diatribe: 'He said to Sir William Scott, "The age is running mad after innovation; all the business of the world is to be done in a new way; men are to be hanged in a new way; Tyburn itself is not safe from the fury of innovation" ' (*BLJ*, iv, 188).

And even more importantly, the idea of the uniformity of human nature seems to be the assumption which prompts all of Johnson's literary theory and criticism. He seems to begin with this premise, which we find in *Idler* 51:

> such is the constitution of the world, that much of life must be spent in the same manner by the wise and the ignorant, the exalted and the low. Men, however distinguished by external accidents or intrinsick qualities, have all the same wants, the same pains, and, as far as the senses are consulted, the same pleasures. The petty cares and petty duties are the same in every station to every understanding, and every hour brings some occasion on which we all sink to the common level. We are all naked till we are dressed, and hungry till we are fed; and the general's triumph, and sage's disputation, end, like the humble labours of the smith or ploughman, in a dinner or in sleep.

It is as if Johnson has just risen from a highly sensitive and sympathetic re-reading of *King Lear*. This instinct for seizing on the broadest common denominator and probing for the real centre of life in those places where life is indisputably common to all— this is very Shakespearian and very Johnsonian, and preoccupations such as these generate Johnson's specific critical response to individual works. His assumption of the uniformity of human nature provides the very basis for his conception of the process of literary transmission from writer to reader, the process by which shapes of ideas and feelings are embodied in a literary construct, as we can see in his famous treatment of the Metaphysical poets in the *Life of Cowley*; the Metaphysicals in general, he says, 'were not successful in representing or moving the affections. As they were wholly employed on something unexpected and surprising, they had no regard for the uniformity of sentiment which enables us to conceive and to excite the pains and the pleasures of other minds.' Here we stand at a far remove from heterodox theories of art as 'self-expression': to Johnson, the way the artist 'feels' or says he feels is of very little consequence; the way he actually works is first to acquaint himself fully with the way other minds operate, and then to find —'invent' is the Latinate Augustan term for it—those 'objective correlatives' which, when presented to the general mind of the apprehender, will invite in him the predictable response which the work requires. The writer's most valuable stock-in-trade, thus, is not a deep fund of new ideas or a profound treasury of personal singularities; it is rather an objective awareness, to be obtained by long study and external observation, of 'that uniformity of sentiment' which all men manifest down underneath their adventitious outer disguises. If the artist is properly principled his task is not impossible, for, as Imlac says in Chapter XVI of *Rasselas*, 'Every man . . . may, by examining his own mind, guess what passes in the minds of others'. A large part of the writer's business is to discover which motifs, ideas, and images are so uniformly gratifying and interesting to general human nature that, given a tactful expression, they almost never fail; as Johnson says in *Adventurer* 108, 'of some images and sentiments the mind of man may be said to be enamoured; it meets them, however often they occur, with the same ardour which a lover feels at the sight of his mistress, and parts from them with the same regret when they can no longer be enjoyed'. Such are the 'images and sentiments' of Gray's *Elegy*, 'images which find a mirrour in every mind, and . . . sentiments to which every bosom returns an echo'. Actually the problem for the writer is a more subtle one than he might think: it is nothing less than to stand at a given moment in history and to mediate between past and future, to avoid the novel for the sake of the genuinely 'new'; in short, to eschew the 'fanciful inventions' which transmit nothing and, at the same time, to avoid outright cliché. Looking always first at 'the mind of man' rather than at literature, Johnson develops a set of literary responses which are for that reason eminently humanistic. No work of literature exists by itself, for only in being experienced by an imagination does it come into being. What the mind does in the face of the work determines its value, and the way the mind actually behaves—rather than the way it ought to behave—is often more important for criticism than merely technical merits or faults in the work itself. In his *Life of Dyer* Johnson goes about his appraisal of 'Grongar Hill' this way: ' "Grongar Hill" is the happiest of his productions: it is not indeed very accurately written; but the scenes which it displays are so pleasing, the images which they raise are so welcome to the mind, and the reflections of the writer so consonant to the general sense or experience of mankind, that when it is once read, it will be read again.'

Since literature addresses itself not to professionals and specialists but to general human nature, it follows that for it to attain its gratifying effects it must look to 'general [human] nature' for its topics and use technical means which accord with the general bent of the uniform human mind. Hence Johnson's key conception of 'general nature', which is perhaps most clearly set forth in the famous passage in the *Preface to Shakespeare*: pointing to Shakespeare's success in portraying general human types, a success proved by the long and universal acceptance of the plays in various ages and environments, Johnson writes in explanation: 'Nothing can please many, and please long, but just representations of general nature. Particular manners can be known to few, and therefore few only can judge how nearly they are copied. The irregular combinations of fanciful invention may delight awhile, by that novelty of which the common satiety of life sends us all in quest; but the pleasures of sudden wonder are soon exhausted, and the mind can only repose on the stability of truth.' The notable thing about this statement is perhaps less the theory of general nature itself, which is a standard humanist possession from Swift to Burke, than the absolutely assured way Johnson talks about the human mind and what its nature requires. The theory of general nature is implicit in *An Essay on Criticism* or *Peri Bathous* or *The Dunciad*, but what gives it distinction here is the profound certainty with which Johnson invokes his findings about the uniformity of human nature to bolster it.

Because, to Johnson, literary works are to be appraised not

by their technical efficiency but rather by their affective appeal, their historical endurance is the only ultimate test of their comparative excellence. The excellence of works of literature, he argues in the *Preface to Shakespeare*, is not 'absolute and definite, but gradual and comparative'. Since that part of the human mind which is gratified by literary motifs and images is unchanging through history, no matter how greatly the extrinsic emotional and intellectual fashions may alter, Johnson's criterion of endurance is humanistically sound: to Johnson it is less a matter of regret than of satisfaction that 'to works not raised upon principles demonstrative and scientifick, but appealing wholly to observation and experience, no other test can be applied than length of duration and continuance of esteem'. This is the criterion that does the most honour to the human mind.

Because the writer performs less for his contemporary audience than for posterity, or rather because he addresses that central element in the contemporary reader which will be the same in future readers, he will do well to avoid the local particulars that will require explanation or annotation in times to come. According to the Johnsonian conception of literature, indeed, explanatory footnotes always imply some degree of disgrace. It is this feeling for the importance of the idea of sheer human continuity that prompts Johnson, in writing *Rasselas*, to eschew local details of the kind which might require future annotation, and it is remarkable that, as a result of Johnson's success in avoiding them, *Rasselas* today requires less explanatory annotation than any other eighteenth-century work of comparable length. We see Johnson's humanistic theory of literature in action when we find him filling the Happy Valley with 'verdure and fertility' rather than with larches or pachysandra, and when we find Imlac procuring 'instruments proper to hew stone and remove earth' rather than mattocks or adzes. We have seen the disgrace which Dryden incurs from his use of nautical jargon in *Annus Mirabilis*, and a similar disgrace awaits all poets who forget that, as Johnson says in *Rambler* 36, 'Poetry has to do rather with the passions of men, which are uniform, than their customs, which are changeable'. The great Johnsonian critical principle of 'the grandeur of generality' involves at bottom a prodigious humanistic faith in the dignity and permanence of the central element in human nature. It is less a critical observation than a moral and philosophic article of belief.

It has undoubtedly distressed some of Johnson's modern admirers that, as he told Boswell, 'what I love most' is 'the biographical part of literature' (*BLJ*, i, 425). It has seemed to suggest a disappointing flatness of mind in Johnson that he admits to preferring biography to, say, some elevated sort of fiction like tragedy or epic. But this preference also seems related to his devotion to the idea of the uniformity of human nature. That kind of instant and deep emotional identification with central humanity which Johnson is always hoping to experience as a reader he finds most readily offered in biography; as he explains in *Rambler* 60, a defence of the dignity of biography, 'there is such an uniformity in the state of man, considered apart from adventitious and separable decorations and disguises, that there is scarce any possibility of good or ill, but is common to human kind'. The depth of Johnson's identifications with persons or characters whose experience seems to take place at the very centre of 'the state of man' can be measured by his astonishing reactions to *King Lear* and to *Othello*. In his 'General Observations' on the plays, he confesses that 'I was many years ago so shocked by *Cordelia*'s death, that I know not whether I ever endured to read again the last scenes of the play till I undertook to revise them as an editor'. An even more interesting response is suggested in his comment on *Othello*, V, ii, the scene in which Desdemona is smothered: 'I am glad', writes Johnson for all to read, 'that I have ended my revisal of this dreadful scene. It is not to be endured.' Far from having too little passion to make an entirely trustworthy critic, Johnson had too much. Only occasionally, perhaps, does his fundamental critical principle of attending to the uniform requirements of the human imagination betray him into a practical critical error, as it does when he assures Boswell that 'Nothing odd will do long. *Tristram Shandy* did not last' (*BLJ*, ii, 449).

Johnson's ultimate criteria for valuing Shakespeare, 'length of duration and continuance of esteem', criteria which depend on the assumption of the uniformity of human nature, are reflected in Reynolds's *Second Discourse* in a passage which can be taken as yet another eighteenth-century reverberation of the seventeenth-century Battle of the Ancients and the Moderns. Implicit in Reynolds's genuflection towards Italian Renaissance painting is the central humanist presupposition of the uniformity of human nature: 'The works of those [painters] who have stood the test of ages, have a claim to that respect and veneration to which no modern can pretend. The duration and stability of their fame, is sufficient to evince that it has not been suspended upon the slender thread of fashion and caprice, but bound to the human heart by every tie of sympathetick approbation.' When we hear Reynolds using such phrases as 'bound to the human heart by every tie of sympathetick approbation', we are carried instantly towards the politics of Burke, and we are reminded again that the *Discourses*, including the *Ironical Discourse*, constitute a mere application to painting of the same principles which, whether expressed in such terms as Johnson's 'general nature' or Burke's 'permanent sense of mankind', inform the whole body of Augustan humanist responses. It would be hard to distinguish between Burke and the Reynolds who says in his preface to the *Ironical Discourse*, where he comments on the folly of assuming that the multitude, as the French Revolution implies, is now, after all these years, suddenly capable of political judgment: 'It is now as it ever has been.' Or the Reynolds who points out in his essay 'On Prejudice' that prejudices are often the very avenues to the heart of the permanent human experience: 'In forming the understanding and judgment to acquire the character of what is called a right-headed man, perhaps no part of our conduct is more necessary to be watched and attended than our prejudices, the difficulty lying in distinguishing between those which are to be eradicated and those which ought to be received with respect and reverence.'

It is the French Revolutionists' rejection of all their 'prejudices', in the humanist sense of the term, that has caused the trouble and brought the humanist ethical world into grave jeopardy. And the fundamental, original crime of the Revolutionists is their questioning the premise of the historical uniformity of human nature. Says Burke in the *Reflections*: 'Those whose principle it is to despise the antient permanent sense of mankind, and to set up a scheme of society on new principles, must naturally expect that such of us who think better of the judgment of the human race than of theirs, should consider both them and their devices, as men and schemes upon their trial.' Burke's large consistency throughout his long career, regardless of whether he is defending against a mechanical tyranny Irish Catholics, Bengalese peasants, or French aristocrats, is suggested by his comment made twenty-five years earlier in his *Tract on the Popery Laws*: 'if our reasons or practices differ from the general informed sense of mankind, it is very moderate to say that they are at least suspicious.' Just as the historical uniformity of human nature is assumed in Swift's satire of the innovating projectors of the Grand Academy of Lagado, so it lies at the base of Burke's assault on the innovating National Assembly. Both assemblages are quite mad with pride and with a perverse desire to distinguish themselves, like Johnson's version of Sir Thomas Browne, from their species. In trying to refine their humanity through novel means, they succeed only in abandoning it.

The humanist satisfaction with the idea of fixed artistic genres is quite consistent with the presupposition of the uniformity of human nature, and as we shall soon see it seems equally consistent with the conception of the depravity of man. The humanist persuaded of the uniformity of human nature reasons on this matter as follows: each unchanging element or capacity of the general human mind naturally has a literary form which 'accords' with its expectations, and, since human nature is historically uniform and since thus the same few basic human actions are played out *ad infinitum*, the genres devised and practised by the ancients should serve for eternity. The part of the mind that relishes gentle melancholy is gratified by elegy; the part that responds to enthusiasm or devotion is gratified by ode; the part that craves ideas of justice is gratified by tragedy or satire or comedy; the part that responds to images of dissipation and irresponsibility is gratified by the song. If the theory were to become rigid and dogmatic, which it does not, it would all be a trifle like the mid-nineteenth-century phrenological chatter about 'amativeness' and 'adhesiveness'. But although the humanist version of this theory of genre is generally flexible, it does carry the implication that, since the ancients were exquisitely aware of the nature of man, the genres they devised to address his central capacities are to be tampered with only at great risk. Thus even Johnson, certainly no rigid genre-monger, goes about his work of justifying Shakespeare's 'mingled drama' —that is, 'tragicomedy'—with a deep theoretical seriousness, conscious of the necessity of arguing the matter carefully and on wholly empirical grounds. Pope is apparently less doubtful of his premises. One of his repeated complaints about Grub-Street is that it is the place where the genres get mixed and confused, the sort of pernicious innovation that cries aloud for satire: as the Goddess of Dulness in *The Dunciad* looks down into Grub Street she beholds the most appalling things—puns, 'motley images', 'Figures ill paired', and other shocking modes of false wit; but perhaps even worse is the miscegenation of the genres which goes on there. She sees

> How Tragedy and Comedy embrace;
> How Farce and Epic get a jumbled race.
>
> (i, 69–70)

In the same way, Pope's gibes at opera in the fourth book of *The Dunciad* are prompted in part by an assumption that an unprecedented mingling of the genres constitutes a dangerous departure from the consecrated constructs of the traditional human imagination. It might even suggest innovations in the theory of man.

One thing that makes Johnson's encounters with Boswell and other wavering humanists so perpetually interesting is that in their disagreements and misunderstandings these indefatigable parlour disputants often play out the larger ethical and aesthetic dialectics of their time. In his instinct for the reality and the force of genre, Johnson's focus is back towards the Renaissance; but Boswell, with his apparent sense that it all doesn't matter very much and with his gay misunderstandings of the requirements of the traditional genres, is like an anticipatory representative of the new world of 'prose poems', 'reveries', 'tales', and 'short stories'. One such misunderstanding speaks volumes, for it seems to suggest how a representative common reader no longer possessed the instinct for considering the satiric as a rhetorical occasion. During the Hebridean tour, as Boswell reports, Johnson 'repeated Pope's four lines in which "Macedonia's madman" comes in, and the conclusion is "farther than his nose". I objected to the last phrase being low. MR. JOHNSON.

F

" 'Tis intended, 'tis satire. The expression is debased to debase the character" ' (*JTH*, 58). Johnson has an instant awareness of those parts of a work which belong to the genre rather than to the individual author, but Boswell—and sometimes his friends as well—is constantly getting mixed up with ideas of 'sincerity' and 'naturalness'. A similar occasion on the tour is Johnson's having to instruct Capt. Lauchlan McLean, who is clearly not an 'ancient', in the necessary or 'known' style of dedication as a genre: 'the known style of a dedication', says Johnson, 'is flattery. It professes to flatter. There is the same difference between what a man says in a dedication and a history, as between a lawyer pleading a cause and reporting it' (*JTH*, 254). We shall soon examine Johnson's sensitivity to the large element of disingenuousness in letter-writing, and we see that he exhibits a similar sophistication about genre when he considers the nature of the memoir as a literary kind. Writing a review of *The Account of the Conduct of the Duchess of Marlborough*, he pauses to consider the rhetorical motive of memoirs and finds that 'the parent of all Memoirs, is the ambition of being distinguished from the herd of mankind, and the fear of either infamy or oblivion'. Urged by such motives, the memoirist will naturally tend to misrepresent actuality and to produce a work which by its very nature is allied to fiction. It would be hard to find before Northrop Frye a critic more sensitive to rhetorical occasion and to the significance of the genres than Johnson.

'Poets do not always express their own thoughts', says Johnson in the *Life of Pope*. This principle he illustrates delightfully in the *Life of Thomson*: 'Savage, who lived much with Thomson, once told me, he heard a lady remarking that she could gather from his works three parts of his character, that he was "a great Lover, a great Swimmer, and rigorously abstinent;" but, said Savage, he knows not any love but that of the sex; he was perhaps never in cold water in his life; and he indulges himself in all the luxury that comes within his reach.'

Such is the power of the genres to say what they rather than their practitioners want to express. To Johnson the feeling for the force of genre is so powerful that he is aware of the amount of convention involved even in occasions which would seem to bear little relation to literature or art. For example, Boswell indicates that Johnson was unusually sensitive to the element of conventionality in 'death-bed scenes': 'he said', Boswell reports, 'that he believed hardly any man died without affectation' (*JTH*, 387). So much for the vulgar belief that willy-nilly a man's dying words reveal his 'ruling passion'.

Thus the artificialities of art, and especially the long existence of the traditional genres, suggest that men are always alike, and perhaps they are nowhere more alike than in their weakness and in their natural depraved leanings towards what is unworthy of their nature. In the humanists' perpetual return to the *all* of humanity we seem to catch an echo of the lament of the un-paradised, humanized Adam of *Paradise Lost*:

> . . . from mee what can proceed,
> But all corrupt, both Mind and Will deprav'd,
> Not to do only, but to will the same
> With me.

(x, 824–7)

Regardless of the cause, man is somehow deeply depraved, and from the premise of his depravity the humanist deduces both a principle of ethics and a theory of literary composition.

4

THE DEPRAVITY OF MAN

NOTHING is more obviously axiomatic to Johnson than that 'the majority are wicked'. Indeed, as he goes on to assert in *Rambler* 175, 'The depravity of mankind is so easily discoverable, that nothing but the desert or the cell can exclude it from notice'. Much of the Augustan humanist enterprise is enlisted in contemplating and articulating this fundamental depravity of man. The notion motivates Swift's contempt for his allegorical spider just as it does Burke's outrage at the deluded exponents of 'The Rights of Man'. It would seem natural for Swift, as a Christian divine of conservative instincts, to imitate in his own lifetime a multitude of medieval and Renaissance Christians who had found man all but hopelessly depraved. As Louis Landa has said, 'Swift probably would have thought an optimistic divine a contradiction in terms'.[1] Hence the general humanistic indignation at such spectacles as the Reverend Laurence Sterne or Dr. Richard Price. Landa illustrates his point by citing the beginning of Swift's sermon 'On the Poor Man's Contentment':

The holy Scripture is full of Expressions to set forth the miserable Condition of Man during the whole Progress of his Life; his Weakness, Pride, and Vanity; his unmeasurable Desires, and perpetual Disappointments; the Prevalency of his Passions, and the Corruptions of his Reason; his deluding Hopes, and his real, as well as imaginary Fears; his natural and artificial Wants; his Cares and Anxieties; the Diseases of his Body, and the Diseases of his Mind; the Shortness of his Life; his Dread of a future State, and his Carelessness to prepare for it: And the wise Men of all Ages have made the same Reflections. . . . all these are general Calamities, from which none are excepted.

[1] *Gulliver's Travels and Other Writings* (Boston, 1960), p. xxi.

Given all this evidence of a profound flaw in man as a natural creature, we can see that the etymology of *Houyhnhnm* as 'the Perfection of Nature' involves a very Christian kind of irony, since to a Christian the natural, participating as it does in the general post-lapsarian curse, can never be entirely perfected, at least while it remains accessible for empirical scrutiny. Perfection would imply the uselessness of moral action as a technique of redemption. No stage of life, neither youth nor age, is exempt from the curse of natural depravity. A Brobdingnagian boy, far removed from the humanizing influence of society which has helped redeem a child like Glumdalclitch, 'naturally' hurls a hazel nut at Gulliver's frail and tiny head; and the longevity of the Struldbrugs simply augments their natural vices: after the age of eighty, they turn 'opinionative, peevish, covetous, morose, vain, and talkative', just like the senile 'suppliant' in *The Vanity of Human Wishes*, who

> Hides from himself his state, and shuns to know
> That life protracted is protracted woe.
>
> (257–8)

The humanistic obligation is to expose the full depths of human depravity, either by homily, satire, or history. Devastating and entirely in the tradition is Swift's irony in the 'Digression on Madness' of *A Tale of a Tub*; assuming something like the role of the benign, anti-satiric Cowper of *The Task*, he 'reasons': 'whatever Philosopher or Projector can find out an Art to sodder and patch up the Flaws and Imperfections of Nature, will deserve much better of Mankind, and teach us a more useful Science, than that so much in Present Esteem, of widening and exposing them . . .'. One thinks of the fatuous sundial uttering 'I count only the sunny hours' in the midst of its perpetually decaying garden. It is impossible here to keep Pound's *Mauberley* from making its comment:

> His true Penelope was Flaubert,
> He fished by obstinate isles;
> Observed the elegance of Circe's hair
> Rather than the mottoes on sun-dials.
>
> (13–16)

By 1775, conservative society had grown so accustomed to neo-Augustinian social talk about the depravity of human nature that even Johnson on occasion hungered for fresher topics. In July of this year Mrs. Thrale attended a very elegant regatta, and Johnson playfully advised her to exploit the experience fully for conversational purposes: 'It is the good of publick life that it supplies agreeable topicks and general conversation. Therefore wherever you are, and whatever you see, talk not of the Punick war [a topic of which Johnson had become thoroughly sick]; nor of the depravity of human nature; nor of the slender motives of human actions; nor of the difficulty of finding employment or pleasure; but talk, and talk, and talk of the regatta . . . ' (*LSJ*, ii, 257). But even though Johnson tired of the topic in social conversation, he seems to have found plenty of room for it in his writings. The *Rambler* essays abound in references to 'the present corruption of mankind' (96), and in the *Adventurer* we are invited to contemplate 'human nature in its present degeneracy and frailty' (111). It is in the degenerate nature of man to lust for sway and to delight in the exercise of tyranny. Thus, offering domestic advice, Johnson suggests to Mrs. Thrale in 1779: 'keep every child, as far as is possible, out of a Nurse's power. A Nurse made of common mould will have a pride in overcoming a child's reluctance. There are few minds to which tyranny is not delightful; Power is nothing but as it is felt, and the delight of superiority is proportionate to the resistance overcome' (*LSJ*, ii, 310).

And he gives Hester Thrale this counsel in 1783: 'strongly entwisted with human nature is the desire of exercising power, however that power be gained or given. Let us pity it in others, and despise it in ourselves' (*LSJ*, iii, 63). Human nature is likewise naturally envious, always secretly appalled and embittered by the good fortune of others. This is why, to Johnson, 'The reciprocal civility of authors is one of the most risible scenes in the farce of life' (*Life of Sir Thomas Browne*). Johnson's awareness of the natural quantum of envy in the human creature also informs his preference, in pedagogy, for corporal punishment instead of the encouragement of emulation. As he tells Langton, 'I would rather . . . have the rod to be the general terrour to all, to make them learn, than tell a child, if you do thus, or thus, you will be more esteemed than your brothers or sisters. The rod produces an effect which terminates in itself. A child is afraid of being whipped, and gets his task, and there's an end on't; whereas, by exciting emulation and comparisons of superiority, you lay the foundation of lasting mischief; you make brothers and sisters hate each other' (*BLJ*, i, 46).

Johnson often rebuked Mrs. Thrale for praising people excessively. Although here his devotion to 'strict veracity' is indeed urging him, he is equally motivated by his consciousness of the dangers to society which reside in the exercise of natural human envy. On one occasion he tells Mrs. Thrale, 'I know nobody who blasts by praise as you do: for whenever there is exaggerated praise, every body is set against a character. They are provoked to attack it' (*BLJ*, iv, 81–82). And as Mrs. Thrale herself attests: 'I do not know for certain what will please Dr. Johnson: but I know for certain that it will displease him to praise any thing, even what he likes, extravagantly' (*BLJ*, iii, 225).

Reynolds is another who seems drawn instinctively to the premise of the depravity of human nature. His whole aesthetic, with its preference for the 'higher' genres in painting, assumes that man is in desperate need of the kind of redemption which is offered in art only by images approaching the heroic. In its natural state the mind is so depraved that it requires all possible institutions to 'soften' and 'humanize' it. Reynolds would agree with Burke that no traditional institution should be jettisoned so long as it retains the slightest capacity for 'raising' man from his naturally depraved state. As he says while praising George III in his *First Discourse*, the members of the Royal Academy 'are patronized by a Monarch, who, knowing the value of science and of elegance, thinks every Art worthy of his notice, that tends to soften and humanise the mind'.

But it is Gibbon who, in the depth of his awareness of the depravity of man, most nearly resembles Swift and Johnson. It is true that, in composing the fifteenth chapter of *The History of the Decline and Fall of the Roman Empire*, Gibbon is motivated by such a very complex satiric design that a given strand is not easily unravelled for inspection; but it is clear at least that his satiric scepticism over the reported achievements of the Roman Christians is the fruit of a commitment to an idea of human depravity which is perhaps less Augustan than Augustinian in its dimensions. He opens his chapter on a note of an almost gay irony which fails wholly to mask his underlying assumptions, which are genuinely dark: 'The theologian may indulge the pleasing task of describing Religion as she descended from heaven arrayed in her native purity. A more melancholy duty is imposed on the historian. He must discover the inevitable mixture of error and corruption which she contracted in a long residence upon earth, among a weak and degenerate race of beings.' And in his sensitivity to 'pride' and the passion for domination as the profoundest springs of the human soul he is also at one with Swift and Johnson. As he observes of the self-satisfaction of the early Christians, 'Every privilege that could raise the proselyte from earth to heaven—that could exalt his devotion, secure his happiness, or even gratify that secret pride, which, under the semblance of devotion, insinuates itself into the human heart—was still reserved for members of the Christian Church.'

Like the self-righteous sectaries in Swift's *The Day of Judgement* or the corrupted Belinda of *The Rape of the Lock*, Gibbon's early Christians are naturally smitten by pride and perverted from their quixotic aim by the all but ineradicable depravity of their secret selves. And if the humble Roman believer was victimized by self-satisfaction, the administrators of the Church were equally at the mercy of their corrupt natures. As Gibbon points out, so instinctive in man is the love of power that '(under the most artful disguises) [it] could insinuate itself into the breasts of bishops and martyrs . . .'. And of Cyprian we are told that he 'had renounced those temporal honours which it is probable he would never have obtained; but the acquisition of such absolute command over the consciences and understanding of a congregation, however obscure or despised by the world, is more truly grateful to the pride of the human heart than the possession of the most despotic power imposed by arms and conquest on a reluctant people'. Here Gibbon is very close to the Johnson who repudiates Soame Jenyns's notion that it is really well for the poor to have little access to education. Looking into his own heart and finding there something quite different from what Sidney expected to find in his, Johnson writes: 'I am always afraid of determining on the side of envy or cruelty. The privileges of education may sometimes be improperly bestowed, but I shall always fear to withhold them, lest I should be yielding to the suggestions of pride, while I persuade myself that I am following the maxims of policy; and under the appearance of salutary restraints, should be indulging the lust of dominion, and that malevolence which delights in seeing others depressed.' 'That malevolence' clearly implies 'that *natural* malevolence', that sadism, indigenous to the human heart, which constitutes a target for major humanist satire all the way from Swift's exposure of the pseudo-mourners in *Verses on the Death of Dr. Swift* to Burke's indignant ridicule of the self-congratulatory regicides of the Revolution.

From this conviction of the depravity of man issues the humanist ethic of restraint, control, and redemption. We have already encountered Johnson's assertion that 'Man's chief merit consists in resisting the impulses of his nature', and we find that his ethical pronouncements seldom depart very far from the assumption that the enemy to be struggled with is deep inside. The dynamics of this struggle Johnson outlines this way: 'We are all envious naturally; but by checking envy, we get the better of it. So we are all thieves naturally; a child always tries to get at what it wants, the nearest way; by good instruction and good habits this is cured, till a man has not even an inclination to seize what is another's; has no struggle with himself about it' (*BLJ*, iii, 271). If left to their own unimproved choices, says Johnson, 'All men will naturally commit fornication, as all men will naturally steal' (*BLJ*, iii, 18). Nor is pity natural to man, for 'Children are always cruel. Savages are always cruel. Pity is acquired and improved by the cultivation of reason' (*BLJ*, i, 437). And anyone may make discoveries like these by purely empirical means. Of Lord Kames's *Sketches of the History of Man* (1774) Johnson observes: 'in this book it is maintained that virtue is natural to man, and that if we would but consult our own hearts we should be virtuous. Now after consulting our own hearts all we can, and with all the helps we have, we find how few of us are virtuous. This is saying a thing which all mankind know not to be true' (*BLJ*, iii, 352).

The vapourings of Shaftesbury and his disciples about 'the moral sense' are thus mere 'romantick fictions', plausible and popular only because they pander to human vanity. Actually, as Johnson notes, 'We are commonly taught our duty by fear or shame, and how can they act upon the man who hears nothing but his own praise?' (*Life of Swift*). So gross indeed is the depravity of man that—as Burke would have it—only a polity assuming mutual checks between numerous depraved estates can guarantee the common safety against the common enemy, man's 'lust of dominion'. And given the degenerate condition of man, scepticism and caution must be the humanist's attitude towards man's apparently disinterested 'projects'. Writing to his friend William Johnson in Connecticut, Johnson comments thus on a proposal for exploring by ship the passages to the North Pole: 'I do not much wish well to discoveries, for I am always afraid they will end in conquest and robbery' (*LSJ*, i, 308). We are reminded of the anti-colonialist Johnson who stunned 'some very grave men at Oxford', as Boswell reports, by proposing the toast, 'Here's to the next insurrection of the negroes in the West Indies' (*BLJ*, iii, 200).

Once we perceive the vigour with which the Augustan humanists commit themselves to the orthodox notion of the depravity of man, we can measure its force in generating the humanist theory of literature, which can be described as em-bracing the following ideas: (1) the idea of the authority of the literary past; (2) the idea of fixed and permanent literary genres useful in part as a curb on the flux of invention; (3) the idea of the objectivity and impersonality of the literary topic; (4) the idea of painstaking rhetorical attention exercised by the artist largely in the process of revision; and (5) the idea that the function of literature is to instruct through the medium of pleasure. Every one of these critical notions assumes a profound self-distrust of the kind which grows out of a prior conviction of the universal depravity of man. That the ideas comprising the humanist theory of literature accord with 'classical' criticism and practice appears perhaps less interesting for our purposes than that they seem to emanate equally from medieval and Renaissance Christian doctrine. In this sense the literature of the eighteenth-century humanist tradition is almost as accu-rately described by calling it 'Christian'—or perhaps even Augustinian—as it is by calling it 'neo-classical'. Indeed, the pre-eminence of great works like *A Tale of a Tub* or *The Dunciad* or *The Life of Johnson*, which would seem to have no classical precedents, may invite us to refine our descriptive terminology and to break away once and for all from such misleading terms as 'neo-classical'.

Self-distrust is one of the conspicuous themes of humanistic criticism of the seventeenth century as well as the eighteenth. Even so self-assured an artist as Milton feels obliged to go through the motions of calling upon his heavenly muse to visit him nightly. When we look back to Ben Jonson we see even more clearly the dependence of humanist literary theory upon the ethics of self-distrust. Jonson's *Timber, or Discoveries* (1641) gives us the essential formulas and provides as well a revealing contrast to such a Shaftesburian, heterodox critical document as the apostate-humanist Edward Young's *Conjectures on Original Composition* (1759). Jonson finds that Shakespeare's only severe fault, his occasionally wayward copiousness, stems from an excessive trust in the integrity of his own conceptions: 'Hee was (indeed) honest, and of an open, and free nature: had an excellent *Phantsie*; brave notions, and gentle expressions; wherein hee flow'd with that facility, that sometime it was necessary he should be stop'd: . . . His wit was in his owne power; would the rule of it had been so too.' But in this fault Shakespeare reflects an all but universal human failing: so vain is man, so fond of his conceptions—most of which in their state of nature are initially deformed and incoherent as a result of their depraved source—that it is morally incumbent upon everyone— and even more upon the writer—to redress and reform that which presents itself to him from his 'Phantsie'. Because of our vanity, 'all that wee invent doth please us in the conception, or birth; else we should never set it downe'. But once we have written it down, we must 'judge of what wee invent; and order what wee approve'. In short, 'Ready writing makes not good writing'. Here we are expatiating in an entirely different moral world from that which appears to sanction theories of unpremeditated art or 'the spontaneous overflow of powerful feelings'. And we experience something akin to moral shock when we turn from Jonson to Young, who takes pains to add the 'modern' injunction 'Reverence thyself' to the orthodox 'Know thyself'. As Young puts it, 'thyself so reverence, as to prefer the native growth of thy own mind to the richest import from abroad'. The spider in *The Battle of the Books* could hardly have expressed it better. And the bee's answer to the spider suggests the degree to which the humanist theory of literature depends on the assumption of the depravity of human nature:

'You boast, indeed, of being obliged to no other Creature, but of drawing, and spinning out all from your self; That is to say, if we may judge of the Liquor in the Vessel by what issues out, You possess a good plentiful Store of Dirt and Poison in your Breast.' A subjective literary aesthetic of the kind which Young urges thus constitutes a direct moral challenge to the orthodox theory of literature; it could be justified, to the humanist, only if man were not originally depraved.

Seventy years after Swift's dramatization of this ethical and artistic crisis through his allegory of the spider and the bee, Reynolds re-enacts in his *Sixth Discourse* the bee's self-distrustful gesture of gathering his artistic materials from the world of permanent universals outside himself. It is for the same work of objective selection rather than subjective 'expression' that Reynolds's ideal artist-critic turns away from his own local singularities towards history and the external world: 'Like a sovereign judge and arbiter of art, he is possessed of that pre-siding power which separates and attracts every excellence from every school; selects both from what is great, and what is little; brings home knowledge from the East and from the West; making the universe tributary towards furnishing his mind and enriching his works with originality, and variety of inventions.' It is notable that it is this paragraph which elicited from Burke, according to James Northcote, the excited comment: 'This is, indeed, excellent, nobody can mend it, no man could say it better.'[2]

The critical theory of Alexander Pope appears to be based squarely on the prior ethical assumption that man is morally obliged to distrust himself while acting in the role of maker. Although we catch a hint of the ethical dimension of Pope's criticism in the well-known lines from the *Essay on Criticism*,

> Be sure *your self* and your own *Reach* to know,
> How far your *Genius*, *Taste*, and *Learning* go;
> Launch not beyond your Depth, but be discreet,
> And mark *that Point* where Sense and Dulness *meet*,

(48–51)

we are conducted to the very moral centre of his critical theory in this delightful passage in the preface to the 1717 edition of his

---

[2] *The Life of Sir Joshua Reynolds* (2nd ed.: London, 1818, 2 vols.), ii, 315–16.

Works: 'I believe no one qualification is so likely to make a good writer, as the power of rejecting his own thoughts; and it must be this (if any thing) that can give me a chance to be one. For what I have publish'd, I can only hope to be pardon'd; but for what I have burn'd, I deserve to be prais'd.' There is great vanity here, to be sure, as there is in most of Pope's public utterances, no matter how 'humble' in dramatic design. But underneath the posturing and the wit we discover a formal ethical theory which all Pope's elegant attitudinizing cannot wholly obscure. What he implies here is a self-contained theory of the ethics of style, a theory in which revision becomes an ethical imperative as well as a mere aesthetic opportunity. And Pope's theory of literary apprehension, like his theory of literary composition, seems to depend as strongly upon the ethics of self-distrust. The whole of *Peri Bathous* assumes man's depraved, natural instinct for the literary high-flown, the bathetic, and the fraudulent. There is of course irony and thus comedy in Pope's formulation, but there is a deep residue of moral—and almost theological—seriousness too: 'The Taste of the Bathos is implanted by Nature itself in the soul of man; till perverted by custom or example, he is taught, or rather compelled, to relish the Sublime. Accordingly, we see the unprejudiced minds of Children delight only in such productions, and in such images, as our true modern writers [i.e. practitioners of the bathetic] set before them.'

It is worth observing that Pope's use of the term 'unprejudiced' in a pejorative sense anticipates Burke's later rehabilitation of the word 'prejudice' to connote something very like 'moral institutions': thus to Burke the established church is a 'prejudice', and so is the British constitution. Perhaps it will not be pushing resemblance too far to find in Pope's critical burlesque something like Burke's *Reflections* writ small. At any rate, when we juxtapose two works like *Peri Bathous* and *Reflections on the Revolution in France*, we appreciate the difficulty of distinguishing 'serious' from 'comic' work among the Augustan humanists: so much of their point seems to call for ironic expression that the comic is always just revealing its dark underside, while the serious is always threatening to burst through into the world of the funny. *The Dunciad* can be taken as an example of the work dubiously comic; certain of the most moral of the *Lives of the Poets*—the *Life of Ambrose Philips* is a good example—illustrate the way irony is constantly undermining the serious.

Like Pope's, Johnson's system of critical responses is largely supported by the premise of human depravity. Literature must instruct because its readers stand in such desperate need of instruction. If we dig deeply enough we find the premise of human depravity in Johnson's suspicion of excessively 'realistic' novels which may confuse the weak reader by 'mingling' vice and virtue (*Rambler* 4); and we find it likewise in his disappointment at having to report, in the *Preface to Shakespeare*, that his author sometimes 'seems to write without any moral purpose'. Sir Richard Blackmore's failure to distrust sufficiently his frail nature arouses Johnson's open indignation. In Blackmore's medical treatises, Johnson says, 'I have observed an affected contempt of the Ancients, and a supercilious derision of transmitted knowledge'; and he goes on to criticize Blackmore's method as a manifestation of 'indecent arrogance' (*Life of Blackmore*). Blackmore's fault, moral as well as intellectual, is a perverse and quite misplaced trust in himself which moves him to abdicate from both history and objective examples. The result is a poetry and a reputation which have been mocked by time.

Johnson's acute sensitivity to genre, his instinct for sensing the conventional obligations laid upon a writer by his selection of a given literary form, also seems related to his assumption of the depravity of human nature. Here our text is a brilliant passage from the *Life of Pope*, a passage which constitutes a *locus classicus* of the humanistic. Johnson has arrived at that point in the *Life* where it is appropriate for him to appraise Pope's moral character. He begins by focusing on Pope's letters and by admitting that we find in them evidence of 'nothing but liberality, gratitude, constancy, and tenderness'. He then examines a popular sentimental cliché: 'It has been so long said as to be commonly believed that the true characters of men may be found in their letters, and that he who writes to his friend lays his heart open before him.' Next, drawing implicit support from his conviction of the depravity of human nature, he proceeds to shatter this naïve cliché: 'But the truth is that such were the simple friendships of the *Golden Age*, and are now the friendships only of children. Very few can boast of hearts which they dare lay open to themselves, and of which, by whatever accident exposed, they do not shun a distinct and continued view; and certainly what we hide from ourselves we do not shew to our friends.' And he concludes with an observation which has large literary as well as psychological relevance: 'There is, indeed, no transaction which offers stronger temptations to fallacy and sophistication [i.e. lying] than epistolary intercourse.' The irony of Johnson's effect here is startling: so far from being the *most* open and 'natural' literary form, the personal letter proves to be exactly the *least*. So faulty, Johnson implies, is literary reasoning which does not base itself firmly on the observed nature of man. What follows suggests how Johnson's feeling for the literary genres as necessarily contrived and controlled artifacts emanates in part from his conviction of the general depravity of the human character: 'In the eagerness of conversation the first emotions of the mind often burst out before they are considered; in the tumult of business [self-]interest and passion have their genuine effect; but a friendly letter [like any kind of literary work] is a calm and deliberate performance in the cool of leisure, in the stillness of solitude, and surely no man sits down to depreciate by design his own character.' We may infer that, just like the 'friendly' letter, no 'kind' of literature can be expected to be 'natural' and 'sincere', especially not those kinds that most ostentatiously proclaim their proximity to the author's genuine feelings. Ironically, then, the song or the Horatian ode probably reflect less accurately an author's 'real' feelings than more 'objective' genres like tragedy and epic.

The fundamental artificiality of the genres can be seen most clearly in a form like the epitaph. And so deep and universal is the depravity of mankind that a literary form like the epitaph, which is obliged to praise, must perforce consist almost entirely of conventional untruths. Speaking once about the degree of 'truth' which an epitaph-writer might permit himself, Johnson asserted: 'The writer of an epitaph should not be considered as saying nothing but what is strictly true. Allowance must be made for some degree of exaggerated praise. In lapidary inscriptions a man is not upon oath' (*BLJ*, ii, 407). Indeed, it would be shocking for an epitaph-writer to tell the truth, for, as we have seen, such is the depth of human depravity that 'very few

can boast of hearts which they dare lay open [even] to themselves'. The depravity of human nature can be gauged by the
rarity of human praises; and, as Johnson points out in the
'Essay on Epitaphs' appended to the *Life of Pope*, 'The scanti-
ness of human praises can scarcely be made more apparent,
than by remarking how often Pope has, in the few epitaphs
which he composed, found it necessary to borrow from himself.
The fourteen epitaphs, which he has written, comprise about an
hundred and forty lines, in which there are more repetitions
than will easily be found in all the rest of his works.' The effect
of Johnson's demonstration is such that the sentimental 'good-
natured man' and the Jacobin 'lover of humanity' will not
know whether to cry, rage, or burst. The genre of the epitaph,
its strained encomiums testifying to the degeneracy of man as
well as the artificiality of art, so amuses Johnson that he often
contemplates it almost with the kind of laughter which nearly
paralysed him when he was informed about Bennet Langton's
having made, with due pomposity, his Last Will.[3] But sometimes a quieter irony is his response to the subject. For example,
in the 'Essay on Epitaphs' he observes that some few genuinely
great and virtuous men are appropriately memorialized by
epitaphs consisting of their names alone. But for the depraved
bulk of humanity advertising is required: 'But to far the greatest
part of mankind a longer encomium is necessary for the publication of their virtues, and the preservation of their memories.'

To the humanist, the assumed existence of a limited number
of specific genres can serve as a hint of man's obligation to rely
on something outside himself; with their predetermined shapes
and conventions, the genres serve as the props and stays provided by the wisdom of the past for the assistance of the present.
They remind both writer and reader of their obligations to
distrust themselves as inventors or critics of forms. Their very
existence and their consecration by long historical use are thus
facts replete with moral meaning.

Like the sympathy—often unconscious—for inherited genres,
the act of satire becomes, in the face of human depravity, something very like a moral obligation. Even though a satire usually
attacks the third rather than the second person, the acute reader

[3] See Walter Jackson Bate, *The Achievement of Samuel Johnson* (New York,
1955), pp. 117–19.

is moved to consider his own fallen state as well as that of the ostensible target; satire by implication exhorts reader as well as target to set about the work of redemption, beginning with the action of self-distrust. To accept the present circumstances of mankind and to 'adjust' to them is to find oneself in the same moral darkness as the Grub-Street speaker in the 'Preface' to *A Tale of a Tub*, who confesses that he has 'neither a Talent nor an Inclination for Satyr': 'On the other side, I am so entirely satisfied with the whole present Procedure of human Things, that I have been for some Years preparing Materials towards *A Panegyrick upon the World*; to which I intended to add a Second Part, entituled, *A Modest Defence of the Proceedings of the Rabble in All Ages.*' But this optimist has been disappointed; he finds that the materials for these works are not so easily available as he once imagined; he has therefore 'chosen to defer them to another Occasion'. His term 'chosen' is rich with ironic suggestions: he fancies that it is his will which is conducting the proceedings, which actually are determined entirely by the natural state of things. Swift often satirizes the mock-logical; here he is satirizing what we can call the mock-volitional.

But such is the depravity of human nature that almost any accurate description of it, especially a description of the correspondence of motives to appearances, tends, at least within the humanist moral climate, to partake of the satiric. Thus Edward Young in the preface to his orthodox satires *The Love of Fame* (1725–28), written a quarter of a century before his recreant *Conjectures*: 'historians . . . may be considered as satirists, and as satirists most severe; since such are most human actions, that to relate, is to expose them'. Gibbon's method in the *Decline and Fall* is implicit here. And in considering a number of humanistic conceptions of the depravity of man, it seems no more than just to let Johnson have the last word. In *Rambler* 131 he reminds the sentimental that we need not look very far for evidence of man's depravity: all we have to do is observe the minuteness and the cunning particularity of contracts and other legal documents. 'Among all the satires to which folly and wickedness have given occasion', says Johnson, 'none is equally severe with a bond or a settlement.'

G

5

THE REDEMPTIVE WILL

DEGENERATE as he is and all but lost, man yet possesses the means for a partial, if largely secular, redemption. Through the exercise of the mysterious and perhaps illusory power of choice which constitutes an assertion of his humanity, he is capable somehow of overcoming his instinctive malevolence and pride and of turning himself towards a more fruitful relation, if not with the supernatural, at least with his fellows and himself. The Augustan humanists inherit the seventeenth-century conviction that, as Richard Hooker asserts in the *Laws of Ecclesiastical Polity*, man's will is entirely in his own command: 'There is in the Will of man naturally that freedom, whereby it is apt to take or refuse any particular object whatsoever being presented unto it' (I, vii). And in *Paradise Lost* the Deity explains how man's 'praise'—that is, his dignity—depends upon his free exercise of will:

> I made [men] just and right,
> Sufficient to have stood, though free to fall . . .
> Not free, what proof could they have giv'n sincere
> Of true allegiance, constant Faith or Love,
> Where only what they needs must do, appear'd,
> Not what they would? What praise could they receive?
> What pleasure I from such obedience paid,
> When Will and Reason (Reason also is choice)
> Useless and vain, of freedom both despoil'd,
> Made passive both, had serv'd necessity,
> Not mee.
>
> (iii, 98–99; 103–11)

Since man's will is conceived of as free, a constant threat to his humanity is a deterministic or mechanistic conception of motive which would persuade him that his power to choose is in any way circumscribed. Hence Swift's moral satire on numerology and deterministic Calvinism in *A Tale of a Tub*; on astrology in the Partridge-Bickerstaff papers; on quantitative social science in *A Modest Proposal*; and on the theory of unpremeditated, 'natural' literary inspiration in *The Battle of the Books*. As a humanist, it is Swift's self-imposed obligation to remind his readers of the loss of humanity—which is to say the inflexibility and rigidity—that attends the abdication of the idea of choice.

Swift's articulation of this old-fashioned commitment is, as we should expect, almost entirely indirect. The mode of fiction through which he consistently operates takes charge and complicates the underlying humanist polemic, as if he were never forgetful of his observations on satiric method in *An Epistle to a Lady, Who Desired the Author to Make Verses on Her, in the Heroick Stile*:

> Bastings heavy, dry, obtuse,
> Only Dulness can produce,
> While a little gentle Jerking
> Sets the Spirits all a working.
>
> (203–6)

The equivalent of 'gentle Jerking' in Swift's humanist performance is his ironic mechanism: instead of contriving fictions which enact the premise of the freedom of the will, he proceeds in the opposite direction and creates fictions and images whose effect is ironically to urge deterministic and mechanistic conceptions. 'Humanism has two enemies', Geoffrey Scott has said, —'chaos and inhuman order.'[1] It is inhuman order that Swift most frequently sets himself to satirize.

In *A Tale of a Tub* the satire on mechanism is as pervasive as it is complex. We find it in both the 'religious' and the 'literary' layers of the whole, in Jack's commitment to predestination as well as in the ideal of the critic ironically recommended in 'A Digression Concerning Criticks', where we are asked to conceive of 'a *True Critick*' as 'a sort of Mechanick, set up with a Stock and Tools for his Trade, at as little Expence as a *Taylor*'. At the moral centre of the religious allegory in the *Tale* stands Martin, distinguished from his two brothers by his ability,

---

[1] *Architecture of Humanism*, p. 244.

through his Anglican free-will, to respond accurately to experience, to play life by ear, as it were: unlike his brothers, he is in command of his passions, and his will is thereby freed for its difficult and subtle work. Jack's slavery to his own fury and Peter's excessive dependence on a vain external tradition ally both of them to another mechanical character in the *Tale*, to whom we are introduced in the 'Digression on Madness': this is 'a certain Great Prince', perhaps to be identified as Henry IV of France, who, imagining that he was making his own choice, 'raised a mighty Army' and then indulged pleasing visions of conquest. Swift's speaker phrases the important question in mechanical terms: 'What secret Wheel, what hidden Spring could put into Motion so wonderful an Engine?' And having momentarily transformed the Prince from a man into a piece of clockwork, the speaker proceeds to metamorphose him one more time, now into a curious man-machine or monstrous sexual timepiece operated by the deterministic humours of an ascendant lubricity: 'It was afterwards discovered, that the Movement of this whole Machine had been directed by an absent *Female*, whose Eyes had raised a Protuberancy, and before Emission, she was removed into an Enemy's Country. . . . the collected part of the *Semen*, raised and enflamed, became adust, converted to Choler, turned head upon the spinal Duct, and ascended to the Brain.' The result of this 'humorous' pressure from below was the Prince's dreams of 'Sieges, Battles and Victories', just as the result of Jack's and Peter's rages was ultimate madness. *A Tale of a Tub* concludes with a final invocation of the image of mechanism, this time literary rather than ethical or doctrinal. As the Grub-Street author rambles to a 'conclusion', he explains that it is the physical pen rather than the will which is conducting the proceedings: 'I am now trying an Experiment very frequent among Modern Authors; which is, to *write upon Nothing*; when the Subject is utterly exhausted, to let the Pen still move on. . . .' But, as Swift says in *The Progress of Beauty*, talking about aging flesh rather than an exhausted topic,

The best Mechanick Hand must fayl
Where Nothing's left to work upon.

(79–80)

If the ironical mechanistic theme pervades *A Tale of a Tub*, it can be said to find an embodiment almost total in *The Mechanical Operation of the Spirit*, where Swift images his moral disgust with deterministic theories of 'motivation' as well as his less profound loathing for the proverbial Puritan vices of oratorical affectation, devotional enthusiasm verging on public sexual ecstasy, and the wearing of greasy hats. Because *The Mechanical Operation of the Spirit* is located climactically at the very end of the 1704 volume, the whole practice of Dissent, set forth here as 'the Phœnomenon of Spiritual Mechanism', illuminates the mechanisms of characters in *A Tale of a Tub*: the moral faults of Jack, Peter, the 'Great Prince', and the mechano-spiritual artists of fraudulent Dissenting oratory merge into one great crime against human nature—the transformation of man into automatic machine.

In the performance of the economic projector who offers *A Modest Proposal* we find a similar satire on mechanism. Here the speaker who humbly offers his final solution to the Irish problem manages to translate the qualitative into the machine-like by the simple technique of applying numeration to matters of moral value. Even the speaker's ostentatious reliance on order and system in his exposition ('First'; 'Secondly'; 'Thirdly') suggests the degree to which he is inspired by the principles of predetermined calculation. The point is all too clear: once divorced from ethics, economics accelerates in the direction of a merely quantitative 'science'. Near the end of *A Modest Proposal* the speaker, dimly conscious of the humanist objection to all this, carefully rejects all the reforms which might result from the action of the humanist will: 'let no man talk to me of other Expedients'. This is mechanism with a vengeance.

The Lilliputian instinct for life as mechanics is less obvious but perhaps almost as expressive. Lilliputian logic carefully omits the one step necessary to redeem mechanical cruelty: Gulliver says of his hosts in Lilliput, 'Sometimes they determined to starve me, or at least to shoot me in the Face and Hands with poisoned Arrows, which would soon dispatch me: But again they considered, that the Stench of so large a Carcase might produce a Plague in the Metropolis, and probably spread through the whole Kingdom.' The implications of the term 'considered' here help define the identity between the one-dimensional logic of the Modest Proposer and that of the Lilliputians: except for the accidental difference in size they are the same moral person. And sometimes Gulliver is made to share their mechanical and non-qualitative response to phenomena. When Gulliver offers the Brobdingnagian monarch the secret of gunpowder, the king rejects the offer with humanist fury. Reasoning like the Lilliputians, Gulliver attributes the king's odd reaction to Brobdingnagian 'ignorance'; he regrets that the Brobdingnagians have not 'hitherto reduced *Politicks* into a *Science*, as the more acute Wits of *Europe* have done'. These 'more acute Wits of Europe' we encounter again, of course, disguised as members of the French National Assembly in Burke's *Reflections*.

In Gulliver's third voyage the satire on mechanism turns more overt and farcical. Here Gulliver meets a professor at The Grand Academy of Lagado who is engaged in 'a Project for improving speculative Knowledge by practical and Mechanical Operations'. By means of this projector's learning machine 'the most ignorant Person at a reasonable Charge, and with a little bodily Labour, may write books in Philosophy, Poetry, Politicks, Law, Mathematicks and Theology, without the least Assistance from Genius or Study'. Farce is also the effect of Gulliver's account of a mathematics master's mechanistic pedagogy at the Grand Academy. Gulliver recounts that 'the Master taught his Pupils after a Method scarce imaginable to us in *Europe*. The Proposition and Demonstration were fairly written on a thin Wafer, with Ink composed of a Cephalick Tincture. . . . As the Wafer digested, the Tincture mounted to [the student's] Brain, bearing the Proposition along with it.' Like the 'Great Prince' of *A Tale of a Tub*, the student here is metamorphosed into a mere vertical tube for the mechanical upward passage of the physical cause of his motive: the body is entirely determining the cast of the mind, which is to say that hierarchy is being grossly violated. A typical humanist response to a situation like this is an image of Pope's in *Peri Bathous*, Chapter XII: 'When a man is set with his head downward, and his breech upright, his degradation is complete: One end of him is as *high* as ever, only that end is the *wrong one*.' The same humanistic disinclination to accept the domination of the intellectual and the volitional by the physical or the mechanical lies at the heart of Reynolds's *Discourses*, and provides indeed the rationale for his high valuation of history-painting, for, as he says in the *Third Discourse*, 'it is not the eye, it is the mind, which the painter of genius desires to address'.

But perhaps the most staggering farce in *Gulliver's Travels* results from Gulliver's mad antics when finally he is forced to return home. Determined to shun the 'chaos' of Yahooism at any cost, he rushes to the other extreme and embraces 'inhuman order'; he now acts with all the mechanical stiffness and rigour characteristic of the protagonist in farce. He reduces himself from a man to a sense-machine when, offended with the imagined stench of the human race—which he confuses always with the Yahoo race—he is careful not to venture out of Don Pedro's Lisbon house without keeping his nose 'well stopped with Rue, or sometimes with Tobacco'. An almost definitive comment on Gulliver's mechanical exclusivism is provided by Burke in his *Letter to the Sheriffs of Bristol*: 'he that accuses all mankind of corruption ought to remember that he is sure to convict only one'.

Another happy Swiftian exhibition of mechanism in action is *A Compleat Collection of Genteel and Ingenious Conversation*, compiled by the 'modern' scholar Simon Wagstaff. To Swift, Wagstaff appears well equipped for his work of reducing human intercourse to mechanical terms, for he has had no acquaintance with the Roman classics in the original; as he tells us, 'I resolved to exceed the Advice of *Horace*, a *Roman* Poet, (which I have read in Mr. Creech's admirable Translation) That an Author should keep his Works Nine Years in his Closet before he ventured to publish them'. Like Burke exposing Dr. Price's apparent innocence of Aristotle's *Poetics*, Swift seems to imply that those moderns unacquainted with the exact contours of the classical texts are especially susceptible to the blandishments of mechanistic procedures. In his introductory instructions for the use of his dialogues of social clichés, Wagstaff reveals that his materials will not work properly until the persons committed to them have managed to become something very like automatic machines; as he says, 'there is hardly a polite Sentence in the following Dialogues which doth not absolutely require some peculiar graceful Motion in the Eyes, or Nose, or Mouth, or

Forehead, or Chin, or suitable Toss of the Head, with certain Offices assigned to each Hand'. Again he tells us: 'I did . . . once intend, for the Ease of the Learner, to set down in all Parts of the following Dialogues certain Marks, Asterisks, or *Nota-Bene's* (in *English, Markwell's*) after most Questions, and every Reply or Answer; directing exactly the Moment when One, Two, or All the Company are to laugh.' But Wagstaff has had to abandon this sort of notation, for he has perceived that such indicators would swell his volume to a size no longer fit for the pocket and for ready consultation.

The word that brings this last passage fully alive is 'exactly', which, like the word 'infallibly' ironically used when nonsense is solemnly being advanced, is one of Swift's favourite stylistic devices for emphasizing the intellectual and moral damage caused by mechanical attempts to be precise where human nature promises no possibilities for precision. 'Exactly' is used with high irony in *The Progress of Beauty*, where, after drawing a comically crude analogy between the Moon and 'rotting' Celia, Swift asserts with a straight face:

> 'Twixt earthly Femals and the Moon
> All Parallells exactly run.
>
> (9–10)

These ironic 'exactly's' and 'infallibly's' constitute a sort of adverbial mock-logic, which Swift offers as a manifestation of the depraved human tendency to transform the complex and the subtle into the simple and, therefore, the mechanical. The tags of traditional formal reasoning, like 'can there be anything more evident?' are often invoked to emphasize the mechanistic stultification which can result from the technique of rigid analogy. Gulliver reports, for example, on the work of a projector in the Grand Academy: 'Whereas all Writers and Reasoners have agreed, that there is a strict universal Resemblance between the natural and the political Body; can there be any thing more evident, than that the Health of both must be preserved, and the Diseases cured by the same Prescriptions?' Thus the health of states is to be safeguarded by the administration to those in power of 'Lenitives, Aperitives, Corrosives, Restringents', and the like. The complex satire here is directed as much at a mechanical mode of 'reasoning' as at the corruptions of the state and the natural fatuity and nastiness of the medical faculty. We can perceive the same humanistic satire of mechanical mock-logic and analogy in all Swift's mock-equations: 'Surely mortal Man is a Broomstick.' And while we are glancing at *A Meditation upon a Broom-Stick*, we should pause to observe Swift's demonstration of the tricks which extrinsically applied rhetorical artifice is likely to play on those whose minds are susceptible to the corruptions of the mechanical. Here in his opening sentence 'Robert Boyle' is betrayed into a preposterous pseudo-parallelism by his habit of mechanical adherence to rhetorical 'systems'. 'This single Stick,' he begins, 'which you now behold ingloriously lying in that neglected Corner, I once knew in a flourishing State in a Forest.' Primed now for his mechanical parallelism, he lets it ring out: 'It was full of Sap, full of Leaves, and full of Boughs.' Thus Swift satirizes those mechanisms of rhetoric which offer the illusion without the reality of choice and which tend to pervert expression in the interest of extrinsic system or symmetry. Swift's omnipresent enemy would seem to be that constant tendency in the human spirit to simplify experience, to collapse into a fatigued acceptance of mechanical shapes and formulas which, initially comforting, are ultimately at odds with the difficult, complex *données* of human nature. It is the almost sacred human will which, once aware of its obligations to resist, becomes man's primary weapon against the natural human impulse to turn automaton. That is, as Swift observes in *Verses on the Death of Dr. Swift*,

His Satyr points at no Defect,
But what all Mortals may correct.

(463–4)

Pope is another who is fond of employing a mechanistic image to invest with a local form the idea of the abdication of will. An impressive antithesis to Burke's figure of 'animated strength' or Johnson's of 'incorporated minds' is Pope's image of the gutless automaton who is the stylish prize poet of *The Dunciad*, Book II; this poet, like the Gulliver who appears on the Lisbon streets with his nose 'well stopped with Rue or . . . Tobacco', has been transformed by the Goddess of Dulness into a sort of junkyard shack stuffed with detritus:

> With pert flat eyes she window'd well its head;
> A brain of feathers, and a heart of lead.

(44–45)

The transformation of the eyes from round to flat is a detail that would not have been lost on readers of William Hogarth, who pointed out in *The Analysis of Beauty* (1753) that 'when the form of the body is divested of its serpentine lines it becomes ridiculous as a human figure . . .'. Colley Cibber is changed from a human being to a similar congeries of machinery in the first book of *The Dunciad*, where Pope contrives that Cibber shall comment thus on the forces that determine his actions:

> As, forc'd from wind-guns, lead itself can fly,
> And pond'rous slugs cut swiftly thro the sky;
> As clocks to weight their nimble motion owe,
> The wheels above urg'd by the load below:
> Me Emptiness, and Dulness could inspire,
> And were my Elasticity, and Fire.

(181–6)

Mechanized here into an air-rifle pellet and a clock is a former human being who has abandoned his inherent power to resist; with the abdication of the will comes an inhuman stiffening of the mind and the person, an absolutely fatal loss of 'Elasticity and Fire'.

If in Swift and Pope the feeling for the freedom of the will customarily takes the form of elaborate mechanical fictions and produces grotesque images of men perverting their nature into the form of farcical machines, Samuel Johnson goes to work in a more direct way. His primary mode here is polemic; his technique tends towards asseveration rather than fictional transmutation. And he spends less energy on satire of the mechanical than on outright, often passionate assertions of the actuality of volitional freedom. His instinct for sensing free-will as the dignifying human attribute is recalled by Frances Reynolds:

Two lines from Pope's *Universal Prayer* I have heard him quote, in very serious conversation, as his theological creed:

> And binding Nature fast in fate,
> Left free the human will.

(*JM*, ii, 254)

This is not to say that Johnson is totally negligent of opportunities for indulging in the mockery of the mechanical; we find him, for example, delicately implying the folly of mechanical criteria when he observes of Frederick the Great, in the *Life of the King of Prussia*, that one of his main ambitions 'was to be master of the tallest regiment in Europe. He therefore brought together from all parts men above the common military standard. To exceed the height of six feet was a certain recommendation to notice, and to approach that of seven a claim to distinction.' With the tone of these sentences in mind we can appreciate fully the traditional moral as well as aesthetic force of Johnson's remark, recalled by Langton, on a contemporary poet (perhaps Joseph Warton): 'Sir, he is an enthusiast by rule' (*BLJ*, iv, 33). Even 'enthusiasm' deserves better than to be subjugated to a tyrannical mechanism. Affectation, perhaps the ultimate mechanism in Johnson's ethical world, finally has the power to deform empirical feeling and to turn men into puppets —like Pope's 'squeaking' Lord Hervey—prompted by their own most self-destructive impulses. To Johnson, Gray, at his worst, appeared 'a mechanical poet', and 'mechanical criticism' is Johnson's satiric butt not only in the whimsical portrayal of Dick Minim in *Idler* 60 and 61 but, more importantly, in the deadly serious scepticism about the dramatic unities in the *Preface to Shakespeare* and in *Rambler* 156. In this latter work Johnson has his customary empirical recourse to actual human responses in the face of literature as his major critical principle and sanction. Here he characterizes the strict view of the unity of time in the drama as an affectation typical of 'mechanical criticism'; and he argues that 'It is rarely observed that minds, not prepossessed by mechanical criticism, feel any offence from the extension of the intervals between the acts'. Minds and wills 'unprepossessed' by extrinsic and deterministic systems and free to respond accurately to experience are the aim of Johnson's literary and ethical criticism alike. So profound is his suspicion of the slightest hint of determinism that we may even be led to infer that a part of his hostility to Scotland results from his sensitivity to the deterministic strain in Calvinism. Although much of his outrage is clearly caused by spectacles of ruined and ill-kept holy places, some of the violence he displayed on the Scottish tour seems hardly explicable except as a doctrinal reaction. His wish that John Knox might have been buried in the highway seems too violent to represent merely Johnson's response to the architectural damage wrought by the Reformers, as does his reporting in the *Journey to the Western Islands* that in Scotland 'The malignant influence of *Calvinism* has blasted ceremony and decency together'.

But even though on occasion he will—like Swift and Pope—exhibit mechanism as either laughable or loathsome, Johnson's humanist energy is largely enlisted in more direct assertions of the absolute freedom of the will and in the practical exhortation of those moderns who are leaning towards determinism. On this question Johnson is always serious; it is the one matter about which he never jests. 'Nature will indeed always operate,' he admits in *Rambler* 151, 'human desires will be always ranging; but', he goes on, 'these motions, though very powerful, are not resistless; nature may be regulated, and desires governed.' Indeed, man's depraved nature *must* be regulated, for his identity, his dignity, and ultimately his redemption depend upon its regulation. As we are told in *Rambler* 185, 'Nothing which reason condemns can be suitable to the dignity of the human mind. To be driven by external motives from the path which our own heart approves, to give way to any thing but conviction, to suffer the opinion of others to rule our choice, or overpower our resolves, is to submit tamely to the lowest and most ignominious slavery, and to resign the right of directing our own lives.' It is poignant to find the Johnson whose difficulties in getting up in the morning have become notorious saying, in *Rambler* 129, something like this: 'It is below the dignity of a reasonable being to owe that strength to necessity which ought always to act at the call of choice, or to need any other motive to industry than the desire of performing his duty.'

Man's frailty and depravity make it inevitable that he will very frequently ascribe to 'external motives' what are really his own defects. That tendency towards oversimplification which Swift is drawn to satirize seems always to prompt man to overestimate the impact on him of external forces. It is Johnson's constant endeavour to recall his readers or addressees to an awareness of their own actual experience in this matter. As he says during a discussion with Boswell, 'All theory is against the freedom of the will; all experience for it' (*BLJ*, iii, 291). And

Johnson's argument seems as frequently directed against the prevalence of abstract 'theory' as against deterministic notions themselves.

One of the 'external motives' which Johnson takes pains to reject again and again is what we can call meteorological determinism, the assumption that weather and climate determine either the kind or the quantity of intellectual production. Here Johnson's stand is against writers like Sir William Temple who had suggested that climate determines national and, by implication, individual character. Johnson perceives that once man contrives to believe that his performance is determined by the weather, he becomes in his own imagination as much a puppet of external forces as Swift's Jack 'predestined' to bump into posts or Soame Jenyns's invalids tortured by a malignant race of higher beings. The human hierarchical superiority to physical nature Johnson asserts vigorously in *Idler* 11: 'Surely nothing is more reproachful to a being endowed with reason, than to resign its powers to the influence of the air, and live in dependence on the weather and the wind, for the only blessings which nature has put into our power, tranquillity and benevolence.' Actually, an excessive sensitivity to the weather is an egregious self-indulgence 'produced only by imagination operating on luxury'. Like the conscious experience of the disappointment of hopes, the very struggle against 'the tyranny of the climate' is conceived by Johnson as an ethical exercise which can toughen the fibres and fit them for more strenuous and important combats: 'Every man,' he continues in *Idler* 11, 'however he may distrust himself in the extremes of good and evil, might at least struggle against the tyranny of the climate, and refuse to enslave his virtue or his reason to the most variable of all variations, the changes of the weather.' Johnson's insistence that men—and especially writers—so manage their imaginations that they may avoid the 'reproach' of living 'in dependence on the weather and the wind' is at the furthest possible remove from the heterodox critical notion, often expressed during Johnson's time and later through the image of the Aeolian lyre or wind-harp, that both man and poet should vibrate at the soft urging of external 'impressions'. As Shelley puts it in *A Defence of Poetry*: 'Man is an instrument over which a series of external and internal impressions are driven, like the alternations of an ever-changing wind over an Aeolian lyre, which move it by their motion to ever-changing melody.' Shelley's 'Man is an instrument', reminding us as it must of 'Robert Boyle's' 'Man is a Broomstick', could hardly be more eloquently expressive of the a-humanistic techniques of false analogy and deterministic figure. It is hardly necessary to observe that to Johnson little could be worse than for man to conceive of himself as the mechanical plaything of the winds, no matter how ravishing the melodies that might be emitted as a by-product. Man's primary business, after all, is not melody: it is action.

Johnson's scepticism about climatological determinism is reflected at crucial points in *The Lives of the Poets*. One of Milton's weaknesses of character, we are told, was his willingness to believe that the spring was the best season for composition. Johnson comments: 'This dependence of the soul upon the seasons, those temporary and periodical ebbs and flows of intellect, may, I suppose, justly be derided as the fumes of vain imagination.' And again he says, 'Another opinion wanders about the world, and sometimes finds reception among wise men; an opinion that restrains the operations of the mind to particular regions, and supposes that a luckless mortal may be born in a degree of latitude too high or too low for wisdom or for wit. From this fancy, wild as it is, [Milton] had not wholly cleared his head, when he feared lest the *climate* of his country might be *too cold* for flights of imagination.' A vulgar error of false analogy is what underlies Milton's erroneous and pernicious opinion: actually the mind is so much its own reality that its operations cannot be compared even remotely with those of physical nature. As Johnson realized, the notion of especially happy moments for composition is really a shrewd device of the depraved consciousness for rationalizing vanity and procrastination. Once at Edinburgh, as Boswell reports, 'Somebody talked of happy moments for composition; and how a man can write at one time, and not at another.—"Nay, (said Dr. Johnson) a man may write at any time, if he will set himself *doggedly* to it" ' (*BLJ*, v, 40). Thomas Gray is another who, in Johnson's view, seized the notion of propitious times and seasons for writing and used it in part to sanction his self-indulgence and to justify the paucity of his production. As

Johnson writes in the *Life of Gray*: '[Gray] had a notion not very peculiar, that he could not write but at certain times, or at happy moments; a fantastick foppery, to which my kindness for a man of learning and virtue wishes him to have been superior.' To Johnson, it is Milton's and Gray's susceptibility to this vulgar deterministic idea that betrays in the moral sphere a similar lapse of command which, in poetry, expresses itself in the impious amalgam of sacred and profane in *Lycidas* and in the gauche pompositics of *The Progress of Poesy* and *The Bard*.

Just as climate and weather must not be conceived of as exercising any notable influence on human action, the externals of time and place are to be resisted as well. Mrs. Thrale reports in her *Anecdotes* that 'nothing more certainly offended Mr. Johnson, than the idea of a man's faculties (mental ones I mean) decaying by time; 'It is not true, Sir (would he say); what a man could once do, he would always do . . . '. Even the memory, commonly thought of by most of Johnson's contemporaries as necessarily a victim of time, is to Johnson quite controllable by will in defiance of the aging process, for, as he argues in *Idler* 74, 'The true art of memory is the art of attention'. And for all his love of London as the seat of British intellectual pleasure and for all his scepticism about the virtues of rural life ('they who are content to live in the country, are *fit* for the country'), he still insists, at least when exhorting Boswell to remain satisfied with Edinburgh, that on a wise man physical place should exercise as little influence as time. He writes Boswell in 1778: 'I wish you would a little correct or restrain your imagination, and imagine that happiness, such as life admits, may be had at other places as well as London. Without asserting Stoicism, it may be said, that it is our business to exempt ourselves as much as we can from the power of external things' (*LSJ*, ii, 251).

Love and sorrow likewise are to be struggled against at the point where they seem to swell into deterministic forces. One of Dryden's moral faults is his commitment to 'the romantick omnipotence of Love' in *All for Love*; in this play, Johnson argues in the *Life of Dryden*, 'he has recommended as laudable and worthy of imitation, that conduct which, through all ages, the good have censured as vicious, and the bad despised as foolish'. The same disinclination to admit the power which love pre-eminently may exercise over the will prompts Johnson, in the *Preface to Shakespeare*, to praise Shakespeare for representing life more accurately than the heroic dramatists:

Upon every other stage the universal agent is love, by whose power all good and evil is distributed, and every action quickened or retarded. To bring a lover, a lady and a rival into the fable; to entangle them in contradictory obligations, perplex them with oppositions of interest, and harass them with violence of desires inconsistent with each other; to make them meet in rapture and part in agony; to fill their mouths with hyperbolical joy and outrageous sorrow; to distress them as nothing human ever was distressed; to deliver them as nothing human ever was delivered, is the business of a modern dramatist. For this probability is violated, life is misrepresented, and language is depraved. But love is only one of many passions, and as it has no great influence upon the sum of life, it has little operation in the dramas of [Shakespeare], who caught his ideas from the living world, and exhibited only what he saw before him. He knew, that any other passion, as it was regular or exorbitant, was a cause of happiness or calamity.

The humanistic eloquence of this statement derives largely from such repetitions as 'nothing human' and from such an expressive parallelism as *probability*: *life*: *language*, an equation which embodies *in petto* the empirical-humanistic theory of literature.

And sorrow is to be guarded against as much as love lest it subtly erode the illusion of free choice. Writing to Mrs. Thrale in 1778 after Henry Thrale's recovery from a stroke, Johnson points out that 'To grieve for evils is often wrong, but it is much more wrong to grieve without them. All sorrow that lasts longer than its cause is morbid, and should be shaken off as an attack of melancholy, as the forerunner of a greater evil than poverty or pain' (*LSJ*, ii, 257). The 'greater evil than poverty or pain' which Johnson alludes to here is insanity, that last and most inhuman determinism which man has it in his power to invite by persuading himself that any force within or without can readily overcome the human will.

Many of Johnson's remarks recorded by Boswell which at first glance seem merely whimsical, comical, or rude prove upon closer examination to issue from this profound concern with volitional freedom. As an example we can regard this little confrontation recorded by Boswell: 'I told him that [music]

affected me to such a degree, as often to agitate my nerves painfully, producing in my mind alternate sensations of pathetick
dejection, so that I was ready to shed tears; and of daring resolution, so that I was inclined to rush into the thickest part of
the battle. "Sir, (said [Johnson],) I should never hear it, if it
made me such a fool" ' (*BLJ*, iii, 197). The moral dynamics
of this interchange are ironic and delightful. Boswell's motive in
his initial announcement is to be taken for a man of feeling, a
person dignified by his exquisite sensibility to external phenomena. We may doubt that the 'pain' with which his 'nerves'
are 'agitated' is excruciating enough to overcome his delight in
imagining that he is distinguished from the bulk of humanity by
such delicacy of sensation. The pleasure he is taking in drama-
tizing the examples of his sensitivity prevents his sensing Johnson's real reaction until it is too late and Johnson's moral
rejoinder breaks over him like a wave. Far from being impressed, as Boswell imagines, Johnson all the while has been
nursing his developing outrage at the satisfaction with which
Boswell apparently is willing to conceive of himself as a mere toy
of external forces, a sort of Scottish Aeolian harp. The collision
between self-satisfied fatuity and serious moral passion could
hardly be more superbly rendered than by Boswell's naïvely
objective version of this scene. And the vigour of Johnson's
reaction suggests how very little sympathy he is going to feel
towards critical theories of natural inspiration, which, in their
deterministic implications, are as morally offensive as Boswell's
misconception of his nature and purpose.

Johnson's quarrel with determinism similarly prompts his
criticism of Pope's *Moral Essay* I (*Epistle to Cobham*), which
advances the theory of the Ruling Passion as the one constant
motive impelling a man's action and revealing his character.
Pope exhorts Cobham to

> Search then the Ruling Passion: There, alone,
> The Wild are constant, and the Cunning known.
>
> (174–5)

In the *Life of Pope* Johnson goes at once to the heart of the moral
problem here; he perceives that a belief in a 'fixed' character
implies a dangerous determinism. He comments: 'This doctrine
[of the Ruling Passion] is in itself pernicious as well as false: its

H

tendency is to produce the belief of a kind of moral predestination, or over-ruling principle which cannot be resisted; he that
admits it is prepared to comply with every desire that caprice or
opportunity shall excite, and to flatter himself that he submits
only to the lawful dominion of Nature, in obeying the resistless
authority of his *ruling Passion.*'

Much of Johnson's correspondence with Boswell has the
object of persuading Boswell that his fancied Ruling Passion—
a tendency to melancholy and a want of intellectual fixity and
focus—is mainly a rationalization contrived by Boswell to justify
his backslidings. In one of his earliest letters to Boswell, Johnson
coyly posits 'a gentleman' who has been idling and affecting
carelessness towards study so long that his bad habit has finally
almost disabled him from changing his posture towards himself.
This young gentleman, Johnson writes, 'wished to return to his
studies; and finding long habits of idleness and pleasure harder
to be cured than he expected, still willing to retain his claim to
some extraordinary prerogatives, resolved the common consequences of irregularity into an unalterable decree of destiny,
and concluded that Nature had originally formed him incapable of rational employment' (*LSJ*, i, 166). Johnson takes
special care to be as explicit as possible with Boswell because he
knows that his fault is akin to Richard Savage's; Savage destroyed himself because, 'having accustomed himself to impute
all [his] deviations from the right to foreign causes, [he] was
upon every occasion too easily reconciled to himself . . .' (*Life of
Savage*).

Even the making of vows and resolutions seems dangerous to
Johnson, for even though their usual purpose is to encourage
virtue, they tend to 'enchain' decision and when violated to
generate feelings of guilt. Writing to Boswell in 1766, he says:
'Your resolution to obey your father I sincerely approve; but do
not accustom yourself to enchain your volatility by vows: they
will sometime leave a thorn in your mind, which you will, perhaps, never be able to extract or eject. Take this warning, it is of
great importance' (*LSJ*, i, 190). Mrs. Thrale receives similar
advice in 1773: 'All unnecessary vows are folly, because they
suppose a prescience of the future which has not been given us.
They are, I think, a crime because they resign that life to
chance which God has given us to be regulated by Reason; and

superinduce a kind of fatality, from which it is the great privilege of our Nature to be free'(*LSJ*, i, 325). The way vows may tend to produce an empty mechanism of character is illustrated in the *Life of Swift*, where Johnson writes that Swift, 'having by some ridiculous resolution, or mad vow, determined never to wear spectacles, could make little use of books in his later years: his ideas therefore, being neither renovated by discourse, nor increased by reading, wore gradually away, and left his mind vacant to the vexations of the hour . . .'. That the man who wrote this hardly let an Easter slip by without solemnly recording a list of resolutions and vows for the coming year is a testimony to the wisdom of Imlac's remark, in Chapter VIII of *Rasselas*, that 'Inconsistencies . . . cannot both be right, but, imputed to man, they may both be true'.

To most people poverty is an evil to be avoided for reasons which are either physical or psychological. But to Johnson it involves a moral evil even worse—it limits the possibilities of choice until the will atrophies from lack of exercise, and the mind, therefore, turns dangerously into something less than a human constituent. To Boswell, who had been falling into debt, Johnson gives this advice: 'Do not accustom yourself to consider debts only as an inconvenience; you will find it a calamity. Poverty takes away so many means of doing good, and produces so much inability to resist evil, both natural and moral, that it is by all virtuous means to be avoided' (*LSJ*, ii, 486). Johnson seldom talks about poverty in any context without managing to imply its tendency towards moral destruction through its circumscribing of choice. In the *Life of Collins*, for example, we find him saying that, although Collins's 'morals were pure, and his opinions pious', yet, 'in a long continuance of poverty, and long habits of dissipation, it cannot be expected that any character should be exactly uniform. There is a degree of want by which the freedom of agency is almost destroyed.' Those like Soame Jenyns who argue that a little decent poverty never hurt anyone receive the total contempt of the Johnson who perceived, in *Rambler* 162, that 'There is no state more contrary to the dignity of wisdom than perpetual and unlimited dependence, in which the understanding lies useless, and every motion [i.e. intention] is received from external impulse'. Because, as Johnson says in the *Life of Dryden*, 'The inevitable consequence of poverty is dependence', Jenyns's suggestions that poverty may conduce to virtue are not only heartless; they are ethically and psychologically erroneous: as Johnson shows in his review of Jenyns's *Free Inquiry*, 'The milder degrees of poverty are sometimes [as Jenyns had argued] supported by hope, but the more severe often sink down in motionless despondence'. Because choice is reason, and because 'Reason is the great distinction of human nature, the faculty by which we approach to some degree of association with celestial intelligences' (*Rambler* 162), the poor are deprived not only of the possibility of moral improvement through the constant exercise of the will; like animals they are thrust away from God almost beyond the hope of redemption. It is possible thus to see Johnson's vigorous answer to Jenyns's complacent acceptance of the *status quo* as embodying a sort of humanist secular theology according to which salvation resides less in the external operation of mysteries such as the Incarnation than in the internal operations of the human capacity to choose. Those who accept the necessity of poverty are not merely condemning men: they are condemning souls. We may observe in passing that the Johnson we see here in this humanist context is quite a different creature from the mere idiosyncratic Tory and the sarcastic conversational sadist so frequently offered us in folklore and so useful for the political and social purposes of a Horace Walpole or a Macaulay. When Johnson has his humanist steam up he often appears closer to a Fabian social reformer of the late nineteenth century than to the reactionaries of his own age with whom he is still sometimes confused.

Readers of the *Life of Johnson* will have noticed that the one subject to which Johnson and Boswell constantly return in conversation is this matter of free will. One reason why this topic occupies so large a part of the *Life* is that Boswell was obsessed with it and sought Johnson's assurances on it at every opportunity. As Boswell attests, 'This is the subject which most of all has perplexed and distressed me at different periods of my life' (*OY*, 46). And many of Boswell's reactions to common experiences proclaim the strength of this obsession. Listening to the advocate Andrew Crosbie discoursing smoothly and well, Boswell has a curious reaction: 'I could not believe that he was a mere *fatal* or *foreknown* machine.' And yet, even though he cannot believe it, he is still disturbed: 'Yet I was uneasy because it *might* be so' (*OY*, 47). Boswell apparently imbibed these odd suspicions about what he calls 'fatality' during his boyhood. Indoctrinated in Calvinism by his mother and by tutors, he had been subjected to innumerable harangues on the subjects of total depravity—to be distinguished from the humanistic concept of *almost*-total depravity—and predestination. Although he managed to break away officially from the stern Calvinism of his youth, first by turning Roman Catholic momentarily and finally by working himself into a generalized if uncertain commitment to Anglicanism, he was haunted throughout his life by the 'gloomy' deterministic images of Scottish Presbyterianism. What he wanted was religious cheer, 'a decent system of mild Christianity'; what he too frequently experienced was the debilitating suspicion that he was somehow not a free agent. Passing through Rome in 1765, he paused at St. Peter's, where, as he recounts, he 'prayed fervent to the unchangeable Father of all to drive away melancholy and keep clouds of Presbyterian Sundays from rendering mind gloomy' (*GT*, 66). As an aspirant humanist, he was constantly appalled by the possibility that, as Calvinism seemed to imply, man might actually turn out to be a determined mechanism. Hence his never letting slip an opportunity to stimulate one of his heroes (Rousseau, Voltaire, Johnson, Hume) to emit portable wisdom in favour of the freedom of the will. But even a continual stream of reassurance from his mentors could not set his spirit at ease. Sir David Dalrymple writes him shrewdly in 1763: 'I find you infatuated with Fatality. Since neither [Dr. Samuel] Clarke nor Johnson has been able to dissipate these clouds which overshadow your mind, how could *I* persuade you that you are a rational being? Tell me, however: when you do good, do you not believe yourself free?' (*H*, 90).

It was during Boswell's stay at Utrecht in 1764 that his doubts about his free will became perhaps most torturous. From Utrecht Boswell offers us dramatic scenes as painful as they are ludicrous. Witness this memorandum: 'You went out to fields, and in view of the tower, drew your sword glittering in the sun, and on your knee swore that if there is a Fatality, then that was also ordained; but if you had free will, as you believed, you swore and called the Great G— to witness that, although you're melancholy, you'll stand it . . . ' (H, 201). Both horrified and disgusted by Boswell's frequent use of his melancholy for purposes of personal publicity, Johnson exhorts him to command it, to drive it away through the exertion of the will. Thus he advises him in 1778: 'When any fit of anxiety, or gloominess, or perversion of mind, lays hold upon you, make it a rule not to publish it by complaints, but exert your whole care to hide it; by endeavouring to hide it, you will drive it away. Be always busy' (LSJ, ii, 272). But Boswell never did achieve a state in which he was entirely convinced that the will was as powerful as Johnson kept saying it was; and the Life frequently portrays confrontations between Johnson's humanism and Boswell's stubborn and often pathetic heterodoxy. At one point Boswell reports Johnson's uttering this bracing little homily which Johnson clearly wants to believe himself: 'A man has from nature a certain portion of mind; the use he makes of it depends upon his own free will. That a man has always the same firmness of mind I do not say; because every man feels his mind less firm at one time than at another; but I think a man's being in a good or bad humour depends upon his will.' Boswell has done his duty in recording and shaping this humanistic utterance for the reader. But moved perhaps by a combination of the masochistic Calvinism of his boyhood and his desire, which we have seen before, to pose as a 'feeler', he is careful to inform the reader immediately: 'I, however, could not help thinking that a man's humour is often uncontroulable by his will' (BLJ, iii, 336). These numerous conflicts between Johnson and Boswell in the Life seem to express something larger than an occasional collision between the mere floating notions of two individuals: despite his personal neurosis, Boswell seems almost an official representative of a new, post-Renaissance urge towards the mechanistic, an urge that Johnson feels always obliged to oppose. The lodgment of this issue within the very fabric of the Life of Johnson seems to suggest its central position at the focus of the eighteenth-century debate between the humanists and the 'moderns'.

The aesthetic of Reynolds is entirely dependent on the Johnsonian assumption of the absolute freedom of the will, and Reynolds makes very clear why humanist aesthetics and ethics can effect no compromise with 'modern' conceptions of natural inspiration or unpremeditated art. In the *Seventh Discourse* he finds not merely pretentious but 'pernicious' all talk of 'courting the muse in shady bowers' or 'waiting the call and inspiration of Genius', not to mention 'attending to times and seasons when the imagination shoots with the greatest vigour'. He goes on: 'To understand literally these metaphors . . . seems to be equally absurd as to conclude, that because painters sometimes represent poets writing from the dictates of a little winged boy or genius, that this same genius did really inform him in a whisper what he was to write, and that he is himself but a mere machine, unconscious of the operations of his own mind.' Blake's marginal comment on this passage, 'How very Anxious Reynolds is to Disprove & Contemn Spiritual Perception', is perhaps more acute than he realizes, for it locates the profound, fundamental basis of the whole humanist aesthetic in Lockean epistemology and might even be taken to succeed in exposing the almost organic alliance between the ethical orthodoxy of eighteenth-century humanism and the empirical psychology of Locke.

Reynolds's *Ironical Discourse*, written in 1791, goes even further in associating the 'modern' theory of unconscious inspiration with mechanism. Like Swift, Reynolds contrives a burlesque modest proposer, who here solemnly advances all the most morally poisonous artistic theories. It is notable that Reynolds's speaker is not merely a devotee of the heresy of unlimited 'inspiration' but also—significantly—that he is designed by Reynolds to represent a British enthusiast for the theory of man manifested in the events of the French Revolution. Reynolds's speaker thus flatters the self-sufficient, 'inspired' student of painting: 'Let the student consider himself whether he is impelled forward by irresistible instinct. He himself is little more than a machine, unconscious of the power which impels him forward to the instant performance of what others learn by the slow method of rules and precepts.' Reynolds's irony, the fruit more of rage than of wit, is almost too broad to work at all. Nevertheless the passage does project the association which Reynolds and the other humanists perceived between the newly stylish theory of artistic inspiration and a mechanistic abdication of freedom. It is ironic that a few years later, with the humanist cause all but lost and in large part even

forgotten, the implications of 'inspiration' were to shift so profoundly that the term could be enlisted directly on behalf of a
new aesthetic 'freedom' from received genres and conventions.

When Gibbon, in his turn, comes to treat the theme of free
will, he seems to glance at Reynolds's shaping of the idea as well
as to hark back not only to the ethical world of Swift's *Mechanical Operation of the Spirit* but that of *Hamlet* as well. The mechanical 'inspiration' he satirizes in the fifteenth chapter of the
Decline and Fall is 'spiritual' rather than artistic, but its ethical
effects and implications are the same. Discussing the alleged
visionary powers of the early Roman Christians, Gibbon writes:

> The divine inspiration, whether it was conveyed in the form of a
> waking or of a sleeping vision, is described as a favour very liberally
> bestowed on all ranks of the faithful, on women as on elders, on boys
> as well as upon bishops. When their devout minds were sufficiently
> prepared by a course of prayer, of fasting, and of vigils, to receive the
> extraordinary impulse, they were transported out of their senses, and
> delivered in ecstasy what was inspired, being mere organs of the
> Holy Spirit, just as a pipe or flute is of him who blows into it.

Gibbon's technique of innuendo here is so brilliant, his tact so
exquisite, that we must pause to try to do this performance
justice. The denigration begins early in the passage with the
exploitation of the contemporary euphemism 'to bestow a
favour liberally', found more frequently in sexual than in
religious contexts; and perhaps a hint of this phrase colours the
meaning of 'impulse' later on, especially if we are mindful of
the Latin sense of an outward 'pushing against'. The innuendo
strengthens as Gibbon plays on the idea of an impious violation
of hierarchy in his phrases 'on women as on elders, on boys as
well as upon bishops'. The necessity of 'a course' of prayer,
fasting, and vigils to bring on what Gibbon hopes to imply are
merely gross hallucinations caused by hunger and hysteria emphasizes the mechanical, deterministic, and fraudulent air of the
proceedings. But the undoubted triumph of the whole passage is
waiting in the word 'inspired': here Gibbon, like Burke with
his epithet 'animated', is relying on the 'ancient' reader's
instinctive awareness of the Latin stem to supply the full ironic
dimension. For these worshippers are being 'blown *upon*', and
they thus earn no merit from what they mechanically 'deliver'.
Their mechanistic, passive role which negates their humanity is

reinforced by the grammatical voice in which their behaviour—
it cannot be called 'action'—is portrayed: all is passive voice
until they 'deliver' what has been blown into them. The Latin
stem of 'inspire' suggests to Gibbon first the image of the organ
pipe—with a side glance, perhaps, at such mechanical internal
organs as bladders and sacs—and then the image of a 'pipe or
flute' being tooted by some ignominious musician who, in the
context of eighteenth-century London, is probably a French or
Italian one at that. Like Swift's Aeolists, the emblems of gassy
Dissent in *A Tale of a Tub*, these early Christian enthusiasts are
transformed by Gibbon's Latinate imagery into mere bags of
wind.

The ethical issue as it strikes Gibbon is very close to that
which appears to obsess Hamlet when he confronts Guildenstern with the flute borrowed from one of the players. Hamlet
asks, 'Will you play upon this pipe?' And when Guildenstern
several times insists that he cannot because he does not know
how, Hamlet answers:

> Why, look you now, how unworthy a thing you make of me! You
> would play upon me; you would seem to know my stops; you
> would pluck out the heart of my mystery; you would sound me
> from my lowest note to the top of my compass; and there is much
> music, excellent voice, in this little organ, yet cannot you make it
> speak. 'Sblood, do you think I am easier to be play'd on than a
> pipe?
>
> (III, ii, 365 ff.)

As both Shakespeare and Gibbon realize, so frail and unstable is man that in any comparison between him and a pipe,
it is not the pipe that will be humanized and glorified but man
who will be diminished and mechanized. In *Hamlet* the figure of
the pipe is used to assert the dignity of the free, honest, and
complicated man in a mechanical, simplified world of 'lying'.
In the *Decline and Fall* the figure, by reversed implication, is
used to suggest a similar freedom and honour which accrue to
those who refuse to surrender their wills to external forces, no
matter how plausibly recommended.

Just as Gibbon's hysterical and 'inspired' Christians recall
Swift's Aeolists, so some of Burke's anti-mechanistic usages seem
reminiscent of the images and techniques of Swift. Because the
whole National Assembly is, to Burke, a merely mechanical

operation—he calls it, indeed, 'the machine now at work in France'—it is to be expected that it will operate by the same vulgar techniques of quantification with which Swift's modest proposer goes to work. In the *Reflections* Burke cites the members of the National Assembly as premising that 'twenty-four millions ought to prevail over two hundred thousand', and he comments: 'True; if the constitution of a kingdom be a problem of arithmetic. This sort of discourse does well enough with the lamp-post [as gallows] for its second: to men who *may* reason calmly, it is ridiculous.' And in its reconstruction of the executive power the National Assembly has betrayed as grave a lapse of humanity as in its management of the legislative. 'Let us now turn our eyes', says Burke, 'to what they have done towards the formation of an executive power. For this they have chosen a degraded king. This their first executive officer is to be a machine, without any sort of deliberate discretion in any one act of his function.' In short, the makers of the Revolution are just as deficient in their conception of what makes a man as the 'profane herd of those vulgar and mechanical [British] politicians', who, believing 'that nothing exists but what is gross and material', had opposed a reconciliation with North America fifteen years before and who had thus become early targets of Burke's contempt in his *Speech on Conciliation with the Colonies*.

All the way from Swift to Burke the humanist sense of the absolute freedom of the will as the basis for ethics seems to oscillate between Christian and Stoical poles. But however close it moves to one pole or the other, the effect is remarkably the same. The point is always that man's happiness is entirely within his own power and the direction of his life entirely within his own command. He and no one else is responsible for what happens to him. In *Sermon* X, written for his old friend Dr. John Taylor, Johnson expresses this point in terms of Anglican Christianity: '[The Devil's] power is so limited by the Governor of the universe, that he cannot hurt us without our own consent; . . . he therefore that yields to temptation has the greater part in his own destruction; he has been warned of his danger, he has been taught his duty; and if these warnings and instructions have had no effect, he may be said voluntarily to desert the right way, and not so much to be deceived by another, as to deceive himself.'

But the Christian formulation here seems not necessarily intrinsic to the idea: it constitutes merely a ready image for articulating the same thing that Swift and Gibbon express through their myths of egregious mechanism. 'Infidel' Gibbon at least would surely approve the 'Roman', stoical tendency of the Johnson of *Rambler* 32, which contains this superb emotional tribute to the nobility of the human will: 'I think there is some reason for questioning whether the body and mind are not so proportioned, that the one can bear all that can be inflicted on the other; whether virtue cannot stand its ground as long as life, and whether a soul well principled will not be separated sooner than subdued.'

It is that kind of commitment to the reality and the power of the will that enables Johnson, tormented by his agonizing illness at the age of 75, to say, 'I will be conquered; I will not capitulate' (*BLJ*, iv, 374). And it is in just that kind of strength that we see the power of the will, as conceived in humanist terms, to redeem human creatures from their drift towards depravity and to redirect them upwards until, for all their unsatisfactoriness, they are capable of imitating something yet higher and thus become fully worthy to be imaged as 'animated strength'.

6

THE PARADOX OF MAN

MAN is thus a mighty curious creature. A flesh-machine of self-destructive depravity fraught with ignorance and vanity, and at the same time inspirited somehow with an *anima* which has it in its power to redeem all defects except, perhaps, mortality, he is a wandering paradox perpetually looking for a place now to hide and now to exhibit himself. He both is and is not like an angel; he both is and is not like a brute. It is his curse and his glory to be at home in a curious moral geography, 'this isthmus of a middle state', as Pope puts it in the *Essay on Man;* and it is his nature that finally it can be suggested only by a series of the most outrageous paradoxes:

> A being darkly wise, and rudely great:
> With too much knowledge for the Sceptic side,
> With too much weakness for the Stoic's pride,
> He hangs between;

Perpetually in doubt, he can commit himself entirely to neither direction in which his dualistic being seems to invite him:

> in doubt to act, or rest,
> In doubt to deem himself a God, or Beast;
> In doubt his Mind or Body to prefer,

—and at this point in Pope's exhibition the pathos which is the usual attendant of the humanist view of man wells up:

> Born but to die, and reas'ning but to err;

Knowledge is of very little use in pointing to a satisfactory direction:

> Alike in ignorance, his reason such,
> Whether he thinks too little, or too much:

There is additional pathos in man's imagining himself 'rational' and orderly, when actually he is only rarely even *capax rationis* and more often is simply a

> Chaos of Thought and Passion, all confus'd;

and whether in a state of ignorance or enlightenment, always his own worst enemy:

> Still by himself abus'd, or disabus'd;

His situation in the general hierarchy of things is both tense and tenuous:

> Created half to rise, and half to fall;

As Adam learns before his Fall, he is the 'Great Lord of all things', and yet, as he discovers just after it, he is 'a prey to all'. In short, he is the 'Sole judge of Truth', but he is also 'in endless Error hurl'd'. Small wonder that to the humanist he is at once

> The glory, jest, and riddle of the world!
>
> (ii, 2–18)

After this demonstration of Pope's, it seems natural that the humanist, when contemplating man, will not know whether to laugh or to weep, and so will do both at once, as at the end of *Gulliver's Travels* or at the end of *The Dunciad*. Pope's version of man sounds familiar and even stale, but one reason why it does is that it occupies so central a position in human experience and in humanistic expression. Pope's 'isthmus' recalls pre-eminently Hamlet's 'sterile promontory', and Hamlet proceeds to lesson Rosencrantz and Guildenstern in a proto-Popian version of man which their mechanistic simplifications show them to be in need of:

> this most excellent canopy, the air, look you, this brave o'erhanging firmament, this majestical roof fretted with golden fire—why, it appeareth no other thing to me than a foul and pestilent congregation of vapours.

Warming to his humanist theme, he proceeds to sketch such a paradoxical picture of man's dualistic capacities that we wonder whether we are being 'abus'd, or disabus'd':

What a piece of work is a man! how noble in reason! how infinite
in faculties! in form and moving how express and admirable! in
action how like an angel! in apprehension how like a god! the
beauty of the world! the paragon of animals!

And yet:

And yet to me what is this quintessence of dust?

(II, ii, 308 ff.)

But familiar as it is, the paradox of the angelic brute is still
capable of giving pause, as it does to poor slow-witted Parson
Adams in *Joseph Andrews*. The parson's son Dick is reading the
story about 'Lennard's' wife: ' "But, good as this lady was, she
was still a woman; that is to say, an angel, and not an angel."
—'"You must mistake, child," cries the parson, "for you read
nonsense." "It is so in the book," answered the son.' This
paradoxical wise child owes something to a fusion of classical
and Christian motifs, suggesting at once the image of the blind
Tiresias being led by a boy and the Christian imagery of the
innocent child leading the dull adults.

The cause of paradox is the juxtaposition of all but irreconcilable dualisms. This is the burden of Erwin Panofsky's definition of 'humanism', which he locates in 'man's proud and tragic
consciousness of self-approved and self-imposed principles, contrasting with his utter subjection to illness, decay and all that is
implied in the word "mortality"'.[1] It seems illuminating that
the humanistic dual view of man as at once angel and beast
appears allied to the paradox of satire in general. Perhaps more
than any other kind of literature, satire transmits a dualistic
vision, for it offers us always a surface of contempt, disparage-
ment, and ridicule masking something quite different, namely,
an implicit faith in man's capacity for redemption through the
operation of choice. Satire works by taxing its targets with
brutishness in order to turn them angelward. In the Augustan
instinct for satire as a favourite literary action we can sense very
powerfully the presence of the dualistic vision of man which in
varying degrees informs all humanist literature of whatever age.

To those aware of the workings of the moral imagination,
dualistic feelings are inescapable, for, as Johnson writes in

[1] *Meaning in the Visual Arts* (New York, 1955), p. 1.

Rambler 169, 'In proportion as perfection is more distinctly conceived, the pleasure of contemplating our own performances
will be lessened.' And it seems to be the strength of his dualistic
instinct that keeps Johnson's view of man, even when highly
satiric in tendency, from ever turning into a mere Mandevillian
cynicism. Thus he writes his friend John Ryland: 'As a being
subject to so many wants Man has inevitably a strong tendency
to self-interest, so I hope as a Being capable of comparing good
and evil he finds something to be preferred in good, and is,
therefore, capable of benevolence . . . ' (*LSJ*, iii, 228). The
subtlety and tenuousness of Johnson's mode of Christianity is
also provided in part by his dualistic habit. He suggests to Mrs.
Thrale that 'It is good to speak dubiously about futurity. It is
likewise not amiss to hope' (*LSJ*, ii, 271).

It would be hard to find a happier emblem of the humanist
dualistic conception of man than the Master Houyhnhnm's
solution to the problem of Gulliver's most appropriate lodging-
place during his first night in Houyhnhnmland. Gulliver could
be sent to harbour with the Yahoos, for he certainly looks rather
like one; or he could remain in the house of the Houyhnhnms,
for he is capable of a form of converse with them. What to do?
Gulliver's master determines on a meaningful compromise:
'When it grew towards Evening, the Master Horse ordered a
Place for me to lodge in; it was but Six Yards from the House,
and separated from the Stable of the *Yahoos*. Here I got some
Straw, and covering myself with my own Cloaths, slept very
sound.' This characteristically empirical, positional image
locates Gulliver just where he belongs, in his proper 'middle
state' from which he is free to move in either direction. It is as if
Swift were mindful of the ancient centaur myth and bent on
domesticating it within the homely eighteenth-century realities
and 'comforts'. Geoffrey Scott observes that what 'nature'
means to the humanist is not what it means to the savage nor
yet what it means to the scientist. Taking Yahoos as loosely
expressive of savagery and Houyhnhnms of science—perhaps
their want of wit qualifies them, at least—we can see that what
Scott says about the humanist's relation to 'nature' illuminates
Gulliver's challenge in Houyhnhnmland, the challenge that he
accepts but bungles so badly. After positing a savage's 'nature'
and a scientist's 'nature', Scott goes on to suggest that 'a third

way is open. [The humanist] may construct, within the world
as it is, a pattern of the world as he would have it. This is the
way of humanism, in philosophy, in life, and in the arts.'[2] But
it is just this 'third way' that Gulliver fails to take, a way which
would make a gesture towards reconciling the dualistic extremes with which he is presented. Given his choice of behaving
like the generous Captain Pedro de Mendez who rescues him or
like the coherent, stable Martin of *A Tale of a Tub*, he decides
instead to play a version of Peter, and the crashing irony is that
he ends a slavering Jack. As Pope says in the *Essay on Man*,
poor man is

> This hour a slave, the next a deity.
>
> (i, 68)

Gulliver sails proudly for home determined to act the deity, and
succeeds only in turning slave.

Two-directional imagery like this image of Gulliver's lodging
we encounter very frequently in Swift, and within the humanist
tradition it seems the most common method for embodying
ethical issues. Once we call it something like the habit of moral
antithesis, it is obvious how it naturally works to shape the
conventions of Augustan sentence structure and the syntactical
and prosodic habits of the heroic couplet. Pope's prefatory
remarks to the *Essay on Man* ('The Design') illustrate the dualistic or antithetical habit in prose: 'If I could flatter myself that
this Essay has any merit, it is in steering betwixt the extremes of
doctrines seemingly opposite, . . . in forming a *temperate* yet not
inconsistent, and a *short* yet not *imperfect* system of Ethics.' Pope
seems remarkably sensitive to the conventional halving of
prayers in epic poetry, and his dualistic habit of mind seems to
move him to recover the image for his own narrative uses. Thus
in *The Rape of the Lock*

> [Lord Petre] begs with ardent Eyes
> Soon to obtain, and long possess the Prize:
> The pow'rs gave Ear, and granted half his Pray'r,
> The rest, the Winds dispers'd in empty Air.
>
> (ii, 43–46)

And complimenting Martha Blount in *Moral Essay* II, Pope
tells her that Phoebus

---

[2] *Architecture of Humanism*, p. 242.

> Averted half your Parents simple Pray'r,
> And gave you Beauty, but deny'd the Pelf
> That buys your sex a Tyrant o'er itself.
>
> (286–8)

It is all quite a bit like Hamlet's similar rhetorical habit. 'Look here upon this picture, and on this', he invites Gertrude, and he proceeds to dichotomize vigorously until even the Queen, gradually moving a step closer to Hamlet's ethical vision, seems to catch the mode. She cries out,

> O, Hamlet, thou hast cleft my heart in twain.

As if encouraged that she has sensed the principle, Hamlet rejoins immediately:

> O, throw away the worser part of it,
> And live the purer with the better half,   (III, iv. 54 ff.)

and he then moves to show her how self-restraint can be developed into an actual habit, almost, in Augustan terms, a 'prejudice'. Dualism is the method of Renaissance ethics, and it is remarkable how profoundly the dualistic habit of mind persists in ethical conservatives through all the political and social vicissitudes of the eighteenth century. Antitheses swarm everywhere: *this* and *that*, wit and judgment, reason and passion, art and nature, city and country, ancient and modern, uniformity and variety, sublime and beautiful. There is even a sense in which it is correct to say that the general method of a standard 'ancient'—that is, moral—eighteenth-century poem is severely dichotomous. An action like the following, from Pope's *Epistle to Miss Blount, on her Leaving the Town, after the Coronation*, is played over and over again, from *Windsor Forest* and *The Day of Judgement* to *The Vanity of Human Wishes*:

> In some fair evening, on your elbow laid,
> You dream of triumphs in the rural shade;
> In pensive thought recall the fancy'd [urban] scene,
> See Coronations rise on ev'ry green;
> Before you pass th' imaginary sights
> Of Lords, and Earls, and Dukes, and garter'd Knights;
> While the spread Fan o'ershades your closing Eyes;
> Then give one flirt, and all the vision flies.
> Thus vanish sceptres, coronets, and balls,
> And leave you in lone woods, and empty halls.
>
> (31–40)

I

It is hard to tell whether the irony of poems like this results from the initial dualism of the ethical assumptions, or whether the ethical assumptions are pushed further in a dualistic direction by the natural operations of irony. But whatever we decide, there can be little doubt that there is an intimate relation between the dualistic method of mind and the humanist obsession with the paradox of man, as especially Samuel Johnson's rhetorical practice indicates.

Indeed, Johnson's habit of conceiving of things dualistically seems to provide him with his basic literary mode, whether he is talking or writing. As Boswell reports: 'He would begin thus: "Why, Sir, as to the good or evil of card-playing—" "Now, (said Garrick,) he is thinking which side he shall take" ' (*BLJ*, iii, 23–24). In looking about him at human actions, Johnson's sense of the depravity of human nature colours dualistic perceptions like this, from *Rambler* 131: 'the race of men may be divided in a political estimate between those who are practising fraud, and those who are repelling it'. In sentence structure a dualism like the following is customary: 'Spring is the season of gaiety, and winter of terror' (*Rambler* 80). Vast stylistic complication occurs, but the dualistic vision remains constant. Here, in the *Journey to the Western Islands*, he is exercising himself on the topic of power and money:

Power and wealth supply the place of each other. Power confers the ability of gratifying our desire without the consent of others. Wealth enables us to obtain the consent of others to our gratification. Power, simply considered, whatever it confers on one, must take from another. Wealth enables its owner to give to others, by taking only from himself. Power pleases the violent and proud: wealth delights the placid and the timorous. Youth therefore flies at power, and age grovels after riches.

In the *Life of Milton* we are given the dualistic view of *Lycidas*, in which 'there is no nature, for there is no truth; there is no art, for there is nothing new'. And we are given the dualistic view of the practice of biography in *Idler* 84: 'He that writes the life of another is either his friend or his enemy. . . .' And when Johnson insists in *Rambler* 4 that virtue and vice be depicted in fiction as clearly distinct and separable, we see the same impulse towards moral dichotomy; we see it too in his advice to Boswell about calling whores by the right name: 'My dear Sir, never accustom your mind to mingle virtue and vice' (*BLJ*, ii, 247). Now and then the dualisms become themselves the agents of irony and wit, as when Johnson says of the Third Letter of Jenyns's *Free Inquiry* that it contains 'a mixture of borrowed truth, and native folly, of some notions just and trite, and others uncommon and ridiculous'. Poor Jenyns!

Johnson conceives of man's paradoxical nature as the product of the conflicting dualisms of which he is constituted. 'While the world was yet in its infancy,' he pronounces in *Rambler* 96, 'TRUTH came among mortals from above, and FALSEHOOD from below.' The result is a hierarchical arrangement of the human faculties which involves a constant struggle between mind at the top and body underneath. The contrary directions in which these two capacities urge him will always produce in man a degree of self-division: as Johnson says in *Adventurer* 120, the mind of the virtuous man, 'however elevated, inhabits a body subject to innumerable casualties'. Part of man's ethical business is to find any means for keeping the mind, the upper part of the hierarchical dualism, in the ascendancy. To Johnson, even so slight an activity as forming virtuoso collections of coins and shells has some ethical value, for, 'by fixing the thoughts upon intellectual pleasures, [it] resists the natural encroachments of sensuality, and maintains the mind in her lawful superiority' (*Idler* 56). The phrase 'lawful superiority' has of course a distinctly old-fashioned ring, recalling as it does such classic Renaissance formulations of moral hierarchy as that in Sir Thomas Elyot's *Book of the Governor* (1531): 'In every thyng is ordre: and without ordre may be nothing stable or permanent: And it may nat be called ordre excepte it do contayne in it degrees, high and base, accordynge to the merite or estimation of the thynge that is ordred.'

Few things are clearer to Johnson than that even in his moral victories man by his nature has been doomed to choose, and thus to reject a treasured part of himself, and thus to be miserable. In *Idler* 52 he writes: 'The general voice of mankind, civil and barbarous, confesses that the mind and body are at variance, and that neither can be made happy by its proper gratifications but at the expence of the other.' And yet man's predicament, ironic as it is, offers him no avenue to satisfaction but to cede to the upper element in his personal hierarchy; Johnson continues: 'And none have failed to confer their esteem on those who prefer intellect to sense, who control their lower by their higher faculties, and forget the wants and desires of animal life for rational disquisitions or pious contemplations.' Self-division is a sad thing, but self-destruction is worse.

Reynolds's image of hierarchy seems, in Elyot's term, to admit more 'degrees' than Johnson's. The end of the *Ninth Discourse* operates in the 'noble' Augustan tradition of fusing artistic taste and moral value. The great use of 'liberal' painting, by which Reynolds means history-painting depicting heroic moral conflicts, is that it may be a vehicle for refining the taste of whole countries. Refinement of taste, he says, 'if it does not lead directly to purity of manners, obviates at least their general depravation, by disentangling the mind from appetite, and conducting the thoughts through successive stages of excellence, till that contemplation of universal rectitude and harmony which began by Taste, may, as it is exalted and refined, conclude in Virtue.' But even though the upward movement from one extreme to another, from 'depravation' to 'purity', necessitates pauses at 'successive stages', we are still conscious of an objective dualism defined by the distance between 'mind' and 'appetite'. As Reynolds confesses in his remarks on Shakespeare, 'If I was to judge from my own experience, the mind always desires to double, to entertain two objects at a time' (*P*, 135).

In Gibbon the dualistic tendency takes the form of an appreciation of something very like duplicity as fundamental to the uniform nature of man. In an observation like the following, from Chapter II of the *Decline and Fall*, we are invited to prefer the disingenuous dualism of the ancient philosophers to the naïve monism ('sincerity') of the early Christians: 'In their writings and conversation the philosophers of antiquity asserted the independent dignity of reason; but they resigned their actions to the commands of law and of custom. Viewing with a smile of pity and indulgence the various errors of the vulgar, they diligently practised the ceremonies of their fathers . . . they approached with the same inward contempt and the same external reverence the altars of the Libyan, the Olympian, or the Capitoline Jupiter.' Dissimulation thus becomes something close to an obligation for those deeply aware of the requirements of human nature. Gibbon's sense of the vast difference between inner and outer corresponds to Johnson's scepticism about literary 'sincerity', and the Gibbonian relation between philosophers and Christians is very like that between the eighteenth-century literary 'ancients' and 'moderns'.

From these examples of the humanist instinct for dualistic images we can gauge the distance of the humanist ethical and rhetorical world from the monistic or transcendental world, with its impulse towards erasing disparities and distinctions rather than asserting and emphasizing them. It is a fundamental humanist assumption that nothing is equal to anything else. It follows as we have seen that man's obligations to the life of value require of him a constant exercise of hierarchical ranking and arranging of the data of experience and the forces of his internal nature. A very frequent humanist action, then, is the hierarchical ordering of the items within the several distinguishable classes of data. The humanist sensibility loves to deal with apparent moral dilemmas and puzzles whose solutions are based upon an apprehension of the proper hierarchical premises. It enjoys considering questions such as these: is Garrick a good actor but a bad man? should Adam have chosen God or Eve? is the just or the expedient action to be preferred? In Chapter II of his *Autobiography* Gibbon exercises his hierarchical sensibility even over the question of the comparative desirability of childhood and age, and, in the process of his reasoning, feels it necessary to reassert the very old-fashioned image of the chain of being. He is doubting the validity of Gray's picture of the joys of youth in *Ode on a Distant Prospect of Eton College*:

I would ask the warmest and most active hero of the playfield whether he can seriously compare his childish with his manly enjoyments, whether he does not feel, as the most precious attribute of his existence, the vigorous maturity of sensual and spiritual powers which nature has reserved for the age of puberty. A state of happiness arising only from the want of foresight and reflection shall never provoke my envy. Such degenerate taste would tend to shrink us in the scale of beings from a man to a child, a dog, and an oyster, till we had reached the confines of brute matter, which cannot suffer because it cannot feel.

The monistic tradition would reject entirely Gibbon's attempt to escape his childhood and to separate it from his maturity. In *Out of the Cradle Endlessly Rocking* it is Whitman's ambition to pass beyond such a distinction and to enact instead the wonder-working fusion of childhood and age. In *Ode: Intimations of Immortality* Wordsworth presents himself in the act of attempting to recover the 'visionary gleam' vouchsafed the child. But Gibbon, inhabiting a moral world where distinction, separation, inequality, and hierarchy are almost self-evident ethical principles, would look upon the performances of both Whitman and Wordsworth as enactments of precisely the kind of 'Dulness' exposed in *The Dunciad*, of which Thomas R. Edwards has observed: 'The aim of Dulness is sameness, the utter absence of the differentiation that makes order possible. . . . In such a state intelligence has no place, for there are no qualitative differences to be discriminated. Dulness melts down and levels off the structural order of "degree" that had been the imagination's dream since the beginnings of thought.'[3]

The distance between the dualistic and the monistic worlds is clearly apparent in the difference between the general theory of metaphor preferred respectively by 'ancients' and 'moderns'. To the humanist, metaphor, which operates like rapid or almost instantaneous simile, does not actually assert that 'a *is* b'; instead it suggests that 'a is *like* b'. Tenor and vehicle are never thought to interfuse; regardless of closeness of resemblance, the two terms in a comparison remain ultimately distinct. This distrust of the 'reality' of metaphor underlies Johnson's point when he tells Boswell: 'I do not approve of figurative expressions in addressing the Supreme Being; and I never use them. Taylor gives a very good advice: "Never lie in your prayers . . ." ' (*BLJ*, iv, 294–5). But within the monistic rhetorical world all the way from Shelley to Wallace Stevens the metaphor is so far from being a 'lie' that instead it becomes the avenue, and often the sole avenue, to reality: the two terms of a figure actually fuse and thus generate a more 'real' third thing.

Johnson's conception of the ultimate frivolity of metaphor suggests his prodigious understanding of the permanent distinctions between form and matter, mind and body; and this under-

[3] *This Dark Estate*, p. 127.

standing prompts his humane perception of the necessary distance between a man's ethical principles and his ethical practice. He is sometimes horrified by the kind of crude, mechanical
assumptions on this question that he encounters. On one occasion he is moved to reprimand 'one who said in his presence'
that 'he had no notion of people being in earnest in their good
professions, whose practice was not suitable to them'. Johnson
explodes: 'Sir, are you so grossly ignorant of human nature as
not to know that a man may be very sincere in good principles,
without having good practice?' (*BLJ*, iv, 396–7). In this
vigorous Johnsonian rejoinder we perceive the truth of Mrs.
Thrale's comment on his dualism: 'all he did was gentle, if all
he said was rough' (*JM*, i, 296).

To the humanist, inconsistency is necessarily man's lot: to
expect consistency from him is to deny by implication the paradoxical dualism that makes him man. Pope reveals his appreciation of this fact about man's nature when, in the *Essay on Man*,
he reasons so that he makes the corrupt passions of man ironically productive of all his virtues. Indeed, the major paradoxical
theme of the poem is

> . . . Man's low passions, [and] their glorious ends.
>
> (iv, 376)

But Pope's attitude towards this subject is complacent when
compared with Johnson's. Johnson seems more empirically
aware than Pope that, as Imlac says in Chapter XVIII of
Rasselas, 'teachers of morality . . . discourse like angels, but . . .
live like men'. And Johnson's perception of the gulf between
principles and practice is pleasantly complicated by an overriding irony and sympathy. So it is in the relation between
Chapters XVII and XVIII of *Rasselas*. The first of these chapters depicts Rasselas's disgust and boredom with the pleasures of
'[Egyptian] young men of spirit and gaiety', whose dissipations
he finds 'gross and sensual' because in them 'the mind had no
part'. In the next chapter, however, determined now to live
according to the promptings of his judgment, Rasselas is
presented with the spectacle of the local Stoic who utters high
principles of self-restraint and intellectual control until his
daughter suddenly dies, whereupon he becomes a man like anyone else and breaks down completely. This Stoic is simply a

bodying forth of Johnson's conviction that 'no man has power of acting equal to that of thinking' (*Rambler* 77).

Johnson's honest and intimate acquaintance with himself—with, for example, his repeated experience of procrastination and violated resolutions—prevents his feeling anything but sympathy for others whose practices diverge grossly from their principles. It goes without saying that one of the sources of the sympathy which emanates from the pages of the *Life of Savage* is Johnson's intimate identification of himself with the character of his subject, whose principles 'were . . . treasured up in his mind rather for shew than use, and operated very little upon his conduct, however elegantly he might sometimes explain, or however forcibly he might inculcate them'. This sympathy with the paradoxical state of man also colours Johnson's interpretation of the character of Pope. In the *Life of Pope* he assures us that despite Pope's indulgence in sceptical levities and indecencies, 'it does not appear that his principles were ever corrupted, or that he ever lost his belief of Revelation'. Pope indeed becomes pleasantly emblematic of Everyman when Johnson explains why it took him so long to translate the *Iliad*; wise after his experience with the *Dictionary*, Johnson comments that 'the distance is commonly very great between actual performances and speculative possibility'. This is to say that a satisfactory monistic synthesis is not within the power of genuinely human creatures, at least in this state, although circumstances may be different elsewhere; as Johnson says, 'The happiness of Heaven will be, that pleasure and virtue will be perfectly consistent' (*BLJ*, iii, 292). But in the sublunary sphere the distance between desire and performance is wide, so wide, in fact, that Johnson feels it necessary to give this advice, in the *Life of Sir Thomas Browne*, to those who would know man: 'The opinions of every man must be learned from himself: concerning his practice, it is safest to trust the evidence of others.'

But all humanists affirm the inconsistency of man: Johnson is simply more deeply immersed in the matter than others. Typical of the whole tradition is Swift's observation in his *Thoughts on Various Subjects*: 'If a Man would register all his Opinions on Love, Politicks, Religion, Learning, and the like; beginning from his Youth, and so go on to old Age: What a Bundle of Inconsistencies and Contradictions would appear at last?' The arch-sin of Pride, indeed, is roughly equivalent to the assumption that human actions can be consistent. And so is the arch-enemy social science. Boswell is fond of exploiting the humanist premise of the inconsistency of man as a pretext for a gratifying self-wonder. He records in his journal in 1762: 'What a curious, inconsistent thing is the mind of man! In the midst of divine service I was laying plans for having women, and yet I had the most sincere feelings of religion' (*LJ*, 54).

In the hands of Reynolds, the conviction of the ludicrous and pathetic inconsistency of man generates a characteristic and little-known humanist document, his fragmentary essay on Shakespeare. 'Arts have little to do with reason', Reynolds observes. And from this Burkean premise he sets out like Johnson to justify Shakespeare's practice of 'mixing tragedy and comedy'. Like Burke and Johnson again, he conceives of his task as in part a skirmish with the 'mechanical' French mind, and like them he turns away from systems and theories to inquire into 'the natural and unsophisticated feelings of mankind'. What the French critics have overlooked is simply that man is not a rational creature:

Theoretical systems . . . go on a supposition that by their precepts and order they can give a different disposition and quality to the mind than nature had thought proper to give, that a man ought totally to keep separate his intellectual from his sensual desires. All this is fine in theory, but—

Man being what he is, an inconsistent being, a professed lover of art and nature, of order, of regularity, and of variety, and who therefore cannot long continue his attention without some recreation; hence it is that the poet relieves the mind of the reader [by variety].

Typical of English humanist criticism from Ben Jonson to T. S. Eliot is the recourse to the actual, experienced operations of the human mind as a basis for literary theory; and typical of the Augustan humanist tradition is Reynolds's sanction of the 'mingled drama' by means of an honest—if compulsively dualistic—look at human realities:

Man is both a consistent and an inconsistent being, a lover of art when it imitates nature and of nature when it imitates art, of uniformity and of variety, a creature of habit that loves novelty. The principles of art must conform to this capricious being. . . .

Critics seem to consider man as too uniformly wise, and in their rules make no account for the playful part of the mind. Their rules are formed for another race of beings than what man really is.

Because the mind works whimsically and inconsistently, and because men are normally as pathetically abstracted and be- mused as the inhabitants of Swift's Laputa, 'The theatre', says Reynolds, 'acts as a flapper and rouses in us for the time a fic- titious feeling of interest and pleasing anxiety.' It is empirically if not theoretically true that, given the inconsistency of the mind, tragicomedy will accord more with that mind's desires than 'purer' and less varied forms (P, 121–38).

'We have', says Johnson, 'less reason to be surprised or offended when we find others differ from us in opinion, because we very often differ from ourselves' (Adventurer 107). Of all the Augustan humanists Johnson remains for us as for his contem- poraries the prime exemplar of a splendid human inconsistency. He has become a pattern for imitation and almost, indeed, a humanist saint. Reynolds noticed that 'From passion, from the prevalence of his disposition for the minute, he was continually acting contrary to his reason, to his own principles' (P, 82). And to Boswell his inconsistency was so interesting because it was so eminently typical of general human nature: 'The heterogeneous composition of human nature was remarkably exemplified in Johnson. His liberality in giving his money to persons in distress was extraordinary. Yet there lurked about him a propensity to paltry saving' (BLJ, iv, 191). Johnson's last days, when he seems to be just exactly as certain of his imminent salvation as he is of his imminent damnation, remind us of those of Abraham Cowley, who uttered near the end this humanist prayer: 'O Lord, I believe: help my unbelief. O Lord, I repent: pardon the weakness of my repentance.' The uneasy partnership between the angelic and the brutal in Johnson's person—that extraordinary spirit in that outrageous body!—seems to project the whole humanist scheme of dualism and inconsistency. And a vignette that embodies all that we have been considering is Boswell's unforgettable portrayal of Johnson, the proud, sarcastical, puffing, heavy bear, lumbering noisily through the City very late at night and gently folding pennies into the hands of the abandoned children asleep in the streets.

What makes the human situation the more pitiful is that man is actually so limited and frail and tiny, especially when viewed next to the heroic images he is pleased to entertain of himself. As Sir Lewis Namier is reputed to have said, 'Conservatism is primarily based on the proper recognition of human limitation.'[4] From the beginning the Augustan conservatives conduct their warfare with the eighteenth-century progressives by insisting on the ineradicable limitations of man. Locke's whole account of the mind stems from his premise that it is much more finite, limited, and frail than had been sometimes thought in the earlier seventeenth century. In the *Theory of Moral Sentiments* Adam Smith hits upon the transformation in the theory of man that has taken place within a couple of centuries; as he perceives, 'Humanity does not desire to be great, but to be loved.' And it desires to be loved because it is secretly conscious of the extent of its 'private infirmities', as Swift calls them in one of his richest comments on the ethical use of the classics. Speaking as if without his customary mask in the 'Digression on Madness' in *A Tale of a Tub*, he says: 'the Brain, in its natural Position and State of Serenity, disposeth its Owner to pass his Life in the common Forms, without any Thought of subduing Multitudes to his own *Power*, his *Reasons* or his *Visions*; and the more he shapes his Understanding by the Pattern of Human Learning, the less he is inclined to form Parties after his particular Notions; because that instructs him in his private Infirmities, as well as in the stubborn Ignorance of the People.' Here Swift, relying on the assumption of the uniformity of human nature, indicates that a primary use of ancient literature ('Human Learning') is to keep man reminded of his limitations and of the irony of his ambitions. Which is to say that the modern perversion of evangelicism, all the way from Puritans to Jacobins, is to be ascribed in part to the modern neglect of classical literature. If the modern Soame Jenyns had been more deeply read in the ancient literature of human limitation, Johnson suggests, he might have imbibed some salutary caution; as it is, says Johnson, Jenyns 'decides too easily upon questions out of reach of human determination, with too little consideration of mortal weakness, and with too much vivacity for the necessary

[4] See Donald J. Greene, 'Is There a "Tory" Prose Style?' *Bulletin of the New York Public Library*, LXVI (Sept. 1962), 453.

caution'. After exposing Jenyns's attempts to reason accurately about the chain of being, Johnson concludes: 'To these meditations humanity is unequal.'

Johnson implies the whole humanist theory of composition—moderns would want to call it 'creation'—in *Rambler* 169, where he argues that a thoroughgoing sense of human weakness is a foremost ingredient of literary genius. The main reason, he says, why the writings of the ancients seem preferable to those of the moderns is not so much that the ancients thought of all the good subjects first or that their language was more polished and subtle, but rather that 'Their sense of human weakness confined them commonly to one study, which their knowledge of the extent of every science engaged them to prosecute with indefatigable diligence.' That is, suspicious of themselves because of their general awareness of human limitations, they judged and revised assiduously, just like Milton and Pope: 'much time, and many rasures, were considered as indispensable requisites; and that no other method of attaining lasting praise has been yet discovered, may be conjectured from the blotted manuscripts of Milton now remaining, and from the tardy emission of Pope's compositions . . .'.

Sometimes Johnson like Swift turns to the overtly physical to enforce the idea of the limitations of human nature. In *Idler* 32, for example, he writes that Alexander,

in the pride of conquests, and intoxication of flattery, . . . declared that he only perceived himself to be a man by the necessity of sleep. Whether he considered sleep as necessary to his mind or body, it was indeed a sufficient evidence of human infirmity; the body which required such frequency of renovation, gave but faint promises of immortality; and the mind which, from time to time, sunk gladly into insensibility, made no very near approaches to the felicity of the supreme and self-sufficient nature.

And Socrates, wiser than Alexander, 'by long observation upon himself and others, discovered the weakness of the strongest, and the dimness of the most enlightened intellect' (*Adventurer* 58). The liability of Gibbon's early Christians to delusion and self-deception suggests the threat to the frail human imagination that attends an excessive will to behold wonders. As it does throughout Chapters XV and XVI of the *Decline and Fall*, Gibbon's word 'extraordinary' means here nothing short of

'incredible' or 'impossible': 'The primitive Christians perpetually trod on mystic ground, and their minds were exercised
by the habits of believing the most extraordinary events. They
felt, or they fancied, that on every side they were incessantly
assaulted by demons. . . .' Gibbon's 'perpetually' and 'incessantly' operate like Swift's 'infallibly' to expose the total preposterousness of these proceedings. What is sacred to Gibbon is
the sense of human limitation: the blasphemy is whatever calls
it into question.

A similar sense of the sacredness of human limitations is the
staple of Burke's whole career in rhetoric and polemic. As he
points out in *Thoughts on French Affairs*, it was the mad pride of
Louis XVI that helped dethrone him. In constraining and
humbling his nobility and clergy, Louis revealed that 'he could
not bear the inconveniences which are attached to everything
human'; he could not bear 'those limits which Nature pre-
scribes to desire and imagination . . .'. What Louis XVI forgot
is precisely what Johnson, with his customary dualistic vision,
sets before us in *Rambler* 178: 'Providence has fixed the limits of
human enjoyment by immovable boundaries, and has set
different gratifications at such a distance from each other, that
no art or power can bring them together. This great law it is the
business of every rational being to understand, that life may not
pass away in an attempt to make contradictions consistent, to
combine opposite qualities, and to unite things which the nature
of their being must always keep asunder.'

The theme of human limitations is admirably 'incorporated'
by Swift in the image of the frailty of Gulliver's body. Indeed,
it is remarkable what happens physically to poor Gulliver during his four voyages. He does far more suffering than acting.
Even though as a surgeon he is more likely than most to dwell
obsessively on his own physical injuries, and even though his
commitment to the ideals of the Royal Society impels him to
deliver his narrative with a comically detailed circumstantiality,
he records a really startling number of hurts. In the voyage to
Lilliput, for example, his hair is painfully pulled, and his hands
and face are blistered by needle-like arrows. During his stay
among the people of Brobdingnag he is battered so badly that
he appears almost accident-prone: his flesh is punctured by
wheat-beards; twice his sides are painfully crushed; he is

shaken up and bruised in a box; his nose and forehead are grievously stung by flies as big as larks; he suffers painful contusions from a shower of gigantic hailstones; he 'breaks' his shin on a snailshell; and he is pummelled about the head and body by a linnet's wings. And during his fourth voyage he is brought again into dire physical jeopardy: his final series of physical ordeals begins as his hand is painfully squeezed by a horse. Finally, as he leaves Houyhnhnmland, Swift contrives that Gulliver shall suffer a wholly gratuitous arrow wound on the inside of his left knee ('I shall carry the Mark to my Grave'). Looking back on the whole extent of Gulliver's experiences before his final return to England, we are hardly surprised that his intellectuals at the end have come unhinged: for years his body has been beaten, dropped, squeezed, lacerated, and punctured. When all is said, the experiences which transform him from a fairly bright young surgeon into a raging megalomaniac have been almost as largely physical as intellectual and psychological. So powerfully does Swift reveal Gulliver's purely mental difficulties at the end of the fourth voyage that we may tend to forget that Gulliver has also been made to undergo the sorest physical trials. During the four voyages he has been hurt so badly that, although he is normally a taciturn, unemotional, 'Roman' sort of person, he has been reduced to weeping three times; so severely has he been injured at various times that at least twenty-four of his total travelling days he has spent recuperating in bed.

In addition to these actual injuries which Gulliver endures, he also experiences a number of narrow escapes, potential injuries, and pathetic fears of physical hurt. In Lilliput the vulnerability of his eyes is insisted upon: an arrow barely misses his left eye, and only his spectacles prevent the loss of both his eyes as he works to capture the Blefuscan fleet. Furthermore, one of the Lilliputian punishments decreed for Quinbus Flestrin is that his eyes be put out. And during the Brobdingnagian trip Gulliver's experience is one of an almost continuous narrow escape from serious injury. He almost falls from the hand of the farmer and off the edge of the table. Stumbling over a crust, he falls flat on his face and barely escapes injury. After being held in a child's mouth, he is dropped, and he is saved only by being miraculously caught in a woman's apron. He is tossed into a bowl of cream, knocked down but not badly hurt by a shower of falling apples, and clutched dangerously between a spaniel's teeth. He is lucky to escape serious injury during a nasty tumble into a mole hill, whereupon he 'coined some Lye not worth remembering, to excuse my self for spoiling my Cloaths'. And during the sojourn at Laputa, he is afraid of some 'hurt' befalling him in his encounter with the magician.

But Gulliver, who acts like a sort of physically vulnerable *Ur*-Boswell on the Grand Tour, is not the only one in the book who suffers or who fears injury: the creatures he is thrown among also endure catastrophes of pain and damage, often curiously particularized by Swift. Thus in Lilliput, two or three of the rope-dancers break their limbs in falls. A horse, slipping part way through Gulliver's handkerchief, strains a shoulder. The grandfather of the Lilliputian monarch, it is reported, as a result of breaking his egg upon the larger end suffered a cut finger. In the same way, the fourth voyage seems busy with apparently gratuitous details of injury and pain: for example, Gulliver carefully tells us that an elderly Houyhnhnm 'of Quality' alighted from his Yahoo-drawn sledge 'with his Hind-feet forward, having by Accident got a Hurt in his Left Forefoot'.

Nor are all the manifold injuries in *Gulliver's Travels* confined to the bodies of Gulliver and his hosts. Gulliver's clothing and personal property suffer constant damage, and when they are not actually being damaged, Gulliver is worrying that at any moment they may be hurt. We are not surprised that a ship-wrecked mariner suffers damage to his clothing and personal effects, but we are surprised that Gulliver constantly goes out of his way to call attention to the damages and losses he suffers: his scimitar, his hat, his breeches—all are damaged in Lilliput, and the damage is punctiliously recounted. In Brobdingnag the familiar process of damage and deterioration begins all over again: a fall into a bowl of milk utterly spoils Gulliver's suit; his stockings and breeches are soiled when he is thrust into a marrow bone; and his suit—what's left of it—is further ruined by being daubed with frog slime and 'bemired' with cow dung. In the third voyage our attention is invited to the fact that his hat has again worn out, and in the fourth voyage we are told yet again by Gulliver that his clothes are 'in a declining Condition'.

Gulliver's clothes and personal effects, in fact, at times seem to be Gulliver himself: this is the apparent state of things which fascinates the Houyhnhnm before whom Gulliver undresses; and this ironic suggestion of an equation between Gulliver and his clothing, reminding us of the ironic 'clothes philosophy' of Section II of *A Tale of a Tub*, Swift exploits to suggest that damage to Gulliver's frail garments is the equivalent of damage to the frail Gulliver. The vulnerability of Gulliver's clothing, that is, is a symbol three degrees removed from what it appears to signify: damage to the clothes is symbolic of damage to the body; and damage to the body is symbolic of damage to Gulliver's complacent self-esteem.

These little incidents of injury and destruction are pervasive in *Gulliver's Travels*, as we are reminded by the recurrence—very striking once we are attuned to it—of words like 'hurt', 'injury', 'damage', 'accident', 'mischief', 'misfortune', and 'spoiled'. When we focus on what is happening physically in *Gulliver's Travels*, we sense the oblique presence of this motif of frailty and vulnerability even in passages which really address themselves to something quite different. For example: 'His Majesty [the Emperor of Blefuscu] presented me . . . with his Picture at full length, which I immediately put into one of my Gloves, to keep it from being hurt.' It is as if Swift were determined not to let us forget that there is a pathetic fragility in all his fictional objects, whether animate or inanimate.

And Swift seems to have provided within his text a key to these pervasive reminders of the vulnerability of man and the fragility of his personal effects. In the second voyage, we are told in a voice which sounds perhaps more Swiftian than Gulliverian of a 'little old Treatise' treasured now only by elderly women and the more credulous vulgar, a copy of which Glumdalclitch has been given by her governess. The burden of this mysterious little book, we are told, is precisely the theme of the physical frailty of man: the book shows 'how diminutive, contemptible, and helpless an Animal . . . [is] Man in his own Nature'. Like Johnson's version of Juvenal in *London*, the book emphasizes man's liability to accident and injury; it argues that 'the very Laws of Nature absolutely required we should have been made in the Beginning, of a Size more large and robust, not so liable to Destruction from every little Accident of a Tile falling from an House, or a Stone cast from the Hand of a Boy, or of being drowned in a little Brook.' Here Swift appears to avail himself of the myth of the Decay of Nature as a fictional surrogate for the Christian myth of the Fall. Although, as Miss Kathleen Williams reminds us, Godfrey Goodman's *The Fall of Man, or the Corruption of Nature* (1616) is perhaps the kind of 'little old Treatise' Swift has in mind,[5] I think we shall not go far wrong if we associate—even though we do not identify— Glumdalclitch's conservative little book with the Bible itself. The theme that Swift realizes by means of the image of Gulliver's physical frailty appears quintessentially humanistic: the theme is the inadequacy of an unassisted self-esteem in redeeming man from his essential frailties of mind and spirit. Swift's conception of Gulliver is close to Pope's feeling for the China jar which is Belinda. And Pope's sense of human frailty in the *Essay on Man* reminds us of Gulliver's fear for his eyes in Lilliput and for his body in Brobdingnag: addressing 'Presumptuous Man', Pope taxes him with being 'so weak, so little, and so blind'. In one of its most significant moods the Augustan humanist mind conceives of man thus as a little delicate cage of bones and skin constantly at the mercy of accidental damage or destruction.

Johnson's sense of man's littleness is such that, if Swift had not already written it, he might himself have been tempted to sketch such a comedy of man diminished as Gulliver enacts in his second voyage. Boswell reports:

I mentioned that I was afraid to put into my journal too many little incidents. JOHNSON. 'There is nothing, Sir, too little for so little a creature as man. It is by studying little things that we attain the great art of having as little misery and as much happiness as possible'.

(BLJ, i, 433)

What Gulliver appears not to learn during his stay with the Brobdingnagians Johnson, in *Idler* 88, indicates that he has mastered completely: 'a little more than nothing is as much as can be expected from [man], who with respect to the multitudes about him is himself little more than nothing'. We think of the preposterousness of poor, foolish Gulliver who imagines that he is doing a great thing in performing on the spinet before the King and Queen of Brobdingnag, pounding on the keys with

[5] *Jonathan Swift and the Age of Compromise* (Lawrence, Kansas, 1958), p. 159.
K

'two round Sticks about the Bigness of common Cudgels'. Says
Gulliver: 'I ran sideling . . . that way and this, as fast as I could,
banging the proper Keys with my two Sticks; and made a shift
to play a Jigg to the great Satisfaction of both their Majesties.'
We may be forgiven if we impute their Majesties' 'Satisfaction'
more to their sense of the ridiculous than to their sense of wonder. Writing Boswell in 1777, Johnson speaks as an educated
and redeemed Gulliver when he refers to the *Lives of the Poets*
this way: 'I am engaged to write little Lives, and little Prefaces,
to a little edition of the English Poets' (*LSJ*, ii, 170). In short,
man's ethical obligation is to learn 'how to become little without becoming mean . . .' (*Rambler* 152).

Reynolds suggests in the *Fifth Discourse* how the assumption of
the littleness of man is the very basis of the practice of heroic
painting, and, by implication, epic poetry: one of Raphael's
weaknesses when he is measured against Michelangelo,
Reynolds argues, is that his 'figures are not so much disjoined
[as Michelangelo's] from our own diminutive race of beings
. . .'. That is, the whole humanist conception of history-painting
depends on a tacit agreement between artist and viewer that
man in his natural state is very tiny: history-painting thus has
the task and the opportunity not of 'representing' man but of
depicting him 'enlarged' and ennobled by his heroic choices.
This is to say that the very existence and appeal of history-
painting presupposes a paradoxical view of man, a view which
sees him as naturally limited, frail, and tiny, and yet capable of
growing to heroism and dignity by willing to imitate images of
the noble.

It may be worth noticing here the similarity between the
humanistic theory of the heroic figure in history-painting and
the humanistic theory of space in classical architecture.
'Reason' and 'logic', deceptive as usual, suggest that, placed
within a very large and open architectural space like a cathedral nave or a palace gallery, man will feel proportionately
diminished and little. But here as elsewhere reason and logic are
wrong. Experience indicates that exactly the opposite is true:
instead of making man feel smaller, large enclosed spaces make
him feel larger, and high ceilings make him feel not shorter, as
we might expect, but taller. Classical architecture, focusing like
all humanistic aesthetic theory on the given nature of man,

exploits the paradoxical capacity of the human imagination to enlarge its vision of itself. It is a curious characteristic of the human imagination that, presented with a very large enclosed space, it somehow operates in such a way as to regard itself as worthy of filling it. The designers of classical temples, theatres, and baths, and of cathedrals and palaces, create ample enclosed space partly, of course, as an index of conspicuous exhibition; but partly too to take advantage of the imagination's power to 'enlarge' itself in the presence of the large. Anyone may make the experiment himself: he may stand in the living-room of a small, low-ceilinged suburban house or in a low-ceilinged bus terminal and then betake himself to something like the central hall of Pennsylvania Station in New York and inquire of himself where he feels the most internal dignity. Sensing that architecture is built *for him* and as a comment *on him*, man will feel flattered and dignified under a high ceiling and insulted and diminished under a low one. It is significant that modern society is rapidly ridding itself of its high ceilings as if to make the point that man's native smallness is unredeemable by art or illusion.[6] Just as the image of the heroic has largely vanished from contemporary literature, so in architecture we are tending to express the same sort of disbelief in heroic redemption which we have already asserted by creating a 'consumer' world. The death of both history-painting and humanistic—that is, heroic —architecture seems thus to reflect a modern erosion of belief in the human paradox, that is, in the vision of man as at once tiny and at the same time capable of dignity.

For despite man's limitations, the humanist holds that he is the only creature capable of dignity, and his being *capax dignitatis* is the ultimate element of the paradox which is his nature. To Locke it is man's capacity for abstraction—for apprehending something like Johnsonian 'general nature'—that constitutes his 'excellency': 'this, I think, I may be positive in', he asserts

[6] It is astonishing the way nature keeps imitating art; or, to put it less pleasantly, the way contemporary life insists upon embodying one's own darkest imagery. When, in 1963, I wrote the passage above, it was still possible to sense the effects of the high stone ceiling of Pennsylvania Station. Now, a year later, the building is rapidly being torn down to provide space for a new low-ceilinged 'concourse' with a stack of profitable low-ceilinged offices on top. The stones of the original structure are being dumped in the nearby New Jersey marshes as 'fill'.

in the *Essay*, 'that the power of abstracting is not at all in [animals]; and that the having of general ideas is that which puts a perfect distinction betwixt man and brutes, and is an excellency which the faculties of brutes do by no means attain to' (II, xi, 9). This 'having of general ideas' is what enables man, as Burke insists, to be largely a creature of his own construction, that is, to take an active role in the formation of his self-image. By the exercise of his power of perceiving 'general nature' man gradually liberates himself from slavery to matter, place, and time, and frees himself to enter history—and thus real life—imaginatively. As Johnson concludes in the *Journey to the Western Islands* after a visit to the sacred island of Icolmkill: 'Whatever withdraws us from the power of our senses; whatever makes the past, the distant, or the future predominate over the present, advances us in the dignity of thinking beings.' And one thing totally inconsistent with human dignity is mechanism of any sort. It is on the free exercise of the will that human dignity depends. 'Reason loses her dignity,' as Johnson says, 'in proportion as she has oftener yielded to temptation' (*Adventurer* 108).

It is this idea of the potential dignity of man, for all his depravity and littleness, that generates a feeling of pathos and tenderness in the humanist, a tenderness born from the perception of the gulf between man as he is and man as he has it in his power to become. Are we wrong to sense, in Swift's account of Gulliver's physical humiliations, a pathos mingling with the wit? Or in Pope's brisk ratiocinations an inexpressible underlying sympathy for man's touching blunders and self-deceptions? It is surely Johnson's exquisite sympathy for the state of man in his 'blunders and puzzles' that impels much of his fury at Soame Jenyns. Outraged by Jenyns's suggestion that the problem of evil can be eased by positing a higher race of beings who torment us for their malignant pleasure, Johnson exposes Jenyns's argument by carrying it both to the point of absurdity and—more important—to the point of pathos:

Many a merry bout have these frolic beings at the vicissitudes of an ague, and good sport it is to see a man tumble with an epilepsy, and revive and tumble again, and all this he knows not why. As they are wiser and more powerful than we, they have more exquisite diversions, for we have no way of procuring any sport so brisk and so lasting as the paroxysms of the gout and stone which undoubtedly must make high mirth, especially if the play be a little diversified with the blunders and puzzles of the blind and deaf.

There is no response to Johnson's quiet, simple, monosyllabic 'and all this he knows not why' except Johnson's own: 'It is not to be endured.' This kind of protective tenderness towards the idea of man, showing itself through all the irony and the satire and the polemic, is a sign that we are close to the living heart of the humanist paradox. 'When [Johnson] would try to repeat the celebrated . . . *Dies Irae*', Mrs. Thrale recalls, 'he could never pass the stanza ending thus, *Tantus labor non sit cassus*, without bursting into a flood of tears' (*JM*, i, 284). There are tears and tears in the eighteenth century, but Johnson's are memorable for being not at all sentimental. They are not Shaftesburian. They are drawn not by namby-pamby lambs and linnets but by the conception of man's conscious precarious location between the fact of mortal dissolution and the hope— always pathetic, for hope deceives—that all God's labour of incarnation and immolation has not been in vain:

> Quaerens me sedisti lassus.
> Redemisti crucem passus:
> Tantus labor non sit cassus.

The frail but noble hope, that is, that so much labour has not been lost, and that such a creature as man shall not in the end find nothing for his efforts at dignity and redemption but a broken promise and an unregarded grave.

PART II

THE REALIZATION OF HUMANISM: IMAGES AND MOTIFS

'The art of literature, vocal or written, is to adjust the language so that it embodies what it indicates.'—ALFRED NORTH WHITEHEAD

7

MORAL WARFARE:
STRATEGY AND TACTICS

SO MANY vulgar errors about eighteenth-century literature are abroad that a critic with a turn for satire could spend a happy lifetime exposing them. One of the most objectionable—because it inhibits the close and attentive reading which we aspire to bring to other kinds of works—is the assumption that this literature somehow operates more 'discursively' than most. That is, that it cosily domesticates itself within the world of 'prose', largely cut off from the 'imaginative' and 'creative' world of metaphor and symbol. It is true that the Royal Society—sometimes mistakenly regarded as a spokesman for most elements of early post-Renaissance society—is said to have tried to purge descriptive and expository language of figure and thus to bring all things as near to the mathematical plainness as it could. But seeking is one thing, succeeding another. To preach the virtues of bare denotation and of descriptive simplicity is one thing; but actually to work with language and perforce to become entangled in its filaments of connotation is quite another. Regardless of the user and regardless of the age in which it is employed, the nature of language is inseparable from symbolic conventions. The eighteenth-century writer does not escape natural symbolic necessity because he wears lace rather than buckskin. One cannot choose to use language symbolically or non-symbolically: the only question is whether one is going to use symbolic conventions well or ill.

The alleged figurative 'thinness' sometimes ascribed to eighteenth-century literature may well be a function less of the things we read than of the expectations we bring to the reading.

Anyone who has read the *Essay on Criticism* with real attention to
figure or who has genuinely attended to the weight of sub-
surface figure in a sentence from *The Rambler* is aware of the
heavy freight of the figurative in the expression of even the most
prosaic of the Augustans. Perhaps the difficulty is that we have
not refined our skill sufficiently in distinguishing, in eighteenth-
century literature, the received metaphor from the dead metaphor, the live traditional symbol from the cliché. Augustan
figures are repetitive and recurrent, as they can be expected to
be in a world dominated by Lockean psychology and the
assumption of the uniformity of human nature. But one reason
why the same figures appear again and again is that Augustan
imagery operates generally as polemic rather than as revelation
or epiphany. What it bodies forth are public moral arguments,
not private apperceptions. And to the Augustan humanist the
subjects of public argument are as few and as traditional as they
are supremely important. Hence in inspecting the figurative
practice through which Augustan humanism embodies itself we
must learn to appreciate how much life really resides in a given
figure rather than assuming that, because the figure of, say,
Justice with her scales is now a cliché, it always has been.

Since the Augustan humanists are writers, they operate in a
world of metaphor just like all writers. And on occasion they
enter the world of metaphor even more readily than later
writers. It is easy to imagine one of us writing the following in
imitation of Johnson's style: 'idleness can scarcely form a wish
which it may not gratify by the toil of others, or curiosity dream
of a toy, which the shops are not ready to afford it'. But Johnson
pushes things further towards absolute metaphor than we
would: 'idleness can scarcely form a wish which she may not
gratify by the toil of others, or curiosity dream of a toy, which
the shops are not ready to afford her' (*Adventurer* 67). Johnson
quite instinctively personifies—which is to say that in a way he
humanizes—wherever possible. 'His mind was so full of
imagery', says Boswell, 'that he might have been perpetually a
poet' (*BLJ*, v, 17). And Boswell's observation is almost equally
true of the other Augustan humanists. Pope's instinct for
absolute precision of figure, his self-consciousness over the
difference between operative and non-operative metaphor, can
be measured in *Peri Bathous*. And Swift's in the wonderfully

successful preposterous, ironic figures of *A Tale of a Tub* or *A Meditation on a Broomstick*. Both are clearly exquisitely practised dealers with metaphor, every bit as brilliant and precise at metaphoric perception as the Johnson who performs thus in the *Life of Addison*:

There is . . . one broken metaphor [in Addison's *Letter from Italy*], of which notice may properly be taken:

> Fir'd with that name—
> I bridle in my struggling Muse with pain,
> That longs to launch into a nobler strain.

To *bridle* a *goddess* is no very delicate idea; but why must she be *bridled*? because she *longs to launch*; an act which was never hindered by a *bridle*: and whither will she *launch*? into a nobler strain. She is in the first line a *horse*, in the second a *boat*; and the care of the poet is to keep his *horse* or his *boat* from *singing*.

Far from suggesting a lack of commitment to metaphor, a critical performance like that, typical of the eighteenth-century attention to mixed figures, bespeaks the most serious literary concern with what figures really say and do. The Augustan humanists want figures to work, which is to say that they want poetry rather than wan reflections of it.

The humanistic myth of dualism, as we have seen, operates by assuming that life at its centre is a perpetual conflict, 'a contention', as Johnson puts it, 'between pleasure and virtue, a struggle which will always be continued while the present system of nature shall subsist: nor can history or poetry exhibit more than pleasure triumphing over virtue, and virtue subjugating pleasure' (*BLJ*, i, 411). And human experience seems to involve two separate sets of dualisms: (1) man's inner convictions are in conflict—or should be—with the practices of a corrupt 'world' outside; and (2) within man himself the inimical elements of his psychic hierarchy, the will and the flesh, conduct with each other an analogous battle. What is more 'natural'—that is, permanently meaningful—than that the Augustan humanist should choose to express these unremitting and all-important conflicts in terms of actual warfare? Both the ethical circumstances and the general imagery available for realizing them are permanent and unchanging, as Johnson suggests when he writes in the *Life of Dryden* that 'Even war and conquest, however splendid, suggest no new images'.

It is a sense of the precariousness of genuine civilization, of the constant menace to civilized values by internal and external powers of disorder and destruction, that seems to lie behind the humanistic habit of expressing ethical imperatives through images of military assault, ambush, and fortification. 'Sources' are too obvious for comment: everybody read epic, everybody read classical history, and everybody read the political and military history of the Civil Wars. Even if an elaborate body of siege symbolism had been unavailable elsewhere, the immense popularity of Pope's Homer and Dryden's Virgil, with their elaborate details of trenches, loop-holes, scaling ladders, ramparts, and palisades, would have been sufficient almost alone to keep the image of the siege fully accessible to the eighteenth-century imagination. What is perhaps worth observing is that the use of military and especially siege imagery to embody ethical principles seems especially a Christian and a humanist habit: we could point to the military imagery in the Pauline epistles, or to literally hundreds of thousands of medieval and Renaissance examples like this one in Spenser's *Faerie Queene*:

> What warre so cruell, or what siege so sore,
>   As that, which strong affections do apply
>   Against the fort of reason euermore
>   To bring the soule into captiuitie:
>
> (II, xi, 1)

What keeps so standard an image from decaying into a dead metaphor is that while it was flourishing so was actual siege warfare: the liveliness of the figure is to be gauged in part by the vividness of contemporary experience of sieges. The siege metaphor, in fact, probably operates more like a cliché when it appears in love poetry, for everyone knows that the besieging of the beloved's body will eventuate in delight, while the internal struggle between body and will resembles more vividly an actual battle because it is so profoundly unpleasant. One use of the figure cannot help being a trifle glib and facile; the other makes a deeper, less merely 'literary' appeal. A 'sally' of thought or wit is, after all, a fully fleshed figure in its proper context of seventeenth and eighteenth-century siege warfare. So is the figure of 'undermining', which has become a dead metaphor only because siege warfare has also died.

Sterne's Uncle Toby is not the only eighteenth-century man whose imagination is a-boil with military images. In an age before the professionalization of warfare, the data of bastions, revelins, hornworks, and curtins were so well known that they can be said to have constituted the common property of all whose social station enabled them to conceive of themselves as potential military commanders or engineers. As a writer Gibbon was perhaps luckier than most: from his 'bloodless and inglorious campaigns' with the Hampshire militia, boring as they were, he imbibed materials useful later on for both literal and metaphorical purposes. As he writes in his *Autobiography*: 'The discipline and evolutions of a modern battalion gave me a clearer notion of the phalanx and the legions, and the captain of the Hampshire grenadiers (the reader may smile) has not been useless to the historian of the Roman empire.' But one need not have gone on manoeuvres to take full possession of contemporary military learning. The obsession with military engineering and tactics seems to run throughout the century in the imaginations of civilians as well as those of active military men. Around 1704 the famous impostor 'George Psalmanazar', at school in southern France, was confronted with an idle teacher whose classes consisted primarily of anecdotal materials

which were neither calculated to improve our minds, nor to make us in love with our books. At length, quite tired, as he seemed, with the drudgery of the college, he took it into his head to teach us heraldry, geography, and fortification, instead of the proper lessons of our class; so that we were forced, in some measure, to exchange books for maps, coats of arms, plans of cities, castles, &c. and, at length, to dabble with him in clay and dirt, in order to make a variety of fortifications, with all their appurtenances. . . .[1]

It is clear that the age spawned its thousands of Uncle Tobys. But Samuel Johnson seems to have been as interested in siege tactics and the techniques of fortification as anyone else. Boswell records this eloquent little scene in 1772: 'Dr. Johnson said, "Pray, General [Oglethorpe], give us an account of the siege of Belgrade." Upon which the General, pouring a little wine upon

[1] *Memoirs of ****. Commonly known by the Name of George Psalmanazar; A Reputed Native of Formosa* (2nd ed.: London, 1765), p. 75.

the table, described every thing with a wet finger: ''Here we were, here were the Turks,'' &c. &c. Johnson listened with the closest attention' (*BLJ*, ii, 181). And in the 1790's the vogue of exact technical knowledge of siege warfare was still lively. In his diary John Byng thus meditates on a personified Death, 'who, by every sly scalade steals in, or mines, or storms: but when we can, let us oppose the monster, and say, "I won't come yet, keep off you fearful rascal" '.[2]

Swift's acquaintance with military weapons and tactics, derived perhaps equally from readings of epic and of seventeenth-century military history, is put to use in *The Battle of the Books*, where the irreconcilable warfare between ancients and moderns is given its first important eighteenth-century embodiment in military terms. Libraries are equated with armories ('magazines'), and we hear (as in *The Vanity of Human Wishes*) of the guarding of passes, as well as of rusty and shining armour, out-guards, sally-ports, cannon-balls and bullets, spears and shields, lances and javelins. One happy irony in *The Battle of the Books* is that the 'modern' spider, replete with nastiness, shows himself to be a master in the art of fortification, an art in which contemporary progressives claimed pre-eminence over the Ancients, and an art whose advances since antiquity the Moderns pointed to as evidence of the validity of the idea of progress. 'The Avenues to his Castle', we are told, 'were guarded with Turn-pikes [spiked barriers], and Palissadoes, all after the *Modern* way of Fortification.' Other Swiftian uses of military imagery are likewise almost entirely put to the service of the moral mock-heroic, as in Section II of *The Mechanical Operation of the Spirit*, which reveals how the Puritan style of oratorical snuffling came into vogue. A 'Banbury Saint', afflicted with the pox, consults his surgeon:

The Surgeon . . . cured the Parts, primarily affected; but the Disease driven from its Post, flew up into his Head; And, as a skilful General, valiantly attack'd in his Trenches, and beaten from the Field, by flying Marches withdraws to the Capital City, breaking down the Bridges to prevent Pursuit; So the Disease repell'd from its first Station, fled before the *Rod of Hermes*, to the upper Region, there fortifying it self; but, finding the Foe making Attacks at the *Nose*, broke down the *Bridge*, and retir'd to the *Head*-Quarters.

[2] *The Torrington Diaries*, ed. C. B. Andrews, abridged by Fanny Andrews (London, 1954), p. 391.

A similar use of military detail on behalf of mock-heroic irony is apparent in the 'Digression in Praise of Digressions' of *A Tale of a Tub*. Here the intellectual and ethical corruption of abridgments and 'study guides' is expressed this way: 'the Army of the Sciences hath been of late, with a world of Martial Discipline, drawn into its *close Order*, so that a View, or a Muster may be taken of it with abundance of Expedition. For this great Blessing we are wholly indebted to *Systems* and *Abstracts* . . .'.

Some of Pope's military figures are playful and mock-heroic like Swift's. In *The Dunciad*, for example, Cibber's followers are depicted as a rabble of infantry

> Light-arm'd with Points, Antitheses, and Puns.
>
> (i, 306)

But other images are more serious ethically. In the *Essay on Man* reason is imaged as a military commander—although a female one—whose obligation it is to safeguard the passions who enlist in her regiment:

> Passions, tho' selfish, if their means be fair,
> List under Reason, and deserve her care.
>
> (ii, 97–98)

But in the Third Epistle of the *Essay on Man* reason takes on a different shape. She is here a kind of sophisticated draft-dodger or unwilling draftee of the psyche, while instinct is imaged as an ingenuous country fellow happy to enlist. When instinct is urging man, says Pope,

> Reason, however able, cool at best,
> Cares not for service, or but serves when prest,
> Stays 'till we call, and then not often near;
> But honest Instinct comes a volunteer.
>
> (85–88)

The dual derivation of most humanist military imagery from the details of epic and from Restoration or contemporary accounts of tactics and fortification seems apparent in Pope's treatment of Belinda's petticoat in Canto II of *The Rape of the Lock*. On the one hand the petticoat is likened mock-heroically to the shield of Achilles and on the other—and this is just hinted —to a sort of eighteenth-century perimeter fortification. Pope's moral point—one based upon the assumption of human frailty —is like Addison's in *Spectator* 127: 'It is most certain that a

Woman's Honour cannot be better entrenched than after this manner, in Circle within Circle, amidst such a Variety of Out-works and Lines of Circumvallation.' Belinda's and Lord Petre's game of Ombre is obviously a military encounter; less obvious perhaps is that their recourse to tea and coffee after-wards constitutes a mock-epic action of 'retreat' in the original sense, that is, a withdrawal of both sides to hills commanding the battlefield at the end of the day.

Pope images the literary 'rules', unlovely as they sometimes are, as necessary weapons against disorder. He writes in the *Essay on Criticism*:

> In grave *Quintilian's* copious Work we find
> The justest *Rules*, and clearest *Method* join'd;
> Thus *useful Arms* in Magazines we place,
> All rang'd with *Order*, and dispos'd with *Grace*,
> But less to please the Eye, than arm the Hand,
> Still fit for Use, and ready at Command.
>
> (669–74)

And in the *Epistle to Bathurst* (*Moral Essay* III) he considers poli-tical bribery in the illuminating terms of siege trench-digging:

> In Vain may Heroes fight, and Patriots rave;
> If secret Gold saps on from knave to knave.
>
> (37–38)

Implied through the image is that bribery is always dangerously 'underground', and also implied is that the 'sap' (trench) is directed at a fortification (the state) which will finally be 'undermined' by corruption. Another fortification image, although a very generalized one, brings us close to Johnson's customary moral use of the fortification figure. Here, in the *Essay on Criticism*, Pope suggests that 'fixed principles' constitute a sort of defensive soldiery safeguarding the psyche against the assaults of external disorder:

> Some praise at Morning what they blame at Night;
> But always think the *last* Opinion *right*.
> A Muse by these is like a Mistress us'd,
> This hour she's *idoliz'd*, the next *abus'd*,
> While their weak Heads, like Towns unfortify'd,
> 'Twixt Sense and Nonsense daily change their Side.
>
> (430–5)

Of all the Augustan humanists, Johnson is undoubtedly the most learned in the exact technical materials of warfare, just as he seems the most ready to exploit them in ethical images. Life is combat to Johnson, and the combat is moral. His writings are busy just below the surface with countless images of parleys, citadels, blockades, invasions, phalanxes, pioneers (i.e. military engineers), saps, sieges, pitfalls, surrenders, cavalry charges, bows and arrows, small arms, artillery batteries, attacks and retreats, conquests and repulses. He began very early both accumulating military details and developing his habit of viewing the moral life in military terms. His Stourbridge school poem *Festina Lentè*, written at the age of sixteen probably to the assigned topic 'Make haste slowly', reveals already many well-developed heroic motifs and figures: we hear of 'commanding' the passions, the 'superiour force' of reason, the 'vengefull dart', and of the 'invaders' and 'troops' driven from Rome by 'cautious Fabius', who had his passions under command. Around 1738, when he was twenty-nine, we find Johnson negotiating with Edward Cave for the preparation and publication of a dictionary of military terms. Although this project never came to fruition, Johnson reveals that he has not wasted his accumulated knowledge of strategy, tactics, fortification, and weapons: it is apparent in his *Miscellaneous Observations on the Tragedy of Macbeth* (1745) as well as in his *Life of* [Admiral Robert] *Blake* and *Life of Sir Francis Drake*, both published in 1740. It is conspicuous in the *Life of the King of Prussia* (1756) and even more so in the *Life of Roger Ascham* (1763), where he exhibits an expert knowledge of Renaissance weaponry.

What is the more remarkable is that Johnson's military knowledge derives mostly from literature and the sympathetic imagination, for, as he confesses in the *Journey to the Western Islands*, '[Fort George] and Fort Augustus are the only two garrisons I ever saw.' Despite his having worked up his knowledge all by himself, his account in the *Journey* of the fortified Hebridean castles reveals an understanding of fortification and the tactical method of investment that is extraordinary. The same can be said of his performance the following year, when, visiting Caernarvon Castle in Wales, he perceives and records in his journal that the purpose of moats was perhaps as much to interdict undermining as to prevent a near approach. And des-

L

pite his limited actual acquaintance with military camps and
garrisons, he is quite serious when he tells Hester Maria Thrale:
'I was in hopes that your letter about the camp would have
been longer, and that you would have considered yourself as
surveying in a camp perhaps the most important scene of
human existence, the real scene of heroick life' (*LSJ*, ii, 260).
Why would Johnson regard a mere military camp as 'perhaps
the most important scene of human existence'? Probably because it has the power to enforce the morally indispensable
ideas of combat and struggle; it generates large, serious, and
even frightening ideas of 'enemy' and 'repulse' which are
requisite to the moral life. It is notable that in the *Rambler*,
military images are very largely confined to those serious ethical
papers written by Johnson himself in his moral *persona* as
Rambler; we find remarkably few military figures in the papers
'contributed' by fictive correspondents: this surely suggests that
when Johnson uses military imagery he is entirely conscious of
what he is about.

But his military outlook is not always sober: in the late spring
of 1758 he devoted many of the *Idler* papers to light mockery of
the British campaign against the French: *Idler* 8 is a good
example. On the other hand, in his facetious, pseudo-Swiftian
A Project for the Employment of Authors (1756), where he suggests
that Britain's excessive population of writers be drafted for
military service to reduce the swarm, there is just a hint of the
kind of deadly seriousness we shall encounter elsewhere: here,
in appearing to hint—if only whimsically—the similarity
between the life of the writer and the life of the soldier or officer,
he seems to glance at the illuminating relation between the
ethical or artistic life and the life of mortal combat.

Speaking of St. Paul in *Rambler* 7, Johnson explains: 'It is not
without reason that the apostle represents our passage through
this stage of our existence by images drawn from the alarms and
solicitude of a military life; for we are placed in such a state,
that almost every thing about us conspires against our chief
interest.' 'Our chief interest' is, of course, redemption, and
redemption is a victory all but impossible to win in a world
'where every step in the progression of existence changes our
position with respect to the things about us, so as to lay us open
to new assaults and particular dangers . . .' (*Rambler* 43). As we

would expect, the *Prayers and Meditations* are full of the imagery of repulse and defence: 'Combat scruples', he exhorts himself. Typical is this prayer which he adapts from *The Book of Common Prayer* and records in 1768: 'Almighty God, who seest that I have no power of myself to help myself; keep me both outwardly in my body, and inwardly in my soul, that I may be defended from all adversities that may happen to the body, and free from all evil thoughts which may assault and hurt the soul, through Jesus Christ our Lord. Amen.'

Life is so serious a combat that reading novels is like going on military manoeuvres. It is the purpose of novels, Johnson asserts in *Rambler* 4, 'to initiate youth by mock encounters in the art of necessary defence . . .'. It is clear that to Johnson *Tom Jones* is not going to serve as a very dependable defensive weapon against the assaults of temptation. Enemies lie waiting on all sides, both within and without. Life correctly lived is a siege painfully but triumphantly withstood.

One of the ironies of moral defence is that the garrison never has enough troops to repel assaults from all quarters at once. Tactical judgment is thus indispensable. In *Rambler* 114, for example, we are told that the policeman normally 'enforces those laws with severity that are most in danger of violation, as the commander of a garrison doubles the guard on that side which is threatened by the enemy'. It is the nature of man that he must focus, and the tactical difficulty is that while he chooses to focus here on his periphery, chaos ensues back there: 'Every condition has its disadvantages. The circle of knowledge is too wide for the most active and diligent intellect, and while science is pursued, other accomplishments are neglected; as a small garrison must leave one part of an extensive fortress naked, when an alarm calls them to another' (*Rambler* 180). But sometimes the garrison is below strength, and then the attack succeeds: 'Such is the state of all mortal virtue, that it is always uncertain and variable, sometimes extending to the whole compass of duty, and sometimes shrinking into a narrow space, and fortifying only a few avenues of the heart, while all the rest is left open to the incursions of appetite, or given up to the dominion of wickedness' (*Rambler* 70).

Another irony incident to moral warfare is that a momentary abdication of vigilance will deliver 'the fortress' to spies—like the forces of advertising for example—whose plausibility can overcome almost all exhausted defences. Johnson writes in *Rambler* 162:

we see often those who never wanted spirit to repel encroachment or oppose violence, at last, by a gradual relaxation of vigilance, delivering up, without capitulation, the fortress which they defended against assault, and laying down unbidden the weapons which they grasped the harder for every attempt to wrest them from their hands. Men eminent for spirit and wisdom often resign themselves to voluntary pupilage, and suffer their lives to be modelled by officious ignorance, and their choice to be regulated by presumptuous stupidity.

'Officious ignorance' and 'presumptuous stupidity' are only two of the enemies which ring the citadel: pain is another, and here defence is never entirely successful, for 'Infelicity is involved in corporeal nature, and interwoven with our being; all attempts therefore to decline it wholly are useless and vain: the armies of pain send their arrows against us on every side, the choice is only between those which are more or less sharp, or tinged with poison of greater or less malignity; and the strongest armour which reason can supply, will only blunt their points, but cannot repel them' (*Rambler* 32).

And some of the arrows propelled by the nature of things are bound to fall within the fortress: in *Adventurer* 120 we are assured that 'the quiver of Omnipotence is stored with arrows, against which the shield of human virtue, however adamantine it has been boasted, is held up in vain: we do not always suffer by our crimes; we are not always protected by our innocence'. But against most attackers the commander of the citadel has ample—but often pathetic—defensive weapons. The *tu quoque* rebuttal, for example, is an ever-ready poisoned arrow. The self-righteous man conscious of his own shortcomings and fully aware of the uniformity of human nature 'triumphs', says Johnson in *Rambler* 76, 'in his comparative purity, and sets himself at ease, not because he can refute the charges advanced against him, but because he can censure his accusers with equal justice, and no longer fears the arrows of reproach, when he has stored his magazine of malice with weapons equally sharp and equally envenomed'.

Occasionally the positions of virtue and vice are reversed,

with vice defending and virtue—or at least good sense—attacking. As Johnson argues in *Rambler* 93, the will must co-operate in any kind of successful literary reception: 'To convince any man against his will is hard, but to please him against his will is justly pronounced by Dryden to be above the reach of human abilities. Interest and passion will hold out long against the closest siege of diagrams and syllogisms, but they are absolutely impregnable to imagery and sentiment; and will for ever bid defiance to the most powerful strains of Virgil or Homer, though they may give way in time to the batteries of Euclid or Archimedes.'

Sometimes it is internal dissension which opens the fort to its enemies. In *Rambler* 83 Johnson discourses on the folly of the learned in weakening their slender defences by internal feuds: the result is an incursion of Goths and the decline and fall of the empire of learning. The learned, writes Johnson, 'have all engaged in feuds, till by mutual hostilities they demolished those outworks which veneration had raised for their security, and exposed themselves to barbarians, by whom every region of science is equally laid waste'. And sometimes within the individual psyche self-division likewise invites destruction, as it does, for example, at a masquerade, where, as we are told in *Rambler* 10, 'all the outworks of chastity are at once demolished'. Belinda's petticoat has broken under assault.

Fortresses and outworks presuppose sentinels, and the image of the sentinel falling asleep or otherwise failing to perform his difficult duty is perennial in Johnson. Even tiny metaphoric sentinels, and even those so non-literally conceived as the 'guards' of 'Chastity', 'Literary Fame', or 'Virtue', are images of real humanity and thus liable to all the standard human frailties. On occasion the sentinels, having been badly treated, betray their commanders out of witty Freudian revenge. Such is the behaviour of the self-interested sentinels of old maids, who simply ape the coyness of their mistresses: old maids, as *Idler* 87 informs us, 'will not easily combine in any plot; and if they should ever agree to retire and fortify themselves in castles or in mountains, the sentinel will betray the passes in spite, and the garrison will capitulate upon easy terms, if the besiegers have handsome sword-knots, and are well supplied with fringe and lace.' But sometimes a weak sentinel can be overcome by a stronger one, and the day can be saved. This is what happens in the *Drury Lane Prologue*, where Johnson, speaking of the Restoration comic dramatists, says that

> their Reign was long;
> Till Shame regain'd the Post that Sense betray'd,
> And Virtue call'd Oblivion to her Aid.
>
> (26–28)

'Virtue' is clearly an officer, and the sentinel she likes to post, as we learn in *Idler* 84, is 'conscience'. Fond old age, careless of the future, is often its own lonely sentinel, as it is in *Rambler* 78, where Johnson writes: 'To neglect at any time preparation for death, is to sleep on our post at a siege; but to omit it in old age, is to sleep at an attack.' It is likely that those most likely to 'sleep at an attack' are the dotards who are fortified only by their own threat of disinheritance: 'This is, indeed, too frequently the citadel of the dotard, the last fortress to which age retires . . .' (*Rambler* 69).

Such is the moral danger of ordinary life. But the standard of human vigilance is occasionally so high that evils sometimes must have recourse to ambush in order to triumph. Johnson is especially inclined to the image of ambush, suggesting as it does the almost unspeakable difficulty of moral action within a world ambitious of destroying virtue. In his delightful short poem *The Ant* he depicts the ambush occurring from the rear. Speaking to the 'sluggard', he warns:

> Amidst the drousy charms of dull delight,
> Year chases year, with unremitted flight,
> Till want, now following fraudulent and slow,
> Shall spring to seize thee like an ambush'd foe.
>
> (13–16)

And the enemy in ambush sometimes waits stationary to surprise his victim as he wanders past. Writing to Mrs. Thrale about her daughter Harriet, who has just been seriously ill, Johnson says: 'I hope to hear again that my dear little girl is out of danger. It will now be pleasing to consider that she and her sister [Cecilia] have past two of the ambushes of life . . .' (*LSJ*, iii, 11). Compared with this off-hand Johnsonian sense of the ambush, which seems to operate quite naturally even in the formal *Vanity of Human Wishes*, Gray's, in his *Ode on a Distant*

Prospect of Eton College, is theatrical and unconvincing, and his spatterings of exclamation points seem to betray his artistic discomfort and to confess that something has failed badly:

> Alas, regardless of their doom,
> The little victims play!
> No sense have they of ills to come,
> Nor care beyond to-day!
> Yet see how all around 'em wait
> The ministers of human fate,
> And black Misfortune's baleful train!
> Ah, show them where in ambush stand
> To seize their prey the murderous band!
> Ah, tell them they are men!
>
> (51–60)

What has failed here is the rhetoric, which is fundamentally a sentimentalist one—the 'Alas' and the 'Ah's' are worthy of Swift's 'Robert Boyle'—and thus a rhetoric quite inappropriate for embodying the all but antithetical humanist attitudes which Gray affects to be entertaining. When we reach the last stanza of Gray's poem we perceive even more clearly the trick that has been played on us, for here the speaker decides *not* to 'tell them they are men' but instead to withhold that liberating knowledge from them, for ' 'Tis folly to be wise'. The end of the poem thus asserts the sentimentalist position which the stanza of the ambush has unsuccessfully attempted to disguise. The difficulty of imagining Johnson's uttering anything like Gray's last line measures Gray's distance from the Augustan humanist tradition. And we may remember a similar use of a military image without its appropriate accompanying ethical substance in a passage we have met before, from the third book of Cowper's *Task*:

> Retreat
> . . . has peace, and much secures the mind
> From all assaults of evil.

Anyone who really believes what Cowper asserts has never earned the right to express himself in images of battle.

In Johnson the ambush image is not merely more subtle than in Gray or Cowper: it is honestly earned. To Johnson, all writers are like combat personnel, since their task is to break down the natural resistance of readers and to work their will on

them. Even Milton is like a soldier hiding in ambush to entrap
the reader: he owes to Homer, says Johnson in the *Life of Milton*, 'all the stratagems that surprise and enchain attention'.
But a writer does not have to be a Milton to operate as a military person: no matter how bad, every writer, even one who
commits only personal letters, is to some degree an assaulter of a
reader. In *Idler* 2 we are presented with a bad and cowardly
writer who is seeking a stupid correspondent to impress, 'as the
young soldiers in the Roman camp learned the use of their
weapons by fencing against a post in the place of an enemy'.
Some kinds of literature, on the other hand, are a heroic contest: satire is one kind which to be successful must always be
conceived in terms of combat. In the *Life of Pope*, Johnson,
speaking of *The Dunciad*, observes that 'The satire which
brought Theobald and Moore into contempt, dropped impotent
from Bentley, like the javelin of Priam'. That Johnson conceived of his conversational bouts in the same way is clear
enough. Victims like Boswell and Sir Alexander MacDonald
and Mrs. Macaulay could derive perhaps a kind of comfort
from Johnson's remarking in the *Life of Cheynel*, 'There is
always this advantage in contending with illustrious adversaries, that the combatant is equally immortalized by conquest
or defeat. He that dies by the sword of a hero will always be
mentioned when the acts of his enemy are mentioned.'

Even in its lesser reaches the writer's mission is like the soldier's. Dryden's delight, we are told in the *Life of Dryden*, 'was
in wild and daring sallies of sentiment . . .'. The critic is one
who assaults obscure texts: in the *Preface to Shakespeare* Johnson
admits that, in trying to illuminate many passages, 'I have
failed, like others; and from many, after all my efforts, I have
retreated, and confessed the repulse'. And in the same work he
justifies his conservative tendency in textual emendation by
explaining, 'I have adopted the Roman sentiment, that it is
more honourable to save a citizen, than to kill an enemy, and
have been more careful to protect than to attack'. And way
down at the very bottom of the eighteenth-century literary
hierarchy, where bad authors put together abysmal poems and
where harmless drudges compile dictionaries, the life of literature is still a mode of battle. In the *Life of Sir Thomas Browne*
Johnson exposes in military terms the stratagem of publishing

genteelly. The author's dodge of printing a manuscript in order only to 'replace' a fictitious 'foul copy' already circulating without his permission enables a new writer, says Johnson, to 'enter the lists', and, at the same time, to 'secure a retreat'. In the same way makers of dictionaries are engaged in a constant battle, sometimes less against a venomous public than against publishers and the whole world of quick and easy profit. Negotiating with the publisher William Strahan over the terms for the *Dictionary*, Johnson images himself as a small but sturdy citadel menaced by powerful but rather dull forces: 'I mean no harm, but . . . my citadel shall not be taken by storm while I can defend it, and . . . if a blockade is intended, the country is under the command of my batteries . . .' (*LSJ*, i, 38–39).

Of all external enemies, disease is perhaps, next to death itself, the worst. One must fortify oneself against it. One must bring to bear his whole armory: 'I will be conquered; I will not capitulate.' Discussing Henry Thrale's condition with Mrs. Thrale, Johnson recommends brave, vigorous defensive measures: 'Gentle purges, and slight phlebotomies are not my favourites, they are popgun batteries, which lose time and effect nothing' (*LSJ*, ii, 394). And in the same terms he enjoins patience and shrewdness as remedies for the gout, 'which seldom takes the fort by a coup-de-main, but turning the siege into a blockade, obliges it to surrender at discretion' (*JM*, i, 276).

Perhaps something of Henry James's retrospective ethical orientation may be deduced from his instinct for similar imagery as he explains, in the Preface to *The Wings of the Dove*, the problems of dealing with the dying Milly Theale: 'the poet essentially *can't* be concerned with the act of dying. Let him deal with the sickest of the sick, it is still by the act of living that they appeal to him, and appeal the more as the conditions plot against them and prescribe the battle. The process of life gives way fighting, and often may so shine out on the lost ground as in no other connexion.'

The way Johnson turns his habit of military figuration to supreme ethical and aesthetic advantage is perhaps best observed in *The Vanity of Human Wishes*, which he conducts as if against a dark but vivid background of slaughters, ambushes, sieges, and military betrayals. The military imagery is deeply interwoven into the texture and thus into the substance of the poem. To alter or remove it—or not to notice it—would be to make quite a different thing from what Johnson has given us. To compare his version with Juvenal's original or with Dryden's translation is to perceive how *The Vanity of Human Wishes* develops an entirely original vigour and weight from its unique dependence on military imagery. In its satire of Hannibal's military career Juvenal's *Tenth Satire* employs lots of literal military matter, and, in its analogous treatment of Sweden's Charles XII, so does Johnson's 'imitation'. But what we look for in vain in Juvenal is Johnson's dimension of military metaphor.

The theme is advanced early in Johnson's poem:

> How rarely reason guides the stubborn choice,
> Rules the bold hand, or prompts the suppliant voice.
>
> (11–12)

The poem is about the ironic—indeed, catastrophic—inappropriateness of most prayers and wishes: what appears to the naïve suppliant to be the most desirable benefit to be hoped for proves upon attainment to have been exactly the cause of his destruction. Which is to say that

> Fate wings with every wish th'afflictive dart,
> Each gift of nature, and each grace of art,
> With fatal heat impetuous courage glows,
> With fatal sweetness elocution flows,
> Impeachment stops the speaker's powerful breath,
> And restless fire precipitates on death.
>
> (15–20)

These are difficult lines. Garrick once said that he found *London* 'lively and easy' but *The Vanity of Human Wishes* 'as hard as Greek': he went on to prophesy that a third Johnsonian satire would prove 'as hard as Hebrew' (*BLJ*, i, 194). The difficulty here resides mainly in the verb 'wings', which means 'hurls'. We can paraphrase the first two lines thus: 'Fate hurls its spear of afflictions along with every wish of a suppliant, whether the wish is for some gift of nature—like courage—or for some grace of art—like fluency.' Each 'gift' carries inseparably allied with it its own horrible disadvantage: courage glows, but with fatal heat: that is, the more brave is a soldier or commander the more he invites his own destruction, impelled as he is by his 'restless fire'. The courageous soldier is like one of those 'heroes of action' in *Rambler* 52, heroes who 'catch the flame [of courage] from one another . . .'. In the same way, the parliamentary orator's gift of fluency is the ironic cause of his self-destruction: in fluency there is power, and power invites impeachment. The uniqueness of the imagery here becomes clear when we consult Juvenal, where we discover that 'impetuous courage' is Johnson's rendering of something like mere 'physical strength'. Juvenal seems to glance at the athlete, and his meaning is close to Housman's reflecting on the athlete's dying young; Johnson, typically, glances at the soldier, and his meaning is the humanist's. Johnson's dual image of the soldier who suffers a fate *like* that of the orator or rhetorician tends to ally the two characters and to suggest the humanist equation between them, which could be phrased this way: 'The expositor or artist is like a military officer. His primary duty is command and victory.'

Among the earliest of Johnson's little *exempla* through which he enacts his theme is that of the poor and therefore cheerful traveller:

> The needy traveller, serene and gay,
> Walks the wild heath, and sings his toil away.

Such a spectacle of a man enjoying himself—especially on Hampstead Heath, notorious for highwaymen—is naturally going to produce a deep envy in the depraved reader, who is next addressed directly:

> Does envy seize thee?

If it does, it is a simple matter to

> crush th' upbraiding joy,

that is, to ruin the joy of the traveller which is tormenting the envious observer. All one has to do is to give the traveller some money:

> Increase his riches and his peace destroy;

At this point Johnson deviates from Juvenal again, and again to introduce military ideas. Now that the traveller's 'peace' has been destroyed, because for the first time he fears thieves, numberless fears 'invade' his little world like an army. Juvenal treats the whole idea of the traveller's ruin in just four lines;

Johnson takes eight, which he needs for the extra 'military' and 'ambush' images:

> Now fears in dire vicissitude invade,
> The rustling brake alarms, and quiv'ring shade,
> Nor light nor darkness brings his fears relief,
> One shews the plunder, and one hides the thief.
>
> (37–44)

Juvenal's Democritus, who watches scenes like this with amused contempt, merely laughs, but Johnson's goes to his satiric work armed with spear and sword: addressing Democritus, Johnson inquires,

> How wouldst thou shake at Britain's modish tribe,
> Dart the quick taunt, and edge the piercing gibe?
>
> (61–62)

A similar 'dart', but this time wielded by the hand of 'Beauty', threatens the career of 'the young enthusiast' of learning. It is to be hoped, says Johnson, that this spear will have had its point blunted against the presumably hard heads of 'fops' before it seeks out the scholar. And the 'young enthusiast', in his turn, is imaged as a soldier in the assault: he proposes to pursue 'Science' up into the mountains until, 'captive', she finally 'yields her last retreat'. These details, like the others, are entirely Johnsonian, with no precedent in Juvenal. The same can be said of the behaviour of 'Famine' and 'Winter' when 'Swedish Charles' sets out on his military expeditions and provides Johnson with an *exemplum* of the vanity of military ambition: here

> Stern Famine guards the solitary coast,
> And Winter barricades the realms of Frost.
>
> (207–8)

Juvenal's dotard, who, like Swift's Struldbrugs, has mistakenly wished for length of life, is the *senex stolidus* of classical comedy; Johnson's becomes a weakened defensive position:

> Unnumbered maladies his joints invade,
> Lay siege to life and press the dire blockade.
>
> (283–4)

Another curse of long life is that even on the virtuous 'her load Misfortune flings'. Friends die and customs change until finally

> Superfluous lags the vet'ran on the stage.
>
> (308)

If we are tempted to imagine that 'veteran' here is insignificant, a glance at Johnson's *Dictionary* will reassure us that the word, in Johnson's day as in ours, means 'an old soldier'.

But when we arrive at Johnson's version of Juvenal's beautiful young people we perceive fully his brilliance in turning all this military imagery to ethical account. Juvenal, satirizing the folly of mothers who wish beauty for their daughters, first instances briefly the corruptions and disasters which female beauty has caused, and then proceeds to a lingering treatment of what his audience undoubtedly found more amusing, the dangers that lie in wait for pretty Roman boys. Johnson eliminates the boys entirely, focuses on female beauty, and, addressing 'Ye nymphs of rosy lips and radiant eyes', asks first:

> What care, what rules your heedless charms shall save,
> Each nymph your rival, and each youth your slave?

He then explains through military images how 'rival' nymphs and 'enslaved' youths can destroy the fortress of virtue and beauty: nymphs ('hate') and youths ('fondness') join forces in the attack, and the one combat team assaults the walls and gate while the other goes more cunningly to work with explosives underground:

> Against your fame with fondness hate combines,
> The rival batters, and the lover mines.

'Virtue' has been appointed sentinel at an outpost, and she warns of the attack, but it proves that she has been positioned too far away for her voice to be heard back at the fortress. Finally exhausted and disgusted, she deserts her position, which faulty communications have already rendered untenable and unstable; and she is replaced by two infinitely corruptible sentinels:

> With distant voice neglected Virtue calls,
> Less heard and less, the faint remonstrance falls;
> Tir'd with contempt, she quits her slipp'ry reign,
> And Pride and Prudence take her seat in vain.

Once Virtue has gone over the hill, the avenues to the fortress are entirely available, despite the presence of the two sentinels-*manqué*. What happens might have been predicted from the first:

> In crowd at once, where none the pass defend,
> The harmless Freedom, and the private Friend.

The two replacement sentinels now yield to superior force—and to bribery—and abandon the positions which they could never be said really to have held:

> The guardians yield, by force superior ply'd;
> By Int'rest, Prudence; and by Flatt'ry, Pride.

All that now remains to the attackers is a mopping-up and looting operation, and the issuing of communiqués and proclamations which will publicize the meaning of the end of the siege:

> Now beauty falls betray'd, despis'd, distress'd,
> And hissing Infamy proclaims the rest.
>
> (329–42)

It is all a little like the siege of the virgin Alma's 'goodly castle' in the second book of the *Faerie Queene*, only the issue of Alma's siege is quite different from that of these eighteenth-century Celias and Belindas.

So far Johnson has conducted much of the poem out of his awareness that the moral life is a battle, and he indicates almost to the very end his unwillingness to relinquish his grip on the military image. Even in the more abstract concluding section, which recommends by way of contrast and 'solution' certain reasonable objects of human wishes, he maintains the pressure of the general military figure. Enjoining sincerity on the suppliant, he exhorts him not to become wholly disillusioned by the massive preceding demonstration of the folly of hoping for things which will undoubtedly turn out to be self-destructive. The suppliant should still

> . . . raise for good the supplicating voice,
> But leave to heav'n the measure and the choice,
> Safe in his pow'r, whose eyes discern afar
> The secret ambush of a specious prayer.
>
> (351–4)

This is complex. Who is setting the ambush? and what exactly does 'specious' mean? 'Pleasing to the view', one of Johnson's definitions in the *Dictionary*, seems to bring us close to 'specious', and if this is the meaning, then we must conclude that the ambush is set by the hopeful but forgetful suppliant himself. We have thus been brought back to the self-delusive world of the orator-commander of lines 15–20, where 'th' afflictive dart' hurled by Fate as an accompaniment of every wish causes a fatal wound which, upon close examination, proves to have been self-inflicted. It is hard to put poor Gulliver, marked forever by his curious arrow wound, out of mind.

After advising the suppliant to pray not for riches, political 'greatness', learning, military glory, length of life, or physical beauty, but rather for 'a healthful mind', 'Obedient passions' (like well-disciplined soldiers), resignation, Christian love, and patience, Johnson concludes by suggesting the most valuable object of prayers, faith. Faith is not merely the agent of redemption but a source of wisdom about the military conditions of life, for just as the humanist poet does, faith considers life to be combat, and it knows that the end of life will signal the end of warfare. 'Pour forth thy fervours', says Johnson,

> For faith, that panting for a happier seat,
> Counts death kind Nature's signal of retreat.
>
> (363–4)

We almost hear the wished-for trumpet-call which heralds the end of the day's battle and sends the man up to his repose on one hill and his enemies—the 'world', his own passions, and perhaps even his own consciousness—to rest on another. We are brought to a kind of peace in these last lines, but we will not forget that we have arrived there through a devastated and ghostly landscape of shattered bodies, ruined fortresses, camouflaged enemies, and betrayed and deserted outposts. Juvenal's poem is vigorous and on occasion indecent; Dryden's translation is comical, self-indulgent, sometimes impudent: Johnson's is frightening and dark, for he has enforced his argument with an imagery rich in connotations of conflict, excitement, and even terror. It would be hard to find a poem of any time or place so instructive in the principles—both strategic and tactical—of moral warfare. A century later and in another

country, Nathaniel Hawthorne, a devotee of Johnson and himself an old-fashioned moralist, finds in writing Chapter XVIII
of *The Scarlet Letter* that a Johnsonian image of military assault
will best serve to embody Arthur Dimmesdale's liability to
another 'fall'. It is hard to imagine that we are not here listening to Johnson himself:

And be the stern and sad truth spoken, that the breach which guilt
has once made into the human soul is never, in this mortal state,
repaired. It may be watched and guarded; so that the enemy shall
not force his way again into the citadel, and might even, in his subsequent assaults, select some other avenue, in preference to that
where he had formerly succeeded. But there is still the ruined wall,
and, near it, the stealthy tread of the foe that would win over again
his unforgotten triumph.

With the military dimension of *The Vanity of Human Wishes* in
mind, we can turn to another great humanist document,
Reynolds's *Second Discourse*, delivered twenty years later, to
measure further the humanist instinct for the military figure.
This Discourse is typical of all fifteen in being primarily a
rhetorical performance: that is, its object is less to tell the bare
truth about something than to move the audience, here, the
impatient young geniuses studying painting at the Royal
Academy, to appropriate moral action, here, self-distrust. Like
the other Discourses, it has less of exposition than of exhortation.
Reynolds begins his work of inspiriting the students by con-
gratulating them on their attainments so far; then, like a skilled
dualist, he carefully lays before them the immense distance they
have to go: 'whilst I applaud you for what has been done, [I]
remind you how much yet remains to attain perfection'. To
gain his hearers' sympathy, he admits that the suggestions he is
about to offer are based in large part on his own youthful mis-
apprehensions and mistakes: 'But the history of errors, properly
managed, often shortens the road to truth.'

He now divides the artist's career into three stages. In the
first the novice masters the mechanical rudiments of drawing,
colouring, and disposing. In the second he 'collects' his
materials—from outside himself, needless to say—amassing 'a
stock of ideas, to be combined and varied as occasion may
require'. In this second period of study, a period of 'subjection
and discipline', it is also his business 'to learn all that has been

known and done before his own time'. Finally, the third period 'emancipates the student from subjection to any authority', except Nature, and now 'the mind that has been thus disciplined, may be indulged in the warmest enthusiasm, and venture to play on the borders of the wildest extravagance'. After outlining these three stages of artistic education, Reynolds informs his audience that they have just entered the second stage, the period of 'collection', and he continues throughout the Discourse to exhort his hearers to a salutary self-distrust. One of his early arguments takes the exact form of the Lockean theory of artistic invention: 'Invention, strictly speaking, is little more than a new combination of those images which have been previously gathered and deposited in the memory: nothing can come of nothing: he who has laid up no materials, can produce no combinations.' Thus 'A Student unacquainted with the attempts of former adventurers, is always apt to over-rate his own abilities; to mistake the most trifling excursions for discoveries of moment, and every coast new to him, for a new-found country.'

The moral is clear: the student arrived at the second stage must 'collect'—that is, select and copy details—from the great masters whose work has demonstrated its equivalence to 'nature' by appealing in every time and place. After warning against idleness, Reynolds returns to his favourite subject in all the early *Discourses*:

You must have no dependence on your own genius. If you have great talents, industry will improve them; if you have but moderate abilities, industry will supply their deficiency. Nothing is denied to well directed labour: nothing is to be obtained without it. Not to enter into metaphysical discussions on the nature or essence of genius, I will venture to assert, that assiduity unabated by difficulty, and a disposition eagerly directed to the object of its pursuit, will produce effects similar to those which some call the result of *natural powers*.

Just as *The Vanity of Human Wishes* proceeds by *exempla*, so does the *Second Discourse* now. Reynolds concludes by developing an elaborate and surprising equation between the artist and the military commander: the point made by the comparison is both disciplinary and Lockean. It is that 'Though a man cannot at all times, and in all places, paint or draw, yet a mind can pre-

M

pare itself by laying in proper materials, at all times, and in all places'. The alertness and vigilance of the artist in the second stage of his development must be those of the military officer: he must not merely accumulate material but dispose it and command it into shape; the things he collects must not manage him or take their own shape—he must manage them. Reynolds's portrait of the artist is the Greek general Philopoemen. Reynolds declares that he will 'quote the passage from LIVY at length, as it runs parallel with the practice I would recommend to the Painter, Sculptor, and Architect.' He then translates from Livy's *Historiarum libri* (XXXV, xxviii):

> PHILOPOEMEN was a man eminent for his sagacity and experience in choosing ground, and in leading armies; to which he formed his mind by perpetual meditation, in times of peace as well as war. When, in any occasional journey, he came to a strait difficult passage, if he was alone, he considered with himself, and if he was in company he asked his friends, what it would be best to do if in this place they had found an enemy, either in the front, or in the rear, on the one side, or on the other. 'It might happen,' says he, 'that the enemy to be opposed might come on drawn up in regular lines, or in a tumultuous body, formed only by the nature of the place.' He then considered a little what ground he should take; what number of soldiers he should use, and what arms he should give them; where he should lodge his carriages, his baggage, and the defenceless followers of his camp; how many guards, and of what kind, he should send to defend them; and whether it would be better to press forward along the pass, or recover by retreat his former station; he would consider likewise where his camp could most commodiously be formed; how much ground he should inclose within his trenches; where he should have the convenience of water, and where he might find plenty of wood and forage; and when he should break up his camp on the following day, through what road he could most safely pass, and in what form he should dispose his troops. With such thoughts and disquisitions he had from his early years so exercised his mind, that on these occasions nothing could happen which he had not been already accustomed to consider.

The 'parallel' here between general and artist is reinforced pleasantly by terms such as 'ground' or 'dispose' or 'passage' or 'lines' which carry both painterly and military meanings. The quotation reminds us irresistibly of the orthodox theory of artistic expression, which proves strikingly similar to theories of both the strategic and the tactical conduct of warfare. The orthodox theory of art—entirely consistent, it should be noted, with Lockean psychology—supposes three distinct, sequential actions: invention, disposition, and expression. In the invention stage the artist *finds* his materials (Lat. *invenio*); the general accumulates troops and matériel. In the disposition stage the artist *arranges* them; the general disposes his troops and weapons. In the expression stage artist and general alike *command* their dispositions into tactical action: they body them forth against disorder. As Reynolds's quotation from Livy makes clear, the worst thing that can befall either the general or the artist is to be surprised—neither must allow materials to dictate the strategic shape of events, no matter how materials may have to dictate minor tactical considerations, such as the disposition of troops or colours. The painter must be as vigilant as the general because the warfare in which each is engaged is supremely serious. *Expertise* is indispensable for the same reason: the most momentous issues—life or death, redemption or accommodation—await the success of minor tactics in either kind of warfare, whether the struggle is against enemy armies or the natural disorder and surprises of actual experience. Reynolds's awareness of this parallel between artist and soldier naturally generates images like this, in the *First Discourse*: 'the impetuosity of youth is disgusted at the slow approaches of a regular siege, and desires, from mere impatience of labour, to take the citadel by storm'. Youth has much to learn from Philopoemen's example. Reynolds's military sense of the artist is not a little like the conception of the artist which belongs naturally to satire. Indeed, it is remarkably like Pope's. To Pope, as Thomas R. Edwards has said, 'The writer is a warrior, as the *Essay [on Criticism]* often implies, and Pope's treatment of him . . . shows indirectly the same fascination with epic more obviously shown in *The Rape of the Lock* and the translations of Homer.'[3] We sense the same obsession with epic—or its parallel genre, history-painting—throughout Reynolds's *Discourses*, and no more so than in his final eloquent, self-deprecatory tribute to Michelangelo, who was not merely sculptor, painter, and architect, but, as Reynolds surely was aware, the designer of the fortifications of Florence.

[3] *This Dark Estate*, p. 16.

The aspirant to learning, as Johnson shows in *The Vanity of Human Wishes*, is beset by as many concealed enemies as the soldier, and the confusions of combat make it likely that he will lose his way on the battlefield. As Gibbon recounts in Chapter III of his *Autobiography*, at Oxford 'The blind activity of idleness urged me to advance without armour into the dangerous mazes of controversy, and at the age of sixteen, I bewildered myself in the errors of the Church of Rome'. But Gibbon is generally so amused by the disparity between actual and literary warfare that, like Swift, he tends to use his military images in a mock-heroic way, suggestive of a refreshing degree of self-deprecation that we do not sense in the literal assertions of the *Autobiography*. In Chapter VII of this work, the controversy awakened by the fifteenth and sixteenth chapters of the *Decline and Fall* is depicted in terms of a battle which employs both epic and modern weapons and techniques. Because his weapons are better than his adversaries', Gibbon's ultimate victory is assured, but he still has some disquieting moments in defence. Upon the publication of the first volume of the *Decline and Fall*, the volume which concludes with the two magnificent chapters, Gibbon realized that an attack was forming: 'the shaft was shot, the alarm was sounded, and I could only rejoice that, if the voice of our priests was clamorous and bitter, their hands were disarmed from the powers of persecution'. But even though they have lost their old and trusted weapon, the enemy troops still possess a sound artillery. It might have given Gibbon some trouble if he had not soon learned that it was either very incompetently aimed or had actually nothing but blanks to fire: 'Let me frankly own that I was startled at the first volleys of this ecclesiastical ordnance. But as soon as I found out that this empty noise was mischievous only in the intention, my fear was converted to indignation. . . .' But the fortress of rectitude and intelligence is so impregnable and so well armed that its commander finds that he need not condescend to notice the feeble assaults: 'every polemic, of either university, discharged his sermon or pamphlet against the inpenetrable silence of the Roman historian'. We cannot help recalling Swift's similar but funnier image in 'An Apology', which introduces *A Tale of a Tub*. Responding likewise to ecclesiastical attacks, Swift reminds his critics that to answer a Book effectually, requires more Pains and Skill, more Wit, Learning, and Judgment than were employ'd in the Writing it. And the Author assures those Gentlemen who have given themselves that Trouble with him, that his Discourse is the Product of the Study, the Observation, and the Invention of several Years, that he has often blotted out much more than he left, and if his Papers had not been a long time out of his Possession, they must have still undergone more severe Corrections; and do they think that such a Building is to be battered with Dirt-Pellets however envenom'd the Mouths may be that discharge them.

And like the Swift of *The Battle of the Books*, Gibbon manages to diminish his attackers by presenting both their assaults and their internal dissensions in mock-epic terms: 'Dr. Priestley threw down his two gauntlets to Bishop Hurd and Mr. Gibbon . . . the dauntless philosopher of Birmingham continued to fire away his double battery against those who believed too little, and those who believed too much . . . his Socinian shield has repeatedly been pierced by the spear of mighty Horsley, and his trumpet of sedition may at length awaken the magistrates of a free country.'

Burke's enactment of military motifs, on the other hand, is anything but mock-heroic. The issue to Burke is the persistence of civilization itself, and the enemy is less to be mocked than extirpated. The most notable single thing about Burke's rhetoric is of course his neo-Renaissance luxuriance of imagery: perhaps he comes as near as anyone outside the seventeenth century to the technique of thinking in figures. James Boswell noticed this characteristic the first time he heard him speak. He writes in 1773, 'I was . . . fortunate enough to hear Mr. Edmund Burke speak twice [in the House of Commons]. It was a great feast to me who have never heard him before. It was astonishing how all kinds of figures of speech crowded upon him. He was like a man in an orchard where boughs loaded with fruit hung around him, and he pulled apples as fast as he pleased and pelted the Ministry' (*BD*, 161). The difference between Boswell's clumsy and self-conscious simile and the typical Burke metaphor indicates—if any such indication is necessary—the subtlety and vigour of the rhetorical world where Burke lives and from which Boswell, for all his touching aspiration and discipleship, is destined to be permanently excluded.

In Burke the humanist inheritance of military imagery is put
to work to suggest the broad menace of revolutionary thought
to the fortress of orthodoxy, whether religious, ethical, or
political. In *A Vindication of Natural Society* he suggests that the
Moderns sometimes go to work underground: readers who expected great things from the posthumous appearance of Bolingbroke's 'philosophical' works were disappointed, and they
'received but a poor recompense for this disappointment, in
seeing every mode of religion attacked in a lively manner, and
the foundation of every virtue, and of all government, sapped
with great art and much ingenuity'. Johnson typically abuses
Bolingbroke in military terms also: 'he was a scoundrel, and a
coward: a scoundrel, for charging a blunderbuss against
religion and morality; a coward, because he had not resolution
to fire it off himself, but left half a crown to a beggarly Scotch-
man [David Mallet], to draw the trigger after his death' (*BLJ*,
i, 268). Burke's *Speech on American Taxation* images the political
battlefield as dark and dangerous: when Lord Chatham led the
passage of the Declaratory Act, Burke writes, 'The allies of
ministry . . . endeavoured to undermine their credit, and to take
ground that must be fatal to the success of the very cause that
they would be thought to countenance . . . everything, upon
every side, was full of traps and mines. . . '. Thus, by the time
of the French Revolution, Burke is already skilled in the
instinctive application of military figures to ethical issues, and
we experience no shock when we find him saying in the *Reflections* that the Revolutionists 'have wrought under-ground a
mine that will blow up, at one grand explosion, all the examples
of antiquity . . .'. But republicans do not always operate underground. Success emboldens them to return to the surface and to
assault the citadel with a potentially disastrous artillery. In
Thoughts on French Affairs we are told that 'The writers of
[republican] papers . . . are either unknown or in contempt, but
they are like a battery, in which the stroke of any one ball
produces no great effect, but the amount of continual repetition
is decisive'. And Burke's military imagery becomes more precise and witty as his career proceeds. Near the end, his imagination heated to fury by the exhibition of actual civil war in
France, he almost turns himself into an actual military en-
gineer. In *A Letter to a Noble Lord*, referring to the revolutionists'

use of old cement and building materials as emergency sources of gunpowder, he delivers this image eloquent of the impending revolutionary destruction of the orthodox principles of hierarchy and discreteness: 'Churches, play-houses, coffee-houses, all alike are destined to be mingled and equalized, and blended into one common rubbish; and, well sifted and lixiviated [mixed with lye], to crystallize into true, democratic, explosive, insurrectionary nitre.' This is brilliant, technical, and passionate. To imagine Cowper, Gray, or Boswell living and breathing for an instant within a world of rhetoric like that, a world stabilized by exact technical detail, is as impossible as imagining any truce between orthodoxy and heterodoxy in the eighteenth century.

Whether employed mock-heroically by Swift and Pope and Gibbon, or heroically by Johnson, Reynolds, and Burke, the military figure, used in an age of actual siege warfare, provides the Augustan humanist imagination with a wonderfully lively —and occasionally terrifying—technique for suggesting a perpetual and dangerous dualism in both internal and external affairs. At the same time it would be silly to leave the impression that military imagery is somehow the sole property of the humanist tradition: images of fortification and combat are uniformly accessible and very broadly applicable to psychological and polemic circumstances. Such images, indeed, reduced to dead metaphors, have become part of the jargon of our day. But it remains true that there is something about a dualistic ethical tradition which cries out for embodiment in images of warfare. A monistic tradition will tend to cleave to figures which imply the process of merging rather than the action of opposition. The open sea or the earthly globe are the monistic figures *par excellence*: Whitman learns the secret of psychic coherence from the sea, and Wordsworth's Lucy is

> Rolled round in earth's diurnal course,
> With rocks, and stones, and trees.

But images of the sea-fight and of land warfare belong to quite another traditional world of rhetoric. A moral world in which self-distrust and self-conquest are the highest virtues and a social world in which redemptive 'Roman' action seems preferable to passion or contemplation will find in the paradigms of the general and the soldier indispensable parallels for the instruction of the artist and the writer. There is a universe of difference between a world in which we loaf and invite our souls and one in which, as Johnson conceives in *Adventurer* 111, combat is the noblest human activity and 'acceptance' the most ignoble: 'To strive with difficulties, and to conquer them, is the highest human felicity; the next is, to strive, and deserve to conquer: but he whose life has passed without a contest, and who can boast neither success nor merit, can survey himself only as a useless filler of existence; and if he is content with his own character, must owe his satisfaction to insensibility.' After an observation like that, we can understand something of what Johnson implies when he tells Boswell that 'Every man thinks meanly of himself for not having been a soldier, or for not having been at sea' (*BLJ*, iii, 265).

8

THE CITY OF LIFE
AND THE CITY OF LITERATURE

THE humanist mind responds with more excitement to the constructions of man than to the creations of nature. Presented with a tree or a shrub, it tends to lose interest quickly, but presented with a work of architecture, it experiences something which begins in curiosity and often ends in moral ecstasy. In the *Life of Congreve* Johnson writes: 'if I were required to select from the whole mass of English poetry the most poetical paragraph, I know not what I could prefer to an exclamation in *The Mourning Bride*'. He then quotes a passage which exploits the relation between the human and the architectural. The setting is 'The Aisle of a Temple'; Almeria speaks to Leonora:

> . . . all is hush'd and still as death.—'Tis dreadful!
> How reverend is the face of this tall pile;
> Whose ancient pillars rear their marble heads,
> To bear aloft its arch'd and ponderous roof,
> By its own weight made stedfast and immoveable,
> Looking tranquillity! It strikes an awe
> And terror on my aching sight; the tombs
> And monumental caves of death look cold,
> And shoot a chillness to my trembling heart.
> Give me thy hand, and let me hear thy voice;
> Nay, quickly speak to me, and let me hear
> Thy voice—my own affrights me with its echoes.
>
> (II, i, 49–60)

Bonamy Dobrée is puzzled by Johnson's delight in this passage: he finds it 'significant of the undramatic mind of the whole of the eighteenth century that Dr. Johnson should have picked out for especial commendation [this] passage, which is the most end-stopped of the whole play, and which strikes the modern reader as being the most unreal, the most filled with artificial imagery, of any he can meet with in the course of the tragedy'.[1] But once we put the matter into its proper context I think we can understand why the passage appeals to Johnson so strongly. First, Almeria's terrifying loneliness in the midst of images of permanence is the sort of universal motif that pleased Johnson likewise in Gray's *Elegy*. He comments here, very much as he does in the *Life of Gray*, 'He who reads these lines enjoys for a moment the powers of a poet; he feels what he remembers to have felt before, but he feels it with great increase of sensibility; he recognizes a familiar image, but meets it again amplified and expanded, embellished with beauty, and enlarged with majesty'. Second, it is likely that the very architectural details delight Johnson, especially, perhaps, the image of the columns humanized, bearing the ponderous roof on their marble heads. Third, Johnson is drawn to the whole paradox and illusion of architecture, to the way, for example, materials of great weight and bulk can assume the illusion of weighing nothing, the way massive and clumsy materials can be made to defy gravity and 'look tranquillity'. Finally, he is probably struck by the moving moral relationship between the human and the architectural: the relation is one between the temporary and the permanent, the frail and the powerful, the puny and the majestic, the living thing that crawls the earth and the cold, lifeless thing that triumphs over gravitation and time. In the face of a temple of the sort in which Almeria is standing, the human imagination both enlarges and contracts, and is thus forced in some way to confront the general paradox of man. Johnson is typical of the Augustan humanists in his excited response to anything architectural. And for Johnson as for others architectural imagery is closely allied with moral ideas. For Keats, the 'magic casements' and the cornices, portals, and porches of *The Eve of St. Agnes* are their own—or their poems'—delightful decorative end, but for the Augustan humanists architectural imagery and moral imperatives seem never very far separated. After a severe illness has made us especially conscious of our mortality, Johnson points out in *Rambler* 17, 'We should then find the absurdity of stretching out our arms incessantly to grasp that which we cannot keep, and wearing out our lives in endeavours to add

---

[1] *Restoration Tragedy: 1660–1720* (Oxford, 1929), p. 170.

new turrets to the fabrick of ambition, when the foundation itself is shaking, and the ground on which it stands is mouldering away.'

One reason why the eighteenth-century imagination is so full of architectural images is that everybody who was anybody was either 'building' or had friends who were. Just as a minimum technical knowledge of fortification was assumed in any civilized person, so anyone of the middle or upper class was expected to possess some technical architectural learning. In his *Account of the Harleian Library* Johnson refers to 'tactics, architecture, and fortification' as 'kindred arts', and all three were assumed to be part of most people's intellectual stock-in-trade. On all sides eighteenth-century London was being torn up and built anew: here and there stone and brick were still being installed to cover the scars left by the Great Fire of 1666, and all London seemed to be a-building. During the early part of the century the last of Wren's churches were being finished. The great town houses like Somerset House, Burlington House, Montagu House, and Buckingham House (today, greatly enlarged and vulgarized, conspicuous as Buckingham Palace) were going up and, what is more important, were being avidly inspected, discussed, and criticized. Mansion House was erected, Newgate Prison rebuilt. The Bank of England was being built just down the street from Johnson's house, and St. Paul's was finally finished in 1710. New squares were laid out, streets were widened, and the London bridges were built or rebuilt: the rebuilding of Westminster Bridge was finished in 1747, and Blackfriars Bridge was completed in 1769. The newly prosperous middle classes were hastening to erect houses all over London, it seemed, and with a uniformity encouraged by the London Building Acts of 1707 and 1708. During all this activity, Rome never diminished as a focus of architectural interest and imitation: works like William Salmon's *Palladio Londinensis* (1755) brought pseudo-Palladian plans to the million, and the discovery of Herculaneum in 1719 and of Pompeii in 1748 generated vast architectural interest. Pope improved his villa, and his friend Lord Burlington built, improved, spent, and patronized. Architects like Kent, Ware, Dance the Younger, the Adam brothers, Paine, Taylor, and Chambers flourished: it was an age as profitable for architects as for portrait painters. Anywhere one chose to look in London one could have seen and studied bricklayers, masons, stone-cutters, and carpenters going about their work, climbing their scaffolding and bawling at their apprentices for mortar and nails. If one had lived in London, the difficult thing would be not to have known a great deal about architecture and build-ing.

The vigour of eighteenth-century architectural activity and images is reflected in some interesting ways. The first formal Grand Lodge of Freemasons, originating as a sort of genteel and Deistic parody of the actual guilds of actual masons, was organized in London in 1717, and the movement soon spread to Caledonia and Hibernia. The notable thing about British Free-masonry as a whimsical and social cult is that, through its symbolism of architecture and building, it manages to project a very orthodox emphasis on self-mastery, restraint, and order. Although the relation of some of them with Freemasonry must have been merely nominal and tenuous, it is striking that all but two of the six great Augustan humanists were Masons—Johnson and Reynolds, for all their clubbability, never joined. But Pope, Swift, Gibbon, and Burke all had the opportunity of extending their natural architectural knowledge by means of the symbolic architectural exercises available at Masonic meetings. In addi-tion, we find that the list of eighteenth-century Masons includes a number of others of a distinctly conservative cast. Perhaps Gay was a member, and Chesterfield certainly was. Frederick, Prince of Wales, was a Mason; so was James Boswell, Esquire. Johnson's friend Richard Savage, William Hogarth, and Dr. Arbuthnot were likewise members of the Craft. British Free-masonry sustains itself by the architectural symbolism derived from the account of Solomon's temple in 1 Kings v–viii, and it seems suggestive of an alliance between images of architecture and ideas of orthodox ethics that it was the conservative but not the rigorously pietistic element in the early eighteenth century that decided to invent Freemasonry. Three notable eighteenth-century poems which can be said to reveal an obsession with architecture are all the work of Masons, Pope's *Temple of Fame*, his *Epistle to Burlington* (*Moral Essay* IV), and Christopher Smart's *Song to David*. It is perhaps worth speculating whether the general conservative sensibility tends to express its moral and artistic ideas through motifs of architecture. Since works of architecture persist and belong to both past and future, they constitute a readily available, indeed an obvious symbol of the persistence of the humanly contrived. We think of Eliot's 'These fragments I have shored against my ruins' as well as of Pound's important distinction between the two materials 'plaster' and 'alabaster' in *Hugh Selwyn Mauberley.*

Another reflection of the Georgian concern with architecture is the plethora of 'building poems', poems celebrating and describing new or famous houses: Robert A. Aubin lists over 130 of them from 1700 to 1798.[2] Samuel Johnson knew so much about architecture that his *Journey to the Western Islands* becomes almost an architectural guidebook: we discover that, for example, when he wants to tell us what a 'range of black rocks' looks like, he says that the rocks 'had the appearance of broken pilasters'. And although Johnson is always extraordinary, there is still something typical in his exhibition of architectural and technical learning in his three letters to the *Gazetteer* (December 1759), where he argues for semicircular instead of elliptical arches in the new Blackfriars Bridge. Here he deploys a precise knowledge of geometrical stresses and strains, of the whole physics and dynamics of architecture, and he supports—he would say 'buttresses'—his argument by reference to the construction of certain famous continental bridges.

To Johnson, the art of the mason is 'one of the principal arts by which reasoning beings are distinguished from the brute' (*Adventurer* 128), and it is a conviction of the nobleness of architecture, considered almost by itself, that prompts Reynolds, in his *Ninth Discourse*, to associate it intimately with 'the dignity of our natures' and 'the excellency of man'. Reynolds's transition in this very short Discourse from architecture to polemic humanism is smooth and instinctive. The Royal Academy has just installed itself in the newly completed Somerset House, designed by Sir William Chambers, and Reynolds begins by inviting the attention of his audience to the building and by praising it and its architect. He then proceeds to exhort the art students to be worthy of the building, and before he has finished he has been conducted by the association of ideas to a passionate

[2] *Topographical Poetry in XVIII-Century England* (New York, 1936), pp. 351–8.

assertion of the potentiality and dignity of the human mind, an
assertion which concludes with a ringing call to redemptive
humanistic action: insisting that it is the nature of painting,
properly considered, to 'raise the thoughts, and extend the
views of the spectator', he goes on to hope that 'its effects may
extend themselves imperceptibly into public benefits, and be
among the means of bestowing on whole nations refinement of
taste: which, if it does not lead directly to purity of manners,
obviates at least their greatest depravation, by disentangling the
mind from appetite, and conducting the thoughts through
successive stages of excellence, till that contemplation of universal rectitude and harmony which began by Taste, may, as it is
exalted and refined, conclude in Virtue.' This passionate and
eloquent credo issues quite naturally from a contemplation of
the mere stones and mortar of Somerset House. The redemptive
assumptions here are like those in Burke's hymn to the values of
the defeated French aristocracy, in the *Reflections*: 'It is gone,
that sensibility of principle, that chastity of honour, which felt a
stain like a wound, which inspired courage whilst it mitigated
ferocity, which ennobled whatever it touched, and under which
vice itself lost half its evil, by losing all its grossness.'

   Like Reynolds, Pope also tends to associate architectural with
redemptive ideas. At the very polemic centre of the *Essay on
Man*, where we are assured that it is the way of heaven to
enable man to redeem his vices into virtues, Pope invokes a
general architectural image. Heaven, he says,

> . . . Virtue's ends from Vanity's can raise,
> Which seeks no int'rest, no reward but praise;
> And build on wants, and on defects of mind,
> The joy, the peace, the glory of Mankind.
>
> (II, 245–8)

The best gloss on 'raise' is Johnson's definition: 'To erect; to
build up'. He illustrates from Joshua viii: 'Take his carcase
down from the tree, cast it at the entering of the gate, and *raise*
thereupon a heap of stones.'

   In this climate of general architectural awareness and enthusiasm, we find John Locke conducting his *Essay Concerning
Human Understanding* in significant architectural terms. He
naturally refers to the Deity as 'the Architect', suggesting there-

by that the universe is a static product put together out of separable, inorganic materials. His account of the mind seems to assume that the human person is like a building, and a building conceived along some very conservative, although undeniably noble, Roman lines. Speaking of the organs of sense, he writes: 'if these organs, or the nerves which are the conduits [i.e. aqueducts, as the term is defined by Johnson] to convey them from without to their audience in the brain—the mind's presence-room (as I may so call it)—are any of them so disordered as not to perform their functions, they have no postern [Johnson: 'A small gate; a little door'] to be admitted by; no other way to bring themselves into view, and be perceived by the understanding' (II, iii, 1). Memory is 'the storehouse of our ideas' (II, x, 2), and initial entry to this storehouse is simpler than has been thought in the past: 'external and internal sensation are the only passages I can find of knowledge to the understanding. These alone, as far as I can discover, are the windows by which light is let into this dark room. For, methinks, the understanding is not much unlike a closet wholly shut from light, with only some little openings left, to let in external visible resemblances, or ideas of things without. . . .' Man is thus like a little building, complete with a water supply, a living-room, a front gate, a storehouse, and a study or bedroom. In such a context as this, what could be more natural than for a humanist like Johnson to turn such suggestions to explicit ethical use, as he does, say, in *Rambler* 20: 'The state of the possesser of humble virtues, to the affecter of great excellencies, is that of a small cottage of stone, to the palace raised with ice by the empress of Russia; it was for a time splendid and luminous, but the first sunshine melted it to nothing'? And in the Lockean context what could be more natural than to proceed one step further and to hint that the separate 'buildings' constitute a sort of social 'city', an urban and urbane complex in which persons are related to each other as houses and public buildings are? Houses and buildings may touch each other, but they never interpenetrate. The inside of one is roughly deducible from the inside of another. They are made not by any mysterious means but by the careful accumulation and arrangement of separable, objective materials. It would be hard to find a more exact emblem of Augustan man.

Locke's architectural imagery is perhaps more traditional than his idea. Renaissance ethical poetry is full of figures of the mind as a room or a set of apartments. Spenser's treatment of mind in *Faerie Queene* II, ix, 45, can be taken as representative. He images mind as the turret of a castle, divided into 'diuerse rooms', the walls of which are 'dispainted' with shapes, colours, and pictures. In one of his self-confident moods when he has persuaded himself momentarily that he is not a victim of 'fatality', Boswell recovers this figure and, in his journal, domesticates it. Where Spenser's 'mind' is a castle turret, Boswell's is a small but respectable town house let to lodgers by a genteel family playing the role of 'will': 'Formerly my mind was quite a lodging-house for all ideas who chose to put up there, so that it was at the mercy of accident, for I had no fixed mind of my own. Now my mind is a house where, though the street rooms and the upper floors are open to strangers, yet there is always a settled family in the back parlour and sleeping-closet behind it; and this family can judge of the ideas which come to lodge' (*BSW*, 137–8).

Boswell's delight in this sort of imagery is clear from his adding 'and sleeping-closet' to 'back parlour': there is no logical reason for providing more 'rooms'—Boswell simply is urged by the sheer fun of imagining the mind to be a Lockean building. Such is the appeal of the architectural image in an age when everybody depended upon Locke for his account of the mind. What has happened since the time of Shakespeare seems clear enough: as Russell A. Fraser says of Shakespeare, 'His greatest single source of imagery he finds in the countryside. When he would body forth human beings, he depicts them most often in terms of plants and trees.'[3] But to turn to an image of Edmund Waller's, in *On the Divine Poems* (1686), is to enter a new world sustained by ideas of property, boundaries, rents, and 'upkeep':

> The soul's dark cottage, batter'd and decay'd,
> Lets in new light through chinks that Time has made.
>
> (13–14)

In Swift the architectural figure is used, now whimsically, now soberly, to embody not persons but large social abstractions

---

[3] *Shakespeare's Poetics* (London, 1962), p. 36.

such as Learning and the State. Even in one of the whimsical figures in *A Tale of a Tub* we perceive the instinctive association which the Augustan mind makes between architectural and military images: it is amazing how frequently the one will seem to give birth to the other. In 'A Digression in Praise of Digressions' the speaker, ironically praising indexes as the proper entrances to learning, says that 'to enter the Palace of Learning at the *great Gate*, requires an Expence of Time and Forms; therefore Men of much Haste and little Ceremony, are content to get in by the *Back-Door*. For, the Arts are all in a *flying* March, and therefore more easily subdued by attacking them in the *Rear*.'

But the architectural figure is sometimes exploited more soberly by Swift, and in a way that moves it in a Burkean direction. At the end of his *Project for the Advancement of Religion and the Reformation of Manners* (1709), he maintains—with a hint of the military motif—that though every commonwealth exhibits its corruptions, 'in a well-instituted State, the Executive Power will be always contending against them, . . . never letting Abuses grow inveterate, or multiply so far that it will be hard to find Remedies, and perhaps impossible to apply them'. Moving on to seek an analogy, Swift resorts to domestic architecture, and his sense of the frailty of houses suggests the same kind of serious irony and pathos that we have seen in his treatment of Gulliver's person and psyche: 'As he that would keep his House in Repair, must attend every little Breach or Flaw, and supply it immediately, else Time alone will bring all to Ruin; how much more the common Accidents of Storms and Rain? He must live in perpetual danger of his House falling about his Ears; and will find it cheaper to throw it quite down, and build it again from the Ground, perhaps upon a new Foundation, or at least in a new Form, which may neither be so safe nor so convenient as the old.'

Swift's architectural delight impels him, like Boswell, to develop the image so fully, almost like an epic simile, that when we finish we have all but forgotten that the decaying house, so moving and interesting an object of sympathy in itself, is emblematic of the untended state.

Where Swift likes to think of buildings as analogues of learning and government, Pope, on one important occasion at least,

N

tends to associate architecture with the human person and to develop a theory of human physical beauty—and of poetry as well—by using an elaborate and brilliant metaphor from architecture. It is not the first time in the *Essay on Criticism* that the figure of a beautiful woman has made its appearance: we have encountered her lurking just below the surface in lines 68–79 ('First follow NATURE'), where we are told that just as '*Art*' from 'that Fund' of Nature 'Works *without Show*', so

> In some fair Body thus th'informing Soul
> With Spirits feeds, with Vigour fills the whole,
> Each Motion guides, and ev'ry Nerve sustains;·
> *It self unseen*, but in th'*Effects*, remains.

That is, the relation of art to nature is that of body to soul: art 'incorporates' nature, and nature is the '*anima*' of art. With his fascinating, complete, beautiful woman before us to 'affect our Hearts', some lines later Pope delivers a related metaphor which is central to the whole argument of the *Essay on Criticism*, and which is indeed central to Pope's whole aesthetic. He uses the metaphor to recommend a total and simultaneous vision of all the elements that constitute a beautiful work of nature or of art. The passage, an invitation to 'Survey the WHOLE', begins:

> In Wit, as Nature, what affects our Hearts,
> Is not th' exactness of peculiar Parts;
> 'Tis not a *Lip*, or *Eye*, we Beauty call,
> But the joint Force, and full *Result* of *all*.

The beautiful lady and a work of art attract us by their arts of coherence, not by their separate, individual beauties. Pope now goes to Michelangelo's dome at St. Peter's Basilica to show us what he means in architectural terms:

> Thus when we view some well-proportion'd Dome,
> (The *World's* just Wonder, and ev'n *thine* O *Rome!*)
> No single Parts unequally surprize;
> All comes *united* to th'admiring Eyes;
> No monstrous Height, or Breadth, or Length appear;
> The *Whole* at once is *Bold*, and *Regular*.

(243–252)

Of all architectural ideas, the dome most perfectly embodies the tension and paradoxical union of vertical and lateral stresses: each seems entirely reconciled to the other; each is so harmonized by the other that, if the dome is perfect, it creates the illusion that stress and weight have been wholly vanquished, and that stone, by some magical reconciliation of contraries, has been transformed into gas or gossamer, that is, that nature has been transmuted into art. But just as the job is done in poetry ('Wit') by learning and technique, and in women by the learned arts of personal coherence, so in architecture it is all done by a sober and extensive technical knowledge for which there is no substitute, and surely not in 'inspiration': the knowledge is that of the weights of stone and of the principles and techniques of physics, dynamics, and engineering. Looking now back at the total figure, and trying to heed Pope's advice to 'Survey the WHOLE', we see that the figure equates the human body, a work of literature, and a work of architecture, and that it implies that all—when in a state of earthly perfection—are 'constructed' in the same dualistic way. 'Boldness' and 'regularity', two opposing forces, must be brought into a harmonious tension in each. Pope calls these two antithetical forces, the forces of danger and safety, by many different names, but a fruitful opposition between them seems to be his ambition everywhere. In the *Essay on Criticism*, where he is talking about literature, they are analogous to Wit (or Invention), which propels, and Judgment, which restrains: these two

> often are at strife,
> Tho' meant each other's Aid, like *Man* and *Wife*.
>
> (82–83)

In the *Essay on Man*, when he is talking about human motives, 'boldness' and 'regularity' are metamorphosed into Passion and Reason, or Self-Love and Social Love. And when he talks about architecture in the *Essay on Man*, 'boldness' and 'regularity' are synonymous with the vertical, downward force and the lateral, outward force. We will not be making a wild mistake, I think, if we take this one figure of the dome in the *Essay on Criticism* to be an important moment in Pope's whole attempt to persuade his readers that they depart dangerously from their humanity if they assume that some one exclusive human quality contains the redemptive secret. For Pope, tension, the result of the interplay and opposition of all man's separate personal

forces, is redemption. It is in this sense of 'stresses and strains'
that man is like a work of architecture, although his being like a
building does not mean that he is simple or easily read from the
outside. As Pope says in the *Epistle to Cobham* (*Moral Essay* I),
men's real characters, as opposed to their affected ones, are
almost impossible to perceive:

> In vain th' observer eyes the builder's toil,
> But quite mistakes the scaffold for the pile.
>
>   (220–1)

All Pope's tensions between polarities constitute his version
of what Lovejoy has called 'the method of counterpoise', that
technique habitual in seventeenth and eighteenth-century
philosophy of reconciling oppositions by balancing them off
against each other. Newtonian astronomy, as Lovejoy points out,
is in essence an imaginative conception very like Pope's sense of
the architectural dome: according to the contemporary popu-
larizations of Newtonian 'celestial mechanics', 'the planets had
within them a centrifugal force which alone would have made
them fly off into space in straight lines, and a centripital force,
which alone would have caused them to fall into the sun;
happily counterbalancing one another, these two otherwise
mischievous forces cause these bodies to behave as they should,
that is, to roll round in their proper orbits'.[4] The theory of
checks and balances embodied in the eighteenth-century
political constitution is as implicit in the Newtonian image of
the heavens as is Pope's vision of human coherence. To Burke as
to Pope, what is wanted is a balance of powers. As Burke puts it
in the *Reflections*, 'To make a government requires no great
prudence. . . . To give freedom is still more easy. It is not
necessary to guide; it only requires to let go the rein. But to
form a *free government*; that is, to temper together those opposite
elements of liberty and restraint in one consistent work,
requires much thought, deep reflection, a sagacious, powerful,
and combining mind.' When we learn that the Houyhnhnms
are 'wholly governed' by reason alone, we are naturally suspicious.

These motifs of the balance of psychological or political
powers create an environment favourable to the imagery of epic

----

[4] *Reflections on Human Nature*, pp. 38–39.

scales readily available in the *Iliad* (viii), the *Aeneid* (xii), and *Paradise Lost* (iv). Although in *The Rape of the Lock* the scales are used conventionally to foretell the issue of the combat, their more frequent appearance is as an image suggesting some ethically enormous imbalance or inequality, some appalling predominance of a 'part' at the expense of a 'whole'. The scales are often imported to realize some ethically hortatory passage, as in the *Essay on Man*: after tempting the reader to condescend to 'the poor Indian', Pope turns to blast the reader himself:

> Go, wiser thou; and in thy scale of sense
> Weigh thy Opinion against Providence.

(i, 113–14)

Again, Pope dares the proud to

> Snatch from [God's] hand the balance and the rod,
> Re-judge his justice, be the GOD of GOD!

(i, 121–2)

The dualist is always seizing opportunities for thrusting forth the scales. Thus Reynolds, in the *Eighth Discourse*: 'An Artist is obliged for ever to hold a balance in his hand. . . .' Thus Burke in *A Letter to a Noble Lord*: 'if the rude inroad of Gallic tumult, with . . . its sword as a make-weight to throw into the scale, shall be introduced into our city by a misguided populace . . ., we shall, all of us, perish and be overwhelmed in a common ruin'. Thus Johnson, in *Rambler* 76, analysing the instincts of the guilty man: 'He easily finds some faults in every human being, which he weighs against his own, and easily makes them preponderate while he keeps the balance in his own hand. . . .' Counterpoise and balance gratify the humanist heart, whether their emblem is beheld figuratively in epic or in traditional sculpture, or literally, parcelling out carrots and beans in the marketplace at Lichfield.

If to some of the Augustan humanists buildings are people, to Samuel Johnson they are likely to be hopes, 'schemes', 'good intentions', governments, or images of 'the world'. Now and then he will imply that men are like buildings, as he does in *Rambler* 89: 'Every man finds himself differently affected by the sight of fortresses of war, and palaces of pleasure; we look on the height and strength of the bulwarks with a kind of gloomy satisfaction, for we cannot think of defence without admitting ideas of danger; but we range delighted and jocund through the gay apartments of the palace, because nothing is impressed by them on the mind but joy and festivity. Such is the difference between great and amiable characters; with protectors we are safe, with companions we are happy.'

But generally Johnson uses his architectural images to enforce implications of instability or frailty, and his buildings, symbolic of the irony of hope or triumph, are often shaky or ruinous, fraught with suggestions of the limitations of human nature. 'He that hopes in the same house to obtain every convenience', he asserts in *Rambler* 134, 'may draw plans and study Palladio, but will never lay a stone'. In *Rambler* 52 'schemes' are imaged ironically: 'it has been found useful . . . to contemplate . . . the various shapes of misery, which . . . when we have built our schemes to the top, ruin their foundations'. Indeed, we might conclude that when Johnson becomes the most ironic, he turns the most architectural. A passage spoken by the character Cali in *Irene* reminds us of Johnson's excitement over the architectural passage in *The Mourning Bride*:

> . . . with incessant Thought laborious man
> Extends his mighty Schemes of Wealth and Pow'r,
> And tow'rs and triumphs in ideal Greatness;
> Some accidental Gust of Opposition
> Blasts all the Beauties of his new Creation,
> O'erturns the Fabricks of presumptuous Reason,
> And whelms the swelling Architect beneath it.

(ii, iii)

Cardinal Wolsey's architectural naïveté in *The Vanity of Human Wishes* illustrates Cali's observation:

> . . . why did Wolsey near the steeps of fate,
> On weak foundations raise th' enormous weight?
> Why but to sink beneath misfortune's blow,
> With louder ruin to the gulphs below?

(125–8)

It is all a little like the actual folly of young William Beckford, who, contriving that his life should imitate art, or at least imagery, built an immense Gothic 'convent' on his grounds at Fonthill. As Geoffrey Scott reports:

Beckford, at Fonthill, finding in the Georgian mansion he inherited no adequate stimulus to the raptures of imagination, instructed his architect Wyatt to design 'an ornamental building which should have the appearance of a convent, be partly in ruins and yet contain some weatherproof apartments'. The scheme at length developed into vast proportions. . . . Five hundred workmen laboured here incessantly, by day, and with torches in the night. But the wind blew upon it, and the wretched structure fell incontinently to the ground. The ideal of a monastic palace 'partly ruined' was ironically achieved.[5]

All kinds of frustrated hopes are like ruined buildings. In the *Life of John Hughes* we are told that Tonson's project to issue a translation of Lucan's *Pharsalia* 'fell to the ground'. In the *Life of Drake*, speaking of the Symerons, an aboriginal tribe encountered by Sir Francis Drake, Johnson says that among them 'he that can temper iron best is . . . most esteemed, and, perhaps, it would be happy for every nation, if honours and applauses were as justly distributed, and he were most distinguished whose abilities were most useful to society. How many chimerical titles to precedence, how many false pretences to respect, would this rule bring to the ground.'

The 'system' erected by Soame Jenyns to explain away evil is as shaky and dangerous as false hopes themselves: Jenyns's system, says Johnson, 'is so ready to fall to pieces of itself, that no great praise can be derived from its destruction'. As if a little bit ashamed of the vigour with which he has demolished his adversary's construction, Johnson concludes his review this way: 'To object is always easy, and it has been well observed by a late writer [the author of *New Practice of Physick*], that *the hand which cannot build a hovel, may demolish a temple.*'

The difference between an architectural 'foundation' and a 'superstructure' provides Johnson with some happy opportunities for imagery suggestive of the Lockean process of knowing through the accumulation of data. Speaking in the *Journey to the Western Islands* of the Scottish students who enter the university, Johnson says that 'they carry with them little fundamental knowledge, and therefore the superstructure cannot be lofty'. And in the *Life of Pope* the image of the superstructure embodies self-esteem. Johnson speculates that Pope's contempt for the world and for the common reader must have been the

[5] *Architecture of Humanism*, p. 50.

result of affectation, for 'How could he despise those whom he lived by pleasing, and on whose approbation his esteem of himself was superstructed?'

Just as Swift's image of the weather-beaten, decaying house suggests Burke's habitual image of the state as a castle, fortress, or temple, so the following doggedly empirical figure from Johnson's *The False Alarm* (1770) likewise seems to point distinctly towards Burke: 'Governments formed by chance, and gradually improved by such expedients, as the successive discovery of their defects happened to suggest, are never to be tried by a regular theory. They are fabricks of dissimilar materials, raised by different architects, upon different plans. We must be content with them as they are; should we attempt to mend their disproportions, we might easily demolish, and difficultly rebuild them.' Implicit here is the historical coherence of past and present, the frailty of institutions, and the equation of alteration with destruction, all notions which will receive their full development through architectural figures in the hands of Burke.

'Fabrick' is one of Johnson's favourite architectural terms. His first definition of the word in the *Dictionary* is 'A building; an edifice'. Men's bodies are thus fortified buildings which, ironically, can be destroyed by their own commanders working either openly or covertly: 'some men ruin the fabrick of their bodies by incessant revels, and others by intemperate studies; some batter it by excess, and others sap it by inactivity' (*Rambler* 48). In a different time or place such an image as the following might suggest weaving or dry-goods, but to Johnson 'fabrick' is architectural: 'Johnson said always', according to Mrs. Thrale, ' "that the world was well-constructed, but that the particular people disgraced the elegance and beauty of the general fabric" ' (*JM*, i, 327). Many eighteenth-century architectural figures have been covered over and hidden from us by successive semantic changes. It would be easy to miss the figure here, for example, in Chapter VII of Gibbon's *Autobiography*: upon Lord North's defeat, says Gibbon, 'The old fabric was dissolved, and the posts of government were occupied by the victorious and veteran troops of opposition'. But when scrutinized, that sentence proves to operate by means of a very precise architectural as well as siege figure. In the same way the term 'basis' is much richer architecturally than we might suspect. The word has declined to a dead metaphor in our time, and, like much military imagery which has lost its vitality, it has been appropriated by the worlds of jargon and cliché. Ironically, one hears 'basis' most often today in the mouths of such arch-enemies of humanism as 'educators' and the less impressive practitioners of 'social science'. But when Johnson speaks in *Rambler* 21 of a student who wants to give the impression of building his happiness 'on a more firm basis' than the heroes of action, he is being very exact, as we can discover by turning to the *Dictionary*: 'BASIS. 1. The foundation of any thing, as of a column or a building.' Thus when, in writing William Strahan, he asserts the distance between will and performance, he constructs an exact architectural figure of a firm, permanent foundation: 'Event is uncertain and fallacious, but of good intention the merit stands upon a basis that can never be shaken' (*LSJ*, iii, 219).

Even Boswell picks up the habit of imaging human affairs in architectural terms. In 1770 he published in the *London Magazine* an observation on the architectural mechanism of acting which has strong dualistic autobiographical overtones: 'my notion is that [an actor] must have a kind of double feeling. He must assume in a strong degree the character which he represents, while he at the same time retains the consciousness of his own character. The feelings and passions of the character which he represents must take full possession as it were of the antechamber of his mind, while his own character remains in the innermost recess' (*BD*, 17).

It is clear that Boswell has been studying his Locke. And when he writes of his own inconsistencies, 'I am truly a composition of many opposite qualities' (*BSW*, 226), his image, if not overtly architectural, certainly suggests a world of building materials and a world in which construction by the accumulation of separable parts seems the most natural way of making something, whether buildings, men, or poems. On one rare occasion Boswell almost departs from the humanistic figurative tradition when he images 'life' in terms of vegetative growth, but even here we see the saving intervention of the human and the arranged. 'Life' is 'a lawn', but it is a lawn laid out and superintended by man: 'After every enjoyment comes weariness or disgust. We never have a large lawn of agreeable life. It is cut to pieces with sunk fences, ha-has, even where it is smoothest' (*BD*, 216).

To Reynolds both man and art are architecture. The young art student becomes a building when, in the *First Discourse,* Reynolds insists that the 'rules' of painting must be mastered by the novice, however he may learn to depart from them as he matures: 'But let us not destroy the scaffold, until we have raised the building.' The mind and imagination are really as little mysterious as a building, he implies in the *Seventh Discourse*: 'My notion of nature', he says, 'comprehends not only the forms which nature produces, but also the nature and internal fabrick and organization, as I may call it, of the human mind and imagination.' A building presupposes rooms, and rooms suggest furniture. Swift's poem 'The Furniture of a Woman's Mind' tells us that the 'objects' furnishing the room run from

A Set of Phrases learn't by Rote

to

the Trick
At proper Seasons to be sick.

But poor Goldsmith is in a worse state even than Swift's society lady: where her mind contains bad pieces and shabby bric-à-brac, his contains nothing at all: as Reynolds says, 'Goldsmith's mind was entirely unfurnished' (*P*, 55). The art of heroic painting is likewise a building. The *Fifteenth Discourse* asks the student to consider 'on what ground the fabrick of our Art is built', and in the *Seventh Discourse* 'the rules' of painting are imaged as a structure erected upon the absolutely trustworthy foundation of uniform human nature: 'What has pleased, and continues to please, is likely to please again: hence are derived the rules of art, and on this immoveable foundation they must ever stand.' To Reynolds, the building of 'ancient taste', resting on the foundation of actual human nature, is just such an edifice as Burke's commonwealth, which, like the actual Bastille, is liable to be stormed, fired, and wrecked by the insurgents of the 'modern'. The speaker in the *Ironical Discourse* exhorts his hearers to 'imitate the great Mirabeau. Set fire to all the pictures, prints, and drawings of Raphael and Michael Angelo. . . . Destroy every trace that remains of ancient taste. Let us pull the whole fabric down at once, root it up even to its foundation.' And corresponding to both 'ancient taste' and the traditional hierarchical commonwealth is Gibbon's 'Roman power'. As he says in Chapter II of the *Decline and Fall*, 'the firm edifice of Roman power was raised and preserved by the wisdom of ages'.

Thus through repeated invocations of the architectural image, the Augustan humanists construct an imaginative city of life, a reflection in terms of bricks and mortar, porches and rooms, columns and capitals, stresses and strains, of the actual world of man, an eminently public, communal, and social world. What the whole image-system seems to do is to direct the focus towards those human qualities which the humanists choose to isolate as important and distinctive human attributes. Just as the military image-system implies the conditions of internal dualism and the unremitting struggle between conscience and a fallen world, so the architectural image-system is a way of realizing the Lockean theory of knowledge and the role of forethought, arrangement, will, and order in the self-construction of the human imagination, as well as suggesting the static and orderly social and political relationships and modes of dependency which belong to urban life. The buildings that constitute the city of life are never 'created'. They are 'constructed', and the theory of construction, we find, also underlies the Augustan sense of art and literature, especially poetry.

If we could learn to pay less attention to what eighteenth-century writers say they are doing and more to what they actually do, I think we should find that instead of being devoted to the Horatian formula *ut pictura poesis*, as they sometimes say they are, they really are much more profoundly committed to the premise *ut architectura poesis*. Boswell records a beautiful little scene which pleasantly dramatizes the eighteenth-century sense of poetic architecture. We may observe in passing that one thing that makes this scene so charming is Goldsmith's judicious and self-confident imitation of Johnson, played for the delectation of the country-boy Boswell:

DODSLEY. 'I think [my anthology of poems] equal to those made by Dryden and Pope'. GOLDSMITH. 'To consider them, Sir, as villages, yours may be as good; but let us compare house with house, you can produce me no edifices equal to the *Ode on St. Cecilia's Day*, *Absalom and Achitophel*, or *The Rape of the Lock*'.　　　　　　(*LJ*, 105)

Poems are thus houses, accumulations of poems are villages, and large assemblages of great poems are cities: as Johnson proclaims in the *Life of Dryden*, 'What was said of Rome, adorned by Augustus, may be applied by an easy metaphor to English poetry embellished by Dryden. . . . He found it brick, and he left it marble.' Johnson's 'easy' does not mean 'facile': it means 'natural', or, as his eighth definition in the *Dictionary* has it, 'Not constrained'. As a house is constructed according to plan by the accumulation and interrelationship of pre-existent, solid, objective materials, so is a poem; and similarly, as a house will not fall or change its nature radically as a result of alterations, neither will a poem necessarily suffer from carefully contrived revisions. The concept of unpremeditated art has as little place in poems as in architecture: collapse will be the most likely eventuality. When one engages to undertake a job of construction, there is no substitute for engineering. At their worst, the 'building materials' of poems in the orthodox tradition may be clichés and *gradus* epithets. But at their best, the materials will be the traditional but eminently lively metaphors 'to which every bosom returns an echo'.

The architectural analogue for suggesting the nature of a poem goes back at least as far as Quintilian. It is revived in Renaissance humanist criticism and transmitted to the eighteenth century without interruption. Ben Jonson on the fable (or plot) of epic is typical. In his *Timber*—the title itself is an architectural metaphor—he invokes the image of an architectural site to illustrate the 'bounds' of an epic plot:

if a man would build a house, he would first appoint a place to build it in, which he would define within certaine bounds: So in the Constitution of a *Poeme*, the Action is aim'd at by the *Poet*, which answers Place in a building; and that Action hath his largenesse, compasse, and proportion. But, as a Court of Kings Palace requires other dimensions than a private house: So the *Epick* askes a magnitude, from other Poems. . . . So . . . wee conclude the fable, to be the *imitation* of one perfect, and intire Action; as one perfect, and intire place is requir'd to a building.

Dryden picks up the architectural image and turns it in an economic direction to explain why his *Fables* is a larger work than he once thought it would be: ' 'Tis with a Poet, as with a man who designs to build, and is very exact, as he supposes, in casting up the cost beforehand; but, generally speaking, he is mistaken in his account, and reckons short of the expence he first intended. He alters his mind as the work proceeds, and will have this or that convenience more, of which he had not thought when he began. So has it happened to me; I have built a house, where I intended but a lodge . . .'. And in the eighteenth century the practice of speaking of works of literature in architectural terms is widespread and not by itself, of course, an index of the humanist critical tradition. Addison reflects the general practice when, in *Spectator* 267, he says, commenting on *Paradise Lost*: 'In poetry, as in architecture, not only the whole, but the principal members, and every part of them, should be great'. The structural assumptions which underlie Addison's image are very close, it would appear, to those which operate when John Gay, in his whimsical 'On a Miscellany of Poems', likens poems to dishes prepared by chefs: the accumulation, combination, and arrangement of pre-existent inert materials constitute the work of the poet. Gay's sense of poems as dishes fit to eat is retained by Leigh Hunt, who, in his tongue-in-cheek tribute to John Pomfret called *The Choice*, conceives of Pomfret as small poetic pastry-cook, and implies thereby that the labours of poet, cook, and architect are essentially allied. Commenting on Pomfret's construction of poetry out of negligible, minor materials, and imaging him by the way as a sort of unpretentious architect, Hunt writes:

> There's a skill
> In pies, in raising crusts as well as galleries.
>
> (5–6)

Where Swift's bee brings home materials for manufacturing honey and wax, the humanist poet ranges as widely and skilfully 'invents' materials to be combined into a useful and pleasing structure. In the hands of William Shenstone the architectural figure becomes so precise and technical as to turn almost fussy. In the essay 'On Writing and Books' he observes that 'Long sentences in a short composition are like large rooms in a little house'; and his theory of the poetic caesura assumes that a poem is 'put together' like the bricks of a wall: in his essay 'Books, &c.', he writes: 'There is a sort of masonry in poetry, wherein the pause represents the joints of building:

which ought in every line and course to have their disposition varied.' This kind of poetic masonry seems precisely what Keats is objecting to in *Sleep and Poetry*, where he specifically accuses the eighteenth-century poets of architectural methods of construction:

> But ye were dead
> To things ye knew not of,—were closely wed
> To musty laws lined out with wretched rule
> And compass vile: so that ye taught a school
> Of dolts to smooth, inlay, and clip, and fit,
> Till, like the certain wands of Jacob's wit,
> Their verses tallied.
>
> (193–9)

But in the eighteenth century prose as well as poetry is architecture. In the Preface to her *Anecdotes of the Late Samuel Johnson, LL.D.* Mrs. Thrale advances the following theory of the Preface as a literary kind: 'the Preface before a book, like the portico before a house, should be contrived, so as to catch, but not detain the attention of those who desire admission. . . '. It is as if she were imitating Swift, whose speaker tells us at the end of the 'Preface' to *A Tale of a Tub*: 'I shall now dismiss our impatient Reader from any farther Attendance at the *Porch*; and having duly prepared his Mind by a preliminary Discourse, shall gladly introduce him to the sublime Mysteries that ensue.' Exhorting Boswell to contract the introductory, historical part of his forthcoming *Account of Corsica*, his friend Lord Hailes counsels him: 'Do not make your vestibule too large for your house . . .' (*BSW*, 13). And Boswell quotes the actor and playwright James Love as saying of the excessive analytical zeal of Lord Kames in his *Elements of Criticism*: 'My Lord Kames is not content if you show him a fine room, perfectly elegant; he wants always to scratch behind the panelling and analyse the plaster of the walls' (*H*, 87).

Some of the significance of this conscious and unconscious architectural imagery becomes very clear if, by way of contrast, we glance at a common literary analogue in romantic criticism. Coleridge seems typical, and what we find in his criticism is not vestibules, porches, and rooms but a crawling tangle of vegetation. As Meyer H. Abrams puts it in *The Mirror and the Lamp: Romantic Theory and the Critical Tradition*:

it is astonishing how much of Coleridge's critical writing is couched in terms that are metaphorical for art and literal for a plant; if Plato's dialectic is a wilderness of mirrors, Coleridge's is a very jungle of vegetation. Only let the vehicles of his metaphors come alive, and you see all the objects of criticism writhe surrealistically into plants or parts of plants, growing in tropical profusion. Authors, characters, poetic genres, poetic passages, words, meter, logic become seeds, trees, flowers, blossoms, fruit, bark, and sap.[6]

Keats operates the same way when he exclaims, in a letter to John Taylor (27 February 1818), 'if Poetry comes not as naturally as the Leaves to a tree, it had better not come at all'. And Wordsworth's sonnet '*A POET!*—He hath put his heart to school' also exemplifies the monistic and Romantic habit of expressing 'organic' artistic imperatives in botanical terms. Addressing a listener who is apparently a young poet-critic, the speaker in Wordsworth's poem enjoins him to write his poems not 'by rule' but instead according to the vegetative analogy:

> How does the Meadow-flower its bloom unfold?
> Because the lovely little flower is free
> Down to its root, and, in that freedom, bold;
> And so the grandeur of the Forest-tree
> Comes not by casting in a formal mould,
> But from its *own* divine vitality.
>
> (9–14)

Both the 'Meadow-flower' and the 'Forest-tree' here are implicitly opposed to the pampered hot-house flower and the artificially shaped tree of the formal garden. Like the charm of the natural flower in the untrimmed meadow—very different from Boswell's 'lawn of life'—the grandeur of the natural tree results not from its being subjected to a preconceived genre-plan or 'formal mould', applied extrinsically by some 'meddling intellect'. Instead the grandeur is generated from the tree's fulfilling its own organic potential. To Wordsworth this 'vitality' is 'divine' because it 'corresponds' to the functioning of the creative, organic human imagination. These botanical images suggest the kind of living shape which Wordsworth expects a poem to assume if it is to be 'vital'. We may pause to observe that the word 'vital', like 'creative' one of the clichés of roman-

[6] (New York, 1953), p. 169.

tic criticism, has gone on to infect the whole modern metaphoric way of regarding the relation of parts to wholes. Here is Woodrow Wilson speaking in defence of the League of Nations Covenant embodied in the Treaty of Versailles; he says in 1919 in New York: 'When that treaty comes back, gentlemen on this side will find the covenant not only in it, but so many threads of the treaty tied to the covenant, that you cannot dissect the covenant from the treaty without destroying the whole vital structure.'[7] It is very probable that, had Wilson spoken in the eighteenth century, his curious image of a sort of living web would have been presented instead as an architectural figure. To Wordsworth, then, with his devotion to the figure of botanical 'vitality', Augustan accumulative or aggregative methods of organization, not to mention the traditionalism of fixed genres and the conventions of received metaphor, are unthinkable. On the other hand, the Augustans, despite frequent lip-service to vaguely Aristotelian ideals of organic unity, reveal by their architectural metaphors as well as by their structural practice a commitment to a wholly different theory of aesthetic structure. Abrams calls it accurately 'the rhetorical and Horatian concept of art' and says that it assumes 'a purposeful procedure, in which the end is foreseen from the beginning, part is fitted to part, and the whole is adapted to the anticipated effect upon the reader'.[8] The ease with which Popian couplets can be detached from context or transposed within it is like the ease with which accumulated bricks and boards may be positioned finally either here or there in architectural construction. General Augustan theory holds, as Abrams says, 'that the inventive process, in its boldest flights, consists in the severance of sensible wholes into parts and the aggregation of parts into new wholes'.[9] It would be hard to find a more accurate description of what is conveyed critically by the architectural image than 'the aggregation of parts into new wholes'. Man is a builder, for he is too limited to be a creator.

Turning now to the Augustan humanist use of the architectural analogue in criticism, we shall sense the way the humanists tend to associate the architectural image with the appropriate

[7] See John Dos Passos, *Mr. Wilson's War* (New York, 1962), p. 470.

[8] *The Mirror and the Lamp*, p. 164.

[9] *ibid.*, p. 161.

moral ideas. A lightweight like Shenstone is skilled in the application of architectural notions to mere technical literary situations: it takes a Swift or a Johnson to perceive the coalescence of literary, architectural, and moral ideas. It is significant that in one of Swift's most humanistic remarks, his famous explanation of what he is trying to do in *Gulliver's Travels*, an assertion of the limitations of man should be associated so intimately with a critical figure from architecture. Swift writes Pope on 29 September 1725: 'I have ever hated all Nations professions and Communityes and all my love is towards individualls. . . . I have got Materials Towards a Treatis proving the falsity of that Definition *animal rationale*; and to show it should be only *rationis capax*. Upon this great foundation of Misanthropy (though not in Timons manner) The whole building of my Travells is erected . . .' (*CAP*, ii, 325). If we attend to the psychological dynamics of this observation, we see that it proceeds from an idea of accumulation ('all Nations', &c.) to a focus on parts ('individualls'). Still focusing on parts ('Materials') it returns to the idea of a whole ('Treatis') as a preparation for arguing that man himself is not complete (*'animal rationale'*) but only partially so (*'rationis capax'*). Just as, to Reynolds, permanent, revealed human nature is the 'foundation' on which the principles of painting are erected, so here, in Swift's transition to his architectural figure, the limitations of universal man provide the 'basis' for the edifice of Swift's realization of human character.

Gulliver's Travels is one of the conspicuous public buildings of the city of literature. So, to Pope, is the work of Shakespeare, although he has chosen to build in the Gothic rather than in the Palladian mode. Pope ends his *Preface to Shakespeare* this way:

I will conclude by saying of Shakespeare, that with all his faults, and with all the irregularity of his drama, one may look upon his works, in comparison to those that are more finished and regular, as upon an ancient majestic piece of Gothic architecture, compared with a neat modern building. The latter is more elegant and glaring [i.e. splendid], but the former is more strong and more solemn. It must be allowed that in one of these there are materials enough to make many of the other. It has much the greater variety, and much the nobler apartments; though we are often conducted to them by dark, odd, and uncouth passages.

o

Pope's terms 'majestic', 'solemn', and 'nobler', together with the ecclesiastical associations of Gothic, seem to provide his observations with an implicit if faint moral dimension. And to Pope even bad poets operate architecturally, just as Shakespeare has built his plays out of 'materials'; he implies as much in Chapter IV of *Peri Bathous*, where he writes gaily, 'We now come to prove, that there is an Art of Sinking in Poetry. Is there not an Architecture of Vaults and Cellars, as well as of lofty Domes and Pyramids? Is there not as much skill and labour in making Dikes, as in raising Mounts?' Pope's 'Domes' as an emblem of great works of literature suggests, when we recall the dome in *Essay on Criticism*, the intersection of Pope's ethical and literary psychologies: great works are made the way coherent people are made, through a tension of opposing forces.

Shakespeare is a building to Johnson as well as to Pope. In his own *Preface to Shakespeare*, Johnson asserts that so vast is Shakespeare's accomplishment that 'he that tries to recommend him by select quotations, will succeed like the pedant in Hierocles, who, when he offered his house to sale, carried a brick in his pocket as a specimen'. Even Shakespeare's crudities can be explained and almost justified by recourse to architectural figure. Defending Shakespeare by placing him in the context of his presumably less-polished age, Johnson says: 'The palaces of Peru or Mexico were certainly mean and incommodious habitations, if compared to the houses of European monarchs; yet who could forbear to view them with astonishment, who remembered that they were built without the use of iron?' And Pope's image of literary transitions as architectural 'passages' Johnson exploits in the *Life of Milton* to justify the weaker parts of *Paradise Lost*: 'In every work, one part must be for the sake of others; a palace must have passages; a poem must have transitions.'

To Johnson poems, like buildings, consist of three essential parts: foundation, 'fabrick', and ornamentation. The foundation must stand immovably upon 'general nature'. *Idler* 59 tells us that *Hudibras* is now so little read because it was based upon temporary materials: 'So vainly is wit lavished upon fugitive topicks, so little can architecture secure duration when the ground is false.' Since the nature of readers is uniform in the future as in the past, writers inattentive to their 'foundations' court oblivion. Every writer, says Johnson in *Rambler* 106, hopes to erect a lasting monument to himself, 'but, among the innumerable architects that erect columns to themselves, far the greater part, either for want of durable materials, or of art to dispose them, see their edifices perish as they are towering to completion, and those few that for a while attract the eye of mankind, are generally weak in the foundation, and soon sink by the saps of time.' Once the foundation has been immovably secured, the writer's task is to make sure that his superstructure is fabricated of materials as durable. Coherence between foundation and fabric is the secret. And in the erection of the fabric (walls, floors, roof) it is important that it be consistently and self-consciously put together. One of the faults of Savage's *The Wanderer* is 'that the whole performance is not so much a regular fabrick, as a heap of shining materials thrown together by accident, which strikes rather with the solemn magnificence of a stupendous ruin, than the elegant grandeur of a finished pile' (*Life of Savage*). Cowley is at fault in his Pindarics because his level of diction is not consistent with his chosen genre: here 'total negligence of language gives the noblest conceptions the appearance of a fabrick august in the plan, but mean in the materials' (*Life of Cowley*). The heroic couplet is the 'fabric' of Pope's poems, as we learn in the *Life of Pope*; and when Johnson speaks of Mark Akenside's versification he likewise employs the architectural image of the 'fabric': 'In the general fabrication of his lines [Akenside] is perhaps superior to any other writer of blank verse' (*Life of Akenside*). With the foundation established firmly on the right kind of ground and the fabric erected upon it, the writer's final task is the selection and disposition of his embellishments, corresponding to architectural details like triglyphs and metopes. These may be altered or renewed from time to time without any organic disturbance of the fabric, as perhaps we may deduce from one of Johnson's comments to Boswell about revising the *Dictionary*: 'Some superfluities I have expunged, and some faults I have corrected, and here and there have scattered a remark; but the main fabrick of the work remains as it was' (*LSJ*, i, 303). And the larger the literary work the less perfect will the details probably be: as Johnson says in the Preface to the *Dictionary*, 'nor can it be expected, that the stones which form the dome of a temple, should be squared and polished like the diamond of a ring'. It is Thomas Gray's misfortune that his ornaments are too often inconsistent with his fabric. Johnson says in the *Life of Gray*: 'These odes are marked by glittering accumulations of ungraceful ornaments.' And it is the nature of the more trivial literary kinds, whether in poetry or prose, that they must appeal through ornament because, like cottages, their fabric is naturally so 'mean': speaking in *Rambler* 152 of trivial personal letters, Johnson points out that 'Trifles always require exuberance of ornament; the building which has no strength can be valued only for the grace of its decorations.' Foundation, fabric, and ornamentation must thus cohere, but they cohere not through any monistic mystery of interpenetration but rather through the objective principle of consistency. The trick is to 'find' the right materials, either by locating them in natural quarries or, like the natives of Renaissance Rome who borrowed their building materials ready-cut from the Forum, by cannibalizing other buildings. The whole process of poetic construction from foundation to ornamentation is brilliantly imaged by Johnson in his Preface to William Lauder's unfortunate *Essay on Milton's Use and Imitation of the Moderns*. Nothing is more worthy of literary study, says Johnson, than 'a retrospection of the progress of this mighty genius [Milton], in the construction of his work; a view of the fabrick gradually rising, perhaps from small beginnings, till its foundation rests in the centre, and its turrets sparkle in the skies; ... to find ... from what stores the materials were collected, whether its founder dug them from the quarries of nature, or demolished other buildings to embellish his own.' Since building materials are always the same stones, bricks, wood, and iron, they can just as well be taken from existing masterpieces as directly from the quarry. There is as little cause for imputations of 'plagiarism' in literature as in architecture, as Johnson explains in *Rambler* 143: 'the author who imitates his predecessors only by furnishing himself with thoughts and elegancies out of the same general magazine of literature, can with little more propriety be reproached as a plagiary, than the architect can be censured as a mean copier of Angelo or Wren, because he digs his marble from the same quarry, squares his stones by the same art, and unites them in the columns of the same orders.'

The whole theory of genre, in literature as in architecture, will guarantee that most poems, like most public buildings, will look somewhat alike: and why should they not, since their function is to please and harmonize men, and since men are always the same? The important thing is less that the materials be 'original' than that they be durable, regardless of their source. The poet's knowledge of his subject is one surety that his materials will persist. In the *Life of Dryden* Johnson observes that Dryden's *Eleonora* is a vague, unsatisfactory poem: 'Dryden confesses that he did not know the lady whom he celebrates. . . . Knowledge of the subject is to the poet what durable materials are to the architect.' And it goes without saying that without 'materials' one can do no building at all. At the age of twenty-two Johnson writes his friend Gregory Hickman to explain why he has not sent a poem which he has apparently promised to write: 'ones own disappointment is no inviting Subject, and . . . though the desire of gratifying You might have prevaild over my dislike of it, yet it proves upon reflection so barren that to attempt to write upon it, is to undertake to build without materials' (*LSJ*, i, 1–2).

Eighteenth-century architectural theory recognized five 'orders' or permanent styles, and this recognition assumes that each order of architecture, like each of the literary genres, is appropriate to one permanent element in human nature. The orders are the Doric, the Ionic, the Corinthian, the Tuscan, and the Composite, and they have a way of corresponding not only to inherited literary genres, styles, or modes, but to the general idiom of the several languages as well. In the Preface to the *Dictionary* Johnson reprobates the stylish contemporary importation of French idiom in these terms: 'No book was ever turned from one language into another, without imparting something of its native idiom; this is the most mischievous and comprehensive innovation; single words may enter by thousands, and the fabrick of the tongue continue the same; but new phraseology changes much at once; it alters not the single stones of the building, but the order of the columns.'

If the natural English 'order' is, say, Ionic, a catastrophe of incoherence will be the result of any attempt to turn it towards, say, Corinthian. And in the *Preface to Shakespeare*, where he is arguing that the 'dramatic unities' are really without any necessary basis in uniform human nature, he imagines a wastefully exhibitionistic architect who becomes the corollary of the playwright concerned with 'the unities': 'He that, without diminution of any other excellence, shall preserve all the unities unbroken, deserves the like applause with the architect, who shall display all the [five] orders of architecture in a citadel, without any deduction from its strength: but the principal beauty of a citadel is to exclude the enemy; and the greatest graces of a play are to copy nature, and instruct life.' Johnson's choice of a 'citadel' here as a vehicle for 'play' seems meaningful: just as the citadel, if properly constructed, will exclude its enemies, so will the play, and the enemies of the play are those of humanism itself—mechanism, brutality, and 'the timely'.

Such is the distance between a man's dualistic halves, his public and his private selves, that those—like Boswell—who burn to collect authors are in for a surprise. In a happy figure in *Rambler* 14, Johnson manages to focus almost simultaneously on the city of literature and the city of life, and his implications prove, characteristically, to be both gay and sombre at once: 'A transition from an author's book to his conversation, is too often like an entrance into a large city, after a distant prospect. Remotely, we see nothing but spires of temples and turrets of palaces, and imagine it the residence of splendour, grandeur, and magnificence; but, when we have passed the gates, we find it perplexed with narrow passages, disgraced with despicable cottages, embarrased with obstructions, and clouded with smoke.' Behind Johnson's image lurks the assumption that only a dualistic view of man will do justice to his complexities: on the one hand, it is sad that his state is such that he appears at his finest only in his literature, but on the other hand it is fortunate that he has invented literature 'to copy nature, and instruct life'.

Reynolds's sense of the architecture of art involves Johnsonian ideas both of 'splendour, grandeur, and magnificence' and of Shakespearian variety. The speaker in the *Ironical Discourse* thus rabble-rouses his hearers: he has been praising the moderns for the innovation of painting statues to 'complete the deception', and he goes on to say, 'This improvement is reserved for this enlightened age, when knowledge is so generally diffused—i.e., when we think for ourselves and dare to reason without prejudices for the opinions of others. We shall soon not leave one stone upon another in the fabric of art. We then rear an edifice not founded on imagination, castles in the air, but on common sense adapted to the meanest capacity' (*P*, 162). From the contemptuously ironical use of 'enlightened' here what could be clearer than that Reynolds—together with the whole tradition for which he is serving as spokesman—has no place in the 'Enlightenment', whatever that is? The assumption of this passage is that it is the work of the imagination that makes man what he is at his best, and that pieces of art which perform the imagination's work for it can have no humanizing function. And it is aesthetic variety which urges the imagination into operation, in literature as in architecture. This is why in literature 'A regular system is not so pleasant as a desultory observation, a regular built city or house as a chance city or improved house. [Addison's] *Cato* is cold; Shakespeare the contrary' (*P*, 123).

With his fellow club-members discoursing all the time in architectural images, it is to be expected that Edward Gibbon will become expert at the habit, the more so because of his profound technical knowledge of the ruins of Rome and his equally profound scepticism about the worth of those materials which people find not among the quarries of nature and history but in their own unassisted wits. It is delightful that Gibbon chooses to present in his *Autobiography* two dramatic vignettes depicting the beginning and the end of his labours on the *Decline and Fall*. And it is not only delightful but significant that the two 'scenes', each of them technically worthy of Boswell himself and each of them suggestive of the great humanistic theme of permanence and dissolution, take place in richly expressive architectural settings. The idea of writing his history came to him, he says, on 15 October 1764: 'It was at Rome, . . . as I sat musing amid the ruins of the Capitol, while the barefooted friars were singing vespers in the temple of Jupiter, that the idea of writing the decline and fall of the city first started to my mind' (Chapter VI). The detail of the friars is a master touch, suggesting as it does Gibbon's whole theme, 'the triumph of barbarism and Christianity'. The end finds him at Lausanne, happy in an unpretentious republic after his years of imaginary residence under despotism, sitting in a garden summerhouse far in both space and time from the ruined splendours of the Forum: 'It was on the day, or rather, night, of the 27th of June 1787,

between the hours of eleven and twelve, that I wrote the last
lines of the last page in a summerhouse in my garden.' He then
takes a short walk which, he asks us to believe, eventuated in
moral reflections. What began amidst the Roman ruins and
came full circle in a Lausanne summerhouse ends in a dualistic
rumination about human frailty: 'I will not dissemble the first
emotions of joy on recovery of my freedom, and perhaps the
establishment of my fame. But my pride was soon humbled, and
a sober melancholy was spread over my mind, by the idea that
I had taken an everlasting leave of an old and agreeable com-
panion, and that whatsoever might be the future date of my
History, the life of the historian must be short and precarious'
(Chapter VIII). *Ars longa, vita brevis.* Routine, perhaps, but
immensely well imagined and superbly re-enacted.

It is Gibbon's deep sense of the social and his instinct for the
magnanimous that impels much of his enthusiasm for Rome as
well as much of his interest in Roman architecture. One of the
things that excites him, when, in Chapter II of the *Decline and
Fall*, he contemplates 'the innumerable monuments of architecture constructed by the Romans' is that 'Many of these works
were erected at private expense, and almost all were intended for
public benefit', like, we may add, eighteenth-century poems
with their public, impersonal themes and their accessible
imagery. To Gibbon, Fielding has succeeded so well in *Tom
Jones* that his public building, as Gibbon asserts in Chapter II
of the *Autobiography*, 'will outlast the palace of the Escorial . . .'.

When we arrive finally at Edmund Burke we can appreciate
the way a very great literary imagination subsumed into his
work a whole century's familiarity with the moral implications
of the architectural image. It is remarkable how deeply Burke's
writings depend upon the architectural figure, much the way
that Johnson's depend upon the military figure. It is safe to say
that if we were to alter the architectural imagery in Burke we
would remove a very large part of the literature: politics in
plenty would remain, but we would be subtracting vastly from
the moral dimension. There is one passage in the *Reflections* that
suggests how much Burke owes to his humanist predecessors in
architectural imagery. Here he embarks on a figure of a
mechanical French formal garden and arrives at the traditional
image of the shabby state tottering on a weak foundation:

The French builders [of the new state], clearing away as mere rubbish whatever they found, and, like their ornamental gardeners, forming every thing into an exact level, propose to rest the whole local and general legislature on three bases of three different kinds . . . they divide the area of their country into eighty-three pieces, regularly square, of eighteen leagues by eighteen. . . . When these state surveyors came to take a view of their work of measurement, they soon found, that in politics, the most fallacious of all things was geometrical demonstration. They had then recourse to another basis (or rather buttress) to support the building which tottered on that false foundation.

This mechanical, geometrical, and therefore inhuman commonwealth is like the Frenchified ornamental garden installed at his pompous villa by Timon in Pope's *Moral Essay* IV (*Epistle to Burlington*), and we may suspect that Burke has actually been remembering Timon's farcical garden when we find him, in the very next paragraph, slightly misquoting Pope's line

But soft—by regular degrees [approach], not yet

(129)

from the *Epistle to Burlington*. Pope's poem is very likely what provides Burke with the lively image he requires of simpleminded mechanism. Timon's house and gardens are alike outsized,

. . . a labour'd Quarry above Ground.

(110)

And the whole is, in Burke's terms, formed into 'an exact level', 'regularly square' according to 'geometrical demonstration' just like the nightmare commonwealth devised by the Jacobins:

No pleasing Intricacies intervene,
No artful wildness to perplex the scene;
Grove nods at grove, each Alley has a brother,
And half the platform just reflects the other.

(115–18)

To see Pope's vulgarly rich Timon and his stupid taste reflected exactly sixty years later in Burke's depiction of the deadly 'ornamental garden' laid out by revolution is to appreciate not merely the technical unity of the Augustan humanist tradition but the similarity of the ethical questions which excite both writers. Pope seems to doubt that a society which generates Timons and urges them to the 'top' can long survive its perverse

values, while Burke, more certain after sixty years, has no
doubts whatever that a society founded on rational, geometrical
principles will end by twisting human nature into monstrosity
and by producing a landscape of uniform hideousness.

Violent reforms, to Burke, are like violent attempts at architectural renovation. Great care must be taken in repealing an
old law, he points out in his *Tract on the Popery Laws*, 'because
laws, like houses, lean on one another . . .'. And to his 'like
houses' many a humanist, as we have seen, would add 'like
people, and like poems'. Those who tear down dilapidated
governments resemble Swift's Puritans in the violence of their
self-righteousness. They are like a London mob demolishing a
bawdy-house. Faced with a faulty government, says Burke in the
Speech on the Plan for Economical Reform, hot-headed reformers
'fall into the temper of a furious populace provoked at the
disorder of a house of ill-fame; they never attempt to correct or
regulate; they go to work by the shortest way: they abate the
nuisance, they pull down the house'. Their innocence about
human nature is just such as that exhibited by Swift's Jack in
A Tale of a Tub, engaged in ripping his coat to shreds rather
than reforming its corruptions gradually. What Burke and Swift
suggest is that any coat, any house, any religion, and any
government, given the deplorable state of man and the world, is
better than none.

Burke's encounter with American affairs prompted early in
his career an obsession with the image of architectural 'cement',
symbolic of the easy cohesion which, given mutual tolerance for
the natural frailties of anything made by human beings, will
hold together political units of such divergent characteristics as
Americans and Britons. Lord Chatham, we learn in the *Speech
on American Taxation*, put together an incoherent ministry:
incoherence of policy was a predictable result. He 'made an
administration so checkered and speckled, he put together a
piece of joinery so crossly indented and whimsically dovetailed,
a cabinet so variously inlaid, such a piece of diversified mosaic,
such a tesselated pavement without cement,—here a bit of
black stone and there a bit of white, patriots and courtiers,
king's friends and republicans, Whigs and Tories, treacherous
friends and open enemies,—that it was, indeed, a very curious
show, but utterly unsafe to touch and unsure to stand on.' The

fantastic energy, the puns ('cabinet', 'a bit of black stone'), and the technique of the apparently endless list suggest that this rhetoric constitutes a revival of Swift's: we will have to return to *A Tale of a Tub* to match it in technique as well as in sheer energetic passion. Just as Lord Chatham's pavement is ruined for lack of cement, so the whole relation between Britain and the Colonies, as Burke informs his countrymen in the speech on *Conciliation*, can be sustained only by the cement of mutual identification and self-interest: 'let it be once understood that your government may be one thing and [the Americans' privileges] another, that these two things may exist without any mutual relation,—the cement is gone, the cohesion is loosened, and everything hastens to decay and dissolution'. Indeed, the gradual dissolution of the parts of the Empire resembles the French revolutionists' later 'dissolving' of the 'fabric' of their commonwealth. The colonial quarrel is like that between Jacobin and Bourbon, bespeaking a decay of the awareness of mutual social dependency. In his *Letter to the Sheriffs of Bristol*, warning against loose, inflammatory anti-American talk, Burke writes: 'Those who do not wish for such a separation [of the Colonies from Britain] would not dissolve that cement of reciprocal esteem and regard which can alone bind together the parts of this great fabric.' Here the 'fabric' is the Empire, but the implication of the image recalls Pope on the architecture of personal coherence, or Johnson on the architecture of poetic.

By 1791, after the Bastille has been reduced and 'dissolved', Burke's imagination, operating now at white heat in the *Reflections* and in *A Letter to a Noble Lord*, seems to turn, if possible, even more architectural. Viewed in the context of the recent siege of the Bastille, the appropriateness and richness of his architectural imagery are now more astonishing than ever. The 'constitution' of the French government is at once a palace and a fortress, he tells the French in the *Reflections*: 'Your constitution, it is true, whilst you were out of possession, suffered waste and dilapidation; but you possessed in some parts the walls, and, in all, the foundations, of a noble and venerable castle. You might have repaired those walls; you might have built on those old foundations.' The Revolutionists share the fault of Swift's spider, Pope's Timon, Dr. Richard Price, Reynolds's Ironical Discourser, and Gibbon's mad Christians: they lack a sense of history, they have no instinct for duration. 'With innovators', says Burke in the *Reflections*, 'it is a sufficient motive to destroy an old scheme of things, because it is an old one. As to the new, they are in no sort of fear with regard to the duration of a building run up in haste; because duration is no object to those who think little or nothing has been done before their time. . . .' Johnson's disquiet over the impact of French idiom on English is mirrored in Burke's concern over the continuance of the architectural 'style' of governments. If he were reforming the British constitution, he tells the French, 'I should follow the example of our ancestors. I would make the reparation as nearly as possible in the style of the building.' And Johnson's attention to the purity and persistence of the five architectural orders resembles Burke's attention to the orders of society. 'Nobility', he says, 'is a graceful ornament to the civil order. It is the Corinthian capital of polished society.'

But the one climactic moment in the history of the humanist architectural imagination is Burke's solemn but ecstatic hymn to Windsor Castle in *A Letter to a Noble Lord*. This is surely one of the most compelling things in all of eighteenth-century literature, and a large part of its effectiveness results from its wise exploitation of a century of architectural figures, figures already fully associated with passionate polemics on behalf of personal, artistic, and social coherence—which is to say, virtue. It is appropriate that the end of Burke's career should bring the architectural figure to its climax, for the end of his career was also the climax of Augustan humanism, doomed to defeat from the start, but violently menaced now by all the new world of revolution, 'inspiration', industrialism, and 'progress'. Burke's appeal to the permanence of Windsor Castle, his desperate attempt to make his image so eloquent that it will melt the hearts even of Jacobins and the Duke of Bedford, has all the pathos and grandeur of any gallantly lost British cause, from Maldon to Arnhem. It is at once noble, pitiful, and entirely interesting.

Windsor Castle is a matchless physical and symbolic object to serve as the climactic focus of humanistic architectural imagery. First of all, it is immense. Its sheer size is what struck William Hogarth, who wrote in *The Analysis of Beauty*: 'Windsor castle is a noble instance of the effect of quantity. The hugeness of its few distinct parts strikes the eye with uncommon grandeur at a distance, as well as nigh. It is quantity, with simplicity, which makes it one of the finest objects in the kingdom, tho' void of any regular order of architecture.' Its immensity and simplicity also make it a perfect stimulus of that emotion called by Burke and others the Sublime, and sublimity is clearly the designed effect of Burke's use of it in his famous image. But it has more of use to the humanistic imagination than its physical appearance of hugeness and permanence. It is a consecrated spot and an object of pilgrimage, as Thomas Otway emphasized in 1685 when, in his lament for Charles II titled *Windsor Castle*, he referred to the castle on its hill as 'Britain's Olympus'. A part of the castle is St. George's Chapel, consecrated to the patriotic devotions of the knights of the Order of the Garter. The primary burial place of Britain's monarchs, it is, as Burke will call it, 'the British Sion'. It is perhaps as close as Britain can come to having a sacred place. It hovers just offstage in Pope's *Windsor Forest*, and that whole poem is dignified by its proximity. The castle was begun by William the Conqueror, and its very idea stimulates Pope to a flurry of loyal sentiments near the end of his poem, as he traces the history of British chivalry from Edward III to Queen Anne. It is on Windsor hill, with the castle looming just behind him, that the speaker positions him-self in Gray's *Ode on a Distant Prospect of Eton College*: both hill and castle became abundantly familiar to imagination and poetry. By Burke's time the castle was fully ripe with associa-tions of the virtuous, the old, the chivalrous, the devout, the powerful, and the splendid, and that is why he employs it as a contrast to Woburn Abbey, the seat of the luckless Francis Russell, fifth Duke of Bedford and Marquis of Tavistock, whose ancestors had received his estate from the inglorious ecclesias-tical rapine—so like that of the Jacobins—of Henry VIII. The Duke of Bedford—'an impetuous but aging youth', W. J. Bate pleasantly calls him[10]—was a parlour radical of Charles James Fox's party who had not merely expressed sympathy with the Jacobins but had attacked Burke's high pension which he had just received as recompense for his parliamentary services. Burke's argument in the *Letter*, which is addressed not as we might assume to the Duke of Bedford but to Burke's friend and

[10] *Edmund Burke: Selected Works* (New York, 1960), p. 36.

younger colleague Lord Fitzwilliam, is perhaps less satisfying than his technique. His point, roughly, is that the Duke of Bedford should stop sympathizing with the Jacobins because, if they were to come to power in England, they would despise him as an aristocrat and instantly destroy him. The *ad hominem* tendency of most of Burke's formal argument seems not quite worthy of him, but the imagery throughout is brilliant, and nowhere more so than in the Windsor Castle passage. Here it is:

> But as to *our* country and *our* race, as long as the well-compacted structure of our church and state, the sanctuary, the holy of holies of that ancient law, defended by reverence, defended by power, a fortress at once and a temple, shall stand inviolate on the brow of the British Sion—as long as the British monarchy, not more limited than fenced by the orders of the state, shall, like the proud Keep of Windsor, rising in the majesty of proportion, and girt with the double belt of its kindred and coeval towers, as long as this awful structure shall oversee and guard the subjected land—so long the mounds and dykes of the low, fat Bedford level will have nothing to fear from all the pickaxes of all the levellers of France.

As Burke himself would say: 'Well!' Translated into discursive prose, this vast sentence says simply that Bedford is safe as long as both Windsor and constitutional monarchy stand; but complete with all its imagery and associations, the sentence bodies forth a whole world of moral and constitutional arguments appropriately surrounded by a full emotional coloration. The very development of the image is a marvel of metamorphosis. We begin by a focus on the abstract principle of coherent compromise between church and state, which gradually turns into the actual Windsor Castle standing inviolate on Windsor hill; while we watch, the castle metamorphoses one more time, this time into constitutional monarchy itself, both limited and protected by the other two orders, lords and commons, just as the castle is both limited in extent and protected from assault by the double protection of its massive towers and walls. By the time we arrive at 'this awful structure', it has taken on the attributes of both the church-state compromise, the physical fortress of Windsor, and the principle of monarchy as one of the three benignly competing 'orders' in a constitutional state; and it is all three of these things that 'oversee and guard' the land below. Bedford is, in effect, being protected by the constitutional compromise of 1689, a compromise divinely consecrated.

One notable thing here is the way the central figure, Windsor Castle as constitutional monarchy, fuses the two traditional architectural images of power, the keep and the temple, suggestive respectively of the claims of the temporal and the eternal. This is a highly traditional way of imaging the dualistic power of the state. For example, we find these two images of fortress and temple engraved on opposite sides of the title-page of the first edition of Hobbes's *Leviathan*, where, as here, they are emblematic of the dualisms of war and peace, action and contemplation; or, to express the dualism in Pope's terms, wit and judgment, passion and reason—or in Johnson's, as we remember *The Vanity of Human Wishes*, military courage and oratory. What Burke's figure of Windsor Castle as *at once* fortress and temple does is to fuse these dualistic oppositions of 'reverence' and 'power' into a kind of coherence, suggestive of the sort of personal coherence exhibited by those who are not Dukes of Bedford but who instead understand and cherish the similar principle of the balance of political powers in the state. Burke's phrase 'a fortress at once and a temple' echoes Tacitus's description of the Temple of Jerusalem, and this echo helps enforce the idea of the sanctity and universality of Burke's point about the balance of power among the 'orders' of the state. The 'cement' image is here, too, in 'well-compacted structure of our church and state', suggesting just such a mutual support between the sacred and the secular as Burke calls for between home and colony in the *Letter to the Sheriffs of Bristol*. So what Burke's figure insists on is that the Duke of Bedford and everyone else is safe so long as the British system of balance and compromise between the three estates persists. So long as the 'awful structure' not of mere monarchy but of *constitutional* monarchy shall at once 'oversee and guard'—like Windsor Forest—the land below, so long peers and commons alike will be secure within the British constitutional system. The enemies of all British classes, high and low alike, are the single-minded demolition experts of France, who, with their vulgar pickaxes, aspire not merely to level Windsor Castle but to sap the whole system of limited monarchy. In jeopardy, therefore, is counterpoise and harmony, the harmony created by the benignly

antagonistic, the beneficently contending forces which constitute the state. According to Burke, the revolutionists because
they are anti-humanists execrate not monarchy or aristocracy
so much as the British constitution itself, conceived by Burke as
an expression of the hard-earned humanistic awareness of the
complexity of man's nature and institutions. One of Burke's
most brilliant achievements in his image is his use of the towers
and walls of Windsor as symbols of peers and commons, and
thus his subtle transformation of the castle from an image of
sheer monarchical power to an image of benign but no less
grand constitutional compromise. As Burke goes on to argue,
with a magnificent rhetorical flourish, as long as the balance of
powers endures,

so long the Duke of Bedford is safe: and we are all safe together—
the high from the blights of envy and the spoliations of rapacity; the
low from the iron hand of oppression and the insolent spurn of contempt. Amen! and so be it: and so it will be,

> Dum domus Æneæ Capitoli immobile saxum
> Accolet; imperiumque pater Romanus habebit.—

'As long as the race of Aeneas dwells on the permanent rock of
the Capitoline Hill, and the father of Rome maintains his
sovereignty.' This emotional recourse to Virgil does dare to
transform George III into Augustus himself, but what matter?
The fusion of Burke's and Virgil's rhythms is so splendid, the
passion so superbly directed and controlled, that logic and
criticism fall back in wonder. Burke's Windsor Castle image,
the chief public building of the Augustan city of life, proves to
be fabricated of the honoured materials found and shaped and
positioned by Burke's humanist predecessors. Burke's figure
apotheosizes Swift's image of the state which will be brought to
ruin like a house if vigilance is remitted as well as Pope's image
of the humane principle visible in the dome of St. Peter's. It
constitutes an architectural and moral climax in every way
consistent with the long, rich tradition of Augustan humanism,
and in every way worthy of it.

9

'THE WARDROBE OF
A MORAL IMAGINATION'

HARDLY any general proposition is more honoured both socially and philosophically in the eighteenth century than that clothes make the man. Compared with our own, it was an age which gave to dress just about all the symbolism it could bear. Although many a modern usage—the handkerchief in the breast-pocket, the buttons on the jacket cuff—survives from the eighteenth century, the equalization of classes and the mass-production of the universal 'suit' have all but deprived contemporary clothing of most of its symbolic value. It is easy to forget now that eighteenth-century costume is conceived with a powerful symbolic dimension. Until around 1780 a 'gentleman' was a man who wore an ornamental sword. A nobleman could be recognized instantly by the star on his breast, and William Shenstone lamented, in his essay 'On Religion': 'It is not now, "We have seen his star in the east," but "We have seen the star on his breast, and are come to worship him." ' General public mourning was common following deaths in the royal family, and everyone who cherished his reputation for affluence appeared in new clothes on the monarch's birthday. Indeed, one measure of the subsequent decay of the eighteenth-century sense of dress is Thoreau's saying, in *Walden*, 'Beware of all enterprises that require new clothes.' Full-dress was worn to some functions, half-dress to others, and at home or in the country one carefully accoutred oneself in un-dress. Clothing could be so emblematic of various specific trades and callings that one could assume a distinct role by appearing at a masquerade dressed as a Quaker, a quack-doctor, a ballad-singer, a clergyman, a tallow-chandler, a Blue-

P

coat boy, or a pimp. Even in folk-eschatology we find a reflection of this sort of symbolism. Peers were hanged with a silken rope, the lesser orders with hemp. When William Cowper essayed suicide, he chose to hang himself in his own garter.

Clothing thus spoke volumes socially, but philosophically it meant even more, for a general premise of the Augustan humanists is that it is clothes which make, not only 'the' man, but man as a distinct species. The Augustan humanists were much closer than we can ever be to King Lear's perceptions about naked, 'unaccommodated' man as bordering on the brute, or to Milton's sense of the immense difference between our first parents naked and clothed. The humanistic obsession with the uniqueness of man invites an imaginative confrontation with clothing and its symbolism. We have already seen Swift concerning himself with the fragility of Gulliver's clothing, and we have seen how much of symbolic moral use Swift derives from that concern. Human frailty is projected in Gulliver's very wearing of clothing in the context of Houyhnhnms and Yahoos in his fourth voyage, for of all living creatures man is the only one whose body is so ill adapted to physical nature that he must rely on the elaborate artifice of clothes just to endure. Gulliver's Houyhnhnm master is sorely perplexed by the fact of Gulliver's clothing. As Gulliver reports, 'He took up all my Cloaths in his Pastern, one Piece after another, and examined them diligently.' Afterwards 'He . . . gave me leave to put on my Cloaths again, for I was shuddering with Cold'. From this evidence the Houyhnhnm concludes—correctly—that there is indeed something gravely the matter with the species of which Gulliver is representative. The Houyhnhnm observes 'that my whole Body wanted a Fence against Heat and Cold, which I was forced to put on and off every day with Tediousness and Trouble'. But in addition to being the only creature whose body is so frail that it requires clothing, man labours under another burden: he is the only creature who requires clothing psychologically, less to satisfy his curious requirements of 'modesty' than to adorn himself and thus to signalize his uniqueness and his worth. His unique capacity for symbolizing and his urge to think well of himself oblige him to use clothing symbolically. Although he distinguishes himself from the brute by wearing symbolic clothing, a dangerous pitfall yawns: always in extremes, man is given to symbolizing either too little or too much. If he oversymbolizes, the clothing seems to become absolutely synonymous with its wearer; and if he undersymbolizes, he approaches the condition of the Houyhnhnm who conceives of man as entirely distinct from clothing and who fails to understand why he wears it. Here as in all else balance is everything.

The extreme of oversymbolizing Swift satirizes in a number of ways. The stylish society to which Peter, Martin, and Jack achieve entry by embellishing their coats equates dress with soul, and in Section II of *A Tale of a Tub* one articulate member of this society utters this mad syllogism: '*That Fellow . . . has no Soul; where is his Shoulder-knot?*' In Section IX the speaker who argues that in all things the outside is preferable to the inside calmly equates skin with clothing, and, in calling attention to both the frailty and the depravity of human nature, at the same time satirizes both his own 'logical' incapacity to distinguish the living from the dead and the urge to oversymbolize externals: 'Last week I saw a Woman *flay'd*, and you will hardly believe, how much it altered her Person for the worse. Yesterday I ordered the Carcass of a *Beau* to be stript in my Presence; when we were all amazed to find so many unsuspected Faults under one suit of Cloaths.' Swift's habitual satire of oversymbolizing—and imprecise analogizing—finds perhaps its most effective images in Section II of *A Tale of a Tub*, which aims at a multifold and complex body of satiric targets, including parochialism, mechanism, 'timeliness', and false analogizing. Taken by itself, Section II, which introduces us to the three brothers and their coats, constitutes an almost self-contained fable of the corruption of virtue by the 'world', here especially the world of externals, fashion, and dress. It is picaresque and novelistic at the same time that it is moral and symbolic. Swift is faced here with the narrative challenge of motivating the brothers' lust to alter their coats, and he rises to this challenge by recreating the Restoration world of foppery and display and by allowing the brothers to be fully seduced by its temptations. In the days when the three brothers came to town, we are told —with the ironic implication that affairs have now altered for the better—the tailor was worshipped as a Creator or 'a sort of Idol'; and indeed the tailor, mechanically parodying the organic act of Creation, 'did daily create Men, by a kind of Manufactory operation'. The worshippers of the tailor naturally adhered to an exclusivist habit of thought and ended by believing the 'Universe to be a large *Suit of Cloaths*'. Availing themselves of the kinds of figures beloved by 'Robert Boyle', they reasoned thus: 'Look on this Globe of Earth, you will find it to be a very compleat and fashionable *Dress*. What is that which some call *Land*, but a fine Coat faced with Green? or the Sea, but a Wastcoat of Watter-Tabby? Proceed to the particular Works of the Creation, you will find how curious *Journeyman* Nature hath been, to trim up the *vegetable* Beaux: Observe how sparkish a Perewig adorns the Head of a *Beech*, and what a fine Doublet of white Satin is worn by the *Birch* . . .'.

This almost unbearably perverse equation of the eternal with the stylish, the beautiful with the pretty, projects the kind of imaginative corruption inevitably wrought by modernism. The activity of mind enacted here is a form of anti-creation like that wrought at the end of *The Dunciad*. Swift's point is reasserted more soberly over seventy-five years later by Johnson in the *Life of Gray*. Criticizing the third stanza of *The Progress of Poesy*, Johnson finds that Gray's phrase 'Idalia's velvet-green' exhibits 'something of cant'. He goes on to generalize: 'An epithet or metaphor drawn from Nature ennobles Art; an epithet or metaphor drawn from Art degrades Nature.' The reason is a matter of elementary humanism: man's works are too frail, tiny, and laughable to be equated with eternal objects and processes. 'Pertness' will be the inevitable effect of such comparisons. And it is perverse miseducation that seduces the soul away from Nature and towards the fashionable. As Pope tells Spence: 'A tree is a nobler object than a prince in his coronation robes.—Education leads us from the admiration of beauty in natural objects, to the admiration of artificial (or customary) excellence.—I don't doubt but that a thorough-bred lady might admire the stars, *because* they twinkle like so many candles at a birth-night.' Swift's '*Journey-man* Nature', like the following century's 'Mother Nature', is worse than a merely vulgar usage: it is distinctly indecent—patronizing and inappropriately self-confident and cosy. The ways of physical nature are not the ways of man, and attempts to pretend that they are end in intellectual dislocation and moral suicide.

As the speaker in Section II proceeds with his clothes philosophy, betraying himself into madder and madder formulations, he stumbles into truth at one point when his cheerful and preposterous false analogies turn suddenly into sinister and accurate symbols:

what is Man himself but a *Micro-Coat*, or rather a compleat Suit of Cloaths with all its Trimmings? As to his Body, there can be dispute; but examine even the Acquirements of his Mind, you will find them all contribute in their Order, towards furnishing out an exact Dress: To instance no more; Is not Religion a *Cloak*, Honesty a *Pair of Shoes*, worn out in the Dirt, Self-Love a *Surtout*, Vanity a *Shirt*, and Conscience a *Pair of Breeches*, which, tho' a Cover for Lewdness as well as Nastiness, is easily slipt down for the Service of both.

But from this ironic apex of perception, which the speaker arrives at innocently, ignorant of the dualistic wisdom he has in his hands, he collapses again into a course of dogged mechanistic 'reasoning': 'These *Postulata* being admitted, it will follow in due Course of Reasoning, that those Beings which the World calls improperly *Suits of Cloaths*, are in Reality the most refined Species of Animals, or to proceed higher, that they are Rational Creatures, or Men.'

After attaining this plateau of error, the speaker goes on to deviate unconsciously again into both truth and wit as he illustrates. Some philosophers, he says,

held that Man was an Animal compounded of two *Dresses*, the *Natural* and the *Celestial Suit*, which were the Body and the Soul: that the Soul was the outward, and the Body the inward Cloathing. . . .

To this System of Religion were tagged several subaltern Doctrines, which were entertained with great Vogue: as particularly, the Faculties of the Mind were deduced by the Learned among them in this manner: *Embroidery*, was *Sheer Wit; Gold Fringe* was *agreeable Conversation, Gold Lace* was *Repartee*, a huge long *Periwig* was *Humour*, and a *Coat full of Powder* was very good *Raillery*.

This is Swift's way of enacting through images of upper-middle-class dress Pope's perception in the *Essay on Criticism*:

> What *woful stuff* this Madrigal wou'd be,
> In some starv'd Hackny Sonneteer, or me?
> But let a *Lord* once own the *happy Lines*,
> How the *Wit brightens*! How the *Style refines*!

(418–21)

Or Johnson's exhibition in *The Vanity of Human Wishes* of the contempt which awaits the portrait of the formerly 'great' man now disgraced:

> . . . now no more we trace in ev'ry line
> Heroic worth, benevolence divine:
> The form distorted justifies the fall,
> And detestation rids th'indignant wall.

(87–90)

There is a pleasant historical irony in Carlyle's furnishing his vitalistic Transcendentalism from the materials of Swift's far- cical, mock-logical universe of macro- and micro-coats. Per- forming in a style which seems to ape that of the Grub Street author of *A Tale of a Tub*, Carlyle inverts the implications of Swift's preposterous clothes philosophy, takes the analogies seriously, and contrives a kinetic scheme of heterodox optimism fraught with the progressivist tones which frequently accom- pany organic and vegetational imagery. As he assures us in Chapter V of *Sartor Resartus*, 'all that Mankind does or beholds, is in continual growth, regenesis and self-perfecting vitality'. Swift's meditations on clothing end in moral farce, but Car- lyle's end in the persuasion that 'Rightly viewed no meanest object is insignificant; all objects are as windows, through which the philosophic eye looks into Infinitude itself'. Too easy, Swift would comment.

Underlying Swift's ironic clothes philosophy is an inherited immemorial folk-contempt for tailors as pusillanimous, avari- cious, hypocritical, and time-serving. Pope deploys a similar traditional contempt for the sort of mock-creation presided over by tailors when, in the Preface to his edition of Shakespeare, he observes that 'Players are just such judges of what is *right*, as tailors are of what is graceful'. And Reynolds attaches himself to the tradition in the *Ironical Discourse*, where his speaker recommends that the statues being carved for St. Paul's exhibit all the particulars of contemporary dress: 'When it shall be determined by the committee that no monumental figure shall be suffered in St. Paul's but in the modern dress, it will be necessary to add to the committee a certain number of the most ingenious tailors, who shall have a voice in regard to fashion.' In the *Seventh Discourse* he exposes the naïve error which has tempted contemporary sculptors to depict their subjects in modern dress. It seems entirely plausible, says Reynolds, 'that a statue which is to carry down to posterity the resemblance of an individual, should be dressed in the fashion of the times, in the dress which he himself wore: this would certainly be true, if the dress were part of the man'. And it would be true too if the dress were expressive of the subject's will rather than representing an adventitious and external symbolism. Contemporary exponents of modern dress for statues are placed by Reynolds's humanistic argument in precisely the position of Swift's devotee of fashion who equates souls with shoulder-knots. The humanist vision, distinguishing always between what is essential to man and what extrinsic and temporary, conceives of sculpture as either nude or draped, and when draped, the drapery is not to look like some identifiable material, which would be to indulge in false wit and to depart from general nature. Drapery, as Reynolds insists, must look like 'drapery' and like nothing else. In painting, indeed, one can identify a style that falls short of the 'grand' by its finicky, merely representational concern with identifiable textures: in the *Fourth Discourse* Reynolds writes: 'It is the inferior stile that marks the variety of stuffs. With [the historical painter], the cloathing is neither woollen, nor linen, nor silk, sattin, or velvet: it is drapery; it is nothing more.' After all, man, not an 'effect', is the object of imitation in humanistic art. Men are made by God and formed by their own wills, not by tailors; works of art are to be achieved only by those whose concern is with man, not with materials, data, or fashions. Rejecting French criticisms of the apparent indecorum of some of Shakespeare's characters, Johnson says in the *Preface to Shakespeare*: 'These are the petty cavils of petty minds; a poet overlooks the casual distinction of country and condition, as a painter, satisfied with the figure, neglects the drapery.' To Johnson it is a defect in Pope's moral character that he succumbs too often to the seductions of the temporary, and, like Swift's three brothers, trims his coat to accord with prevailing fashion. As Johnson says in the *Life of Pope*, 'When Pope murmurs at the world, and when he professes contempt of fame, . . . he certainly does not express his habitual and settled sentiments, but either wilfully disguises his own character, or, what is more likely, invests himself with temporary qualities, and sallies out in the colours of the present moment.' As usual in humanistic responses, all this imagery of clothing seems to suggest a commitment to values of natural-ness and a suspicion of affectation, of 'theory', 'logic', and 'intellect'. Alfred North Whitehead seems to suggest what Swift, Reynolds, and Johnson imply about their contemporaries when he says, 'Intellect is to emotion as our clothes are to our bodies; we could not very well have civilized life without clothes, but we would be in a poor way if we had only clothes without bodies.'[1]

To the humanists, indeed, clothes are to the body as architec-tural details are to the 'fabrick'. Although neither is to be neglected, one is surely less consequential than the other, and confusion and disaster are likely to be the result if the one is mistaken for the other or if they are not coherently 'cemented'. And as clothes to body or embellishment to fabric, so in writing expression or style is conceived of as the 'dress' of thought, a presentable and appropriate costume superimposed by will from without rather than emerging instinctively and organically from within the 'body' of an idea. It is important to perceive the distinctly inorganic implications of the clothing image when applied to expression. Clothing differs from skin in being static, conventional, and alterable. Unlike actual coats, those given the three brothers by their omnipotent Father are magical in their longevity and their organic quality; they are the garments of folk-tale rather than real life. As the Father says in Section II of *A Tale of a Tub*, 'these Coats have two Virtues contained in them: One is, that with good wearing, they will last you fresh and sound as long as you live: The other is, that they will grow in the same proportion with your Bodies, lengthening and widening of themselves, so as to be always fit'. But when we leave the regions of fancy for those of actuality, we return to a world in which clothing, unlike skin, is static and inorganic, and it is this quality of it that is important in the humanistic conception of 'style as the dress of thought'. Like clothing, style is largely a matter of convention: what one wants to do with it is less important than what others are going to think about it. Furthermore, if style is the dress of thought, then a thought can

[1] *Dialogues of Alfred North Whitehead, as Recorded by Lucien Price* (Boston, 1954), p. 232.

appear in any number of dresses, some of which will be more appropriate than others but all of which will at least save it from a naked indecency. Styles, like clothes, can be changed, altered, put on, discarded, mended, and refurbished. That is, revision is to the writer what renovation is to the housewife.

Thus it is that the indispensability of rhetoric is one imperative which is realized by the image of 'dressed' thoughts. Because they always issue from a depraved source, ideas themselves are naked, raw, crude: they must be shaped, presented, and delivered—in short, redeemed—to suit them for introduction into a social audience. Erasmus Darwin, in his *Loves of the Plants*, sums up the orthodox theory this way: 'The Muses are young ladies, we expect to see them dressed.' He is merely echoing Pope's assertion in the *Essay on Criticism* that 'Nature', dressed to advantage, becomes 'True Wit' (297).

But just as convention dictates the mode of costume, so in writing general expectation regulates the kinds of styles which are the appropriate dresses of various thoughts. If an author is well principled, he will permit his own personal whimsies to have as little force in determining the kinds of garments his ideas assume in public as he permits them to have in his dress. Because the symbolic system of language is public property, in writing public criteria take precedence over private. In *Tatler* 230, for example, Swift reprehends the use of novel elisions in prose, rejecting usages like 'I can't do't'. 'In this last Point', he says, 'the usual Pretence is, that they spell as they speak: A noble Standard for Language! To depend upon the Caprice of every Coxcomb; who, because Words are the Cloathing of our Thoughts, cuts them out, and shapes them as he pleases, and changes them oftner than his Dress.' We think of the Puritans, whose prose style is as novel and eccentric as their dress and demeanour: both betray the distance of the Puritan from the centre of general human nature.

Thus public rhetorical expectation rather than private impulse is what provides the criteria of appropriateness for the various styles. Pope gives the idea its classical formulation in the *Essay on Criticism*:

> Expression is the *Dress* of *Thought,* and still
> Appears more *decent* as more *suitable*;

We should probably resist the temptation to find a pun in 'suitable'. The passage continues with precise illustrations from the decorum of social dress:

> A vile Conceit in pompous Words exprest,
> Is like a Clown in regal Purple drest;

'Clown' is, of course, as Johnson defines it, 'a rustick fellow', and the image is thus less one of a masquerade than of an indecent, scandalous, and illegal imposture: the image is moral as well as literary and social. Just as the three general degrees of formality in costume—un-dress, half-dress, and full-dress—are appropriate to degrees of social formality, so in writing the three general styles—low, middle, and high—are appropriate to three kinds of materials and audiences:

> For diff'rent *Styles* with diff'rent *Subjects* sort,
> As several Garbs with Country, Town, and Court.
>
> (318–23)

The relation to the theory of style as dress to the theory of architecture is implicit in Pope's exhortations to Burlington in *Moral Essay* IV: appropriateness to a universal human social situation is the chief criterion of both. In all building, Pope enjoins,

> . . . let Nature never be forgot.
> But treat the Goddess like a modest fair,
> Nor over-dress, nor leave her wholly bare.
>
> (50–52)

Johnson's whole theory of dictional decorum, best expressed, perhaps, in the *Life of Cowley*, seems largely an inverse variation played on Pope's image of the rustic ill-clothed in regal purple: 'Language is the dress of thought: and as the noblest mien, or most graceful action, would be degraded and obscured by a garb appropriated to the gross employments of rusticks or mechanicks; so the most heroick sentiments will lose their efficacy, and the most splendid ideas drop their magnificence, if they are conveyed by words used commonly upon low and trivial occasions, debased by vulgar mouths, and contaminated by inelegant applications.' Two things are especially noteworthy here: the first is Johnson's use of the word 'efficacy' where we would naturally say 'effectiveness'. Heroic sentiments have a productive *use*, and a moral one—they 'raise' the reader and forward his process of redemption. The second important thing here is the way Johnson's explanation assumes a relation not organic but social between ideas and words: their relation is not that of skin to body but of garments to body. Johnson's variation on Pope's image of the rustic disguised as king generates an image of a king in disguise as a rustic. King Lear comes to mind: we are already moving steadily towards Burke.

Since ideas can be separated from their momentary styles, one way to measure their real weight and shape is to strip them of their dress, like Swift's beau, and scrutinize them in the nude. When subjected to this test—suggestive of Reynolds's way of apprehending the classical human form—the ideas of the *Essay on Man* prove disappointing. As Johnson asks in the *Life of Pope*, 'When ... the doctrine of the Essay, disrobed of its ornaments, is left to the powers of its naked excellence, what shall we discover?' Little more than the clichés of the most elementary moral instruction: 'The reader feels his mind full, though he learns nothing; and, when he meets it in its new array, no longer knows the talk of his mother and his nurse.' Such is the power of dress to dignify commonplace materials. It is amusing to contemplate James Boswell's ingenuous use of the humanist proposition 'style is the dress of thought' for purposes of boyish moral self-improvement. He tells his journal in 1763: 'Style is to sentiment what dress is to the person. The effects of both are very great, and both are acquired and improved by habit. When once we are used to it, it is as easy to dress neatly as like a sloven; in the same way, custom makes us write in a correct style as easily as in a careless, inaccurate one' (*LJ*, 186–7).

Typically Boswellian too is his homely rendering of the classical idea of stylistic appropriateness. Longinus had used the image of a child's face covered by a tragic mask to argue for decorum in style, and Frank Brady and F. A. Pottle suggest that the Longinian image is perhaps lurking behind Boswell's defence of Johnson's presumed stylistic pomposities.[2] Boswell explains Johnson's formal (or 'high') style: 'He gives large words because he has large ideas. ... The late King of Prussia's tall regiment looked very stately with their large grenadier caps. If [Archibald] Campbell [author of *Lexiphanes*, a "ridicule" of Johnson's style] had taken these caps and clapped them on the

[2] *Boswell in Search of a Wife: 1766–1769* (New York, 1956), p. 151, n. 2.

heads of a parcel of blackguard children in the streets it would be highly ridiculous, but does that prove anything against the caps when properly applied?' (*BSW*, 151).

Thus even in the hands of Boswell the figure of style as clothing implies public, social appropriateness, as well as the roles of artifice and conscious will in expression. As often as not, style is conceived of as a social symbol like clothing which derives from a sort of public wardrobe (like the public 'armory' which contains the 'weapons' of expression and moral struggle). The stylistic clothing is deliberately chosen to accord with an occasion: it is then 'placed over' the thought, much as clothing is placed over the body. The distinction between the orthodox and the heterodox theories of style is that the orthodox theory feels no impulse to imagine the clothing as being at one with the body. Their relation is not organic—they express and imply each other without any vital dependence upon each other. Romantic criticism is more likely to image the relation between idea and style in terms of body and skin, or stem and leaves. To the Augustan humanist, clothes, like buildings, are static, public, social, completely controllable, and devoid of mysteries. They constitute thus an almost inevitable image for suggesting the humanist sense of the nature and purpose of expression.

The Augustan humanists seem given to perceiving that it is the general poverty and frailty of unadorned man that justify the eighteenth-century decorative values of elegance, richness, and splendour. We make a mistake, I think, if we assume that phenomena like Blenheim or gold lace express merely a vulgar passion for the showy, a devotion to external exhibition for its own sake. In these things it is less the grandeur and self-sufficiency of man that is being expressed than the littleness and frailty of his nature, which *needs* such elegant ornamentation. Anything that will help him conceive of himself as distant from the animal will gradually produce in him—so the humanists think—a more or less habitual motive of noble and social action. Mrs. Thrale reports that Johnson 'was no enemy to splendour of apparel or pomp of equipage—"Life (he would say) is barren enough surely with all her trappings; let us therefore be cautious how we strip her" ' (*JM*, i, 345). Although Johnson was usually attired in a simple, almost puritanical, brown suit, Boswell testifies that his imagination was not averse to luxuriating in images of quite another kind: 'when talking of dress, he said, "Sir, were I to have any thing fine, it should be very fine. Were I to wear a ring, it should not be a bauble, but a stone of great value. Were I to wear a laced or embroidered waistcoat, it should be very rich" ' (*BLJ*, v, 364). As we shall see, there is a sense in which all these gaudy eighteenth-century waistcoats, wigs, embroideries, and gilded chairs express not self-satisfaction, as the practice of conspicuous exhibition in succeeding eras might tempt us to assume, but quite its opposite. These items of 'magnificence' constitute the trappings which man, small, plain, and unsatisfactory as he is, needs if he is to think of himself as fully human and fully capable of willed, virtuous, and therefore splendid action. These items are yet another index of the precariousness of civilization and the frailty of man.

Burke is the fortunate inheritor of all this clothing imagery, and of the six great humanists he is the one destined to exploit it to illuminate the ethical dimension in politics. The image of the rustic garbed as a monarch, a traditional conservative image of misrule, is used in Pope's hands to sanction stylistic decorum, but under Burke's management it is inverted and deployed to insinuate the Duke of Bedford's madness in dressing himself as a republican. In a tone of mock-apology Burke explains: 'If I should happen to trespass a little [on the Duke's dignity] . . . let it always be supposed, that a confusion of characters may produce mistakes; that, in the masquerades of the grand carnival of our age, whimsical adventures happen. . . .' For a duke to come forward in the garb of a *sans-culotte* is as monstrous a perversion of order as for an abbé to appear in the role of a haberdasher with a cunning instinct for the mode of the moment. Warning Bedford that his person and feudal properties are by no means safe from republican designs upon them, Burke writes that

Abbé Sieyès has whole nests of pigeon-holes full of constitutions ready-made, ticketed, sorted, and numbered, suited to every season and every fancy: some with the top of the pattern at the bottom, and some with the bottom at the top; some plain, some flowered; . . . some in long coats, and some in short coats; some with pantaloons, some without breeches. . . . So that no constitution-fancier may go unsuited from his shop, provided he loves a pattern of pillage, oppression, arbitrary imprisonment, confiscation, exile, revolutionary judgment, and legalized premeditated murder, in any shapes into which they can be put.

But dukes and abbés are not alone in putting on dresses which suit them ill. 'Never before this time', says Burke, 'was a set of literary men converted into a gang of robbers and assassins. Never before did a den of bravoes and banditti assume the garb and tone of an academy of philosophers.'

These images of clothing draw vigour and detail from Swift and Pope, just as the passionate figure of Windsor Castle accumulates, fuses, and revitalizes a whole tradition's moral images of architecture. In an important passage in the *Reflections* likewise Burke takes an affectionate retrospective view of the usages of his humanist predecessors and seizes upon their kind of moral figures as the most telling and appropriate devices —because the most ennobled by moral associations—for moving his readers to reconsider the consequences of innovation and revolution. Swift's Jack ripping up his coat in a frenzy of revenge and Lemuel Gulliver standing naked and forlorn before the perplexed Houyhnhnm lend life and substance to many of Burke's images in the *Reflections*. At one point, contrasting French and English modes of reform, he writes: 'Many of our men of speculation, instead of exploding general prejudices, employ their sagacity to discover the latent wisdom which prevails in them. If they find what they seek, and they seldom fail, they think it more wise to continue the prejudice, with the reason involved, than to cast away the coat of prejudice, and to leave nothing but the naked reason.'

One of the 'prejudices' which has served the English well is Established Christianity, which, admittedly frail as it is, at the very least has the merit of 'filling the mind' and occupying the 'place' which otherwise might be filled by some predisposition destructive of personal and social coherence. Burke writes: 'if . . . we should uncover our nakedness, by throwing off that Christian religion which has hitherto been our boast and comfort . . ., we are apprehensive . . . that some . . . pernicious, and degrading superstition might take place of it'. Like the dogma of the Rights of Man, for example.

As buildings lean upon one another and thus complicate simpleminded attempts to reform them, so anything human is a complex object, just as complex as the relation—physical and psychological at once—of man to his clothing. 'I cannot stand forward', says Burke, 'and give praise or blame to anything which relates to human actions, and human concerns, on a simple view of the object, as it stands stripped of every relation, in all the nakedness and solitude of metaphysical abstraction.' The very trappings and associations and even the garments of royalty and aristocracy—the social correspondences of images of the noble in history-painting or epic poetry or public archi-tecture—are a part of the 'decent drapery of life' and are torn away and discarded at grave risk of imaging human life in terms so simplistic and one-dimensional as to bring it near the brutal, not to mention the Yahoo. A passage in the *Reflections* fit almost to rank next to the Windsor Castle performance in *A Letter to a Noble Lord* is Burke's poignant lamentation on the downfall of the French royal family. The rhetoric here is so gorgeous, the effect so commandingly contrived, the issues so central to the conduct of human life that the passage deserves to be excerpted, bound in limp black leather, and appointed to be read in churches on Sundays.

After abusing Dr. Price for 'exulting' over the spectacle of the downfall of the royal family when, as a man capable of learning that *humani nihil a me alienum*, his nature calls upon him to experience fear and pity, Burke turns to congratulate the king and queen on their fortitude under imprisonment and calumny. The king he praises for his sympathy towards his murdered guards and for his sad solicitude towards his mis-guided subjects: this solicitude 'derogates little from his forti-tude, while it adds infinitely to the honour of his humanity'. The queen he praises likewise for bearing her trials 'in a manner suited to her rank and race, and becoming the offspring of a sovereign [Maria Theresa] distinguished for her piety and her courage'; and he goes on to say that he hears, and rejoices to hear, 'that she feels with the dignity of a Roman matron; that in the last extremity she will save herself from the last disgrace, and that if she must fall, she will fall by no ignoble hand'.

Entertaining thus these shocking ideas of Marie Antoinette's actually being obliged perhaps to kill herself with a dagger to escape 'the last extremity' of being outraged and torn apart by the mad populace, Burke is moved to recover through memory a very different scene. His reminiscence takes the form of a delicate and finely drawn image of the nineteen-year-old dauphiness alighting years ago at Versailles surrounded like the morning star with auspices of delightful promise. The image is so subtle that it may prompt us to apply to Burke what Johnson says of Dryden: 'Next to argument, his delight was in wild and daring sallies of sentiment, in the irregular and eccentric violence of wit. He delighted to tread upon the brink of meaning, where light and darkness begin to mingle; to approach the precipice of absurdity, and hover over the abyss of unideal vacancy.'

Johnson's definition of *morning-star*—'The planet Venus when she shines in the morning'—suggests the superb appropriateness of Burke's image for evoking sensations of both delight and promise: 'It is now sixteen or seventeen years since I saw the queen of France, then the dauphiness, at Versailles; and surely never lighted on this orb, which she hardly seemed to touch, a more delightful vision. I saw her just above the horizon, decorating and cheering the elevated sphere she just began to move in,—glittering like the morning-star, full of life, and splendor, and joy.' What this image does is to equate the French court with the heavens themselves, but the assonance and the rhythm—especially the dying fall of 'the elevated sphere she just began to move in'—distract us beautifully from what in another mood we should reject as either blasphemy or sheer snobbery. From this rich and lovely recollection of the past, Burke undertakes a sudden transition to the hideous present of revolutions and Dr. Price: 'Oh! what a revolution! and what a heart must I have, to contemplate without emotion that elevation and that fall!' He next laments the decay of French chivalry, which might have protected her and saved her from the necessity of carrying like Cleopatra 'the sharp antidote against disgrace concealed in that bosom'. Sixteen or seventeen years ago things might have been different: 'I thought', he says, 'ten thousand swords must have leaped from their scabbards to avenge even a look that threatened her with insult.' But not now: 'the age of chivalry is gone.—That of sophisters, œconomists, and calculators has succeeded; and the glory of Europe is extinguished forever.' 'The glory of Europe' here— 'extinguished' like a bright star fading out—is exactly the chivalric spirit generated by an aristocracy protective at

once of the rights of the commons and the rights of the
monarch.

Burke has now arrived at a point where it is appropriate for
him to trace the history of European knighthood, and this he
does in a paragraph in which he locates the essence of European
imagination and polity in the institution of hereditary chivalry.
Even until very recently, he argues, the chivalric institution has
left its legacy of gentleness, elegance, and manners. 'But now
all is to be changed. All the pleasing illusions, which made
power gentle, and obedience liberal, which harmonized the
different shades of life, and which, by a bland assimilation,
incorporated into politics the sentiments which beautify and
soften private society, are to be dissolved by this new conquering
empire of light and reason.' And here, in this passionately
elegiac mood, his imagination heated and his heart saddened by
visions of the collapse of whole civilizations, Burke chooses to
proceed to the heart of his argument by means of a clothing
figure: 'All the decent drapery of life is to be rudely torn off.
All the superadded ideas, furnished from the wardrobe of a
moral imagination, which the heart owns, and the understanding ratifies, as necessary to cover the defects of our naked,
shivering nature, and to raise it to dignity in our own estimation,
are to be exploded, as a ridiculous, absurd, and antiquated
fashion.'

This passage is so rich in accumulated strands of humanistic
ideas, gestures, and images that to analyse it satisfactorily would
be simply to repeat all that has been said so far. We must just
note that the chief premise upon which the passage rests is the
frailty and depravity of man which urge him to 'furnish' himself with images and ideas of noble possibility lest he identify
himself with the brute he resembles and so destroy himself. We
must also observe the important Lockean and architectural
implications of the 'wardrobe' which holds the moral ideas,
collected like furniture in a house. We must note finally the
concern of the passage with the distinction between the permanent and the timely, its concern with the very serious obligation of man to inquire what it is that makes him human and
connects him thus with the past and with reality. By focusing on
the universal discomfort and shame of man when naked, the
passage makes an appeal to the reader's deepest attributes and

Q

thus enlists him willy-nilly as a participant in its rhetoric. In the insistence of the passage that the 'superadded ideas'—ideas of aristocracies, courtesy, and virtue—derive from 'a *moral imagination*', we find the traditional humanistic devotion to ethics as a mode of secular redemption; and in the heart's recognition of the justice and necessity of such ideas we find the traditional humanistic recourse to something like the educated instinct of the instructed heart—Burke carefully accuses the Jacobins of 'cold hearts'—as distinctly preferable to all the systems, abstractions, and rationalisms by which men frequently proclaim that they live but which only the Jacobins have been so foolish, so naïve, so simpleminded as to base a whole polity upon.

But now that the once correspondent ideas of courtesy, elegance, virtue, and redemption have been divorced and 'dissolved' by Jacobin reasoning, Europe is destined for a new scheme of things: 'On this scheme of things, a king is but a man; a queen is but a woman; a woman is but an animal; and an animal not of the highest order. All homage paid to the sex in general as such, and without distinct views, is to be regarded as romance and folly. Regicide, and parricide, and sacrilege, are but fictions of superstition, corrupting jurisprudence by destroying its simplicity. The murder of a king, or a queen, or a bishop, or a father, are only common homicide . . .'.

This nightmare world in which kings become merely men and queens turn into animals is the world of *King Lear*, a play that seems never to have been very far from Burke's mind. His enemy Thomas Paine seems to have sensed something important about his method. He observes in *The Rights of Man*: 'I cannot consider Mr. Burke's book in any other light than a dramatic performance; and he must, I think, have considered it in the same light himself, by the poetical liberties he has taken of omitting some facts, distorting others, and making the whole machinery bend to produce a stage effect.' The state of the tragic theatre in Burke's time was such that Nahum Tate's cheerful version of *King Lear*, with the amended ending which manages to evade all the tragic consequences of the initial action, was still the standard text for performance. From this evidence we might be led to assume that the tragic spirit was dead in the eighteenth century. But such an assumption would imply that human nature is temporarily alterable, which would seem highly doubtful. Actually the spirit of tragedy is very much alive in the century: together with its attendant experience of irony, it has fled a commercialized and vulgarized theatre and lodged in humanist prose like Johnson's, Gibbon's, and Burke's, just as in our own time it has been driven by melodrama from Broadway and the West End to lodge in fiction, lyric, and works of history.

King Lear does a multitude of things at once, but one of the chief things it does is to enact a fable of human needs. Behind the rages and the storms, the mistakes and the betrayals, runs a constant question, and it is the humanistic question: what is the nature of man, and what does he need to be fully human? The answer available in the action of the play is to be sought perhaps more in the entanglings of the plot in the middle of the action than in their unravellings at the end. From an exchange in Act II, scene ii, it is clear that whatever man is he is not to be manufactured by tailors. Quarrelling with Oswald, Kent asserts that 'nature disclaims in thee; a tailor made thee'. Cornwall, puzzled, says, 'Thou art a strange fellow. A tailor make a man?' And Kent answers, 'Ay, a tailor, sir. A stonecutter or a painter could not have made him so ill, though he had been but two hours at the trade' (59–65). And Edgar's soliloquy in Act II, scene iii, suggests that man, as he is the more deprived, comes the closer to beast. Meditating his form of disguise, Edgar says:

> Whiles I may scape
> I will preserve myself; and am bethought
> To take the basest and most poorest shape
> That ever penury, in contempt of man,
> Brought near to beast.
>
> (5–9)

But it is Lear himself who provides the most illuminating answers to the humanist question. In scene iv of Act II, as he dickers with Goneril and Regan over the number of his train, he breaks through his quantitative silliness to arrive at the humanist perception that man's psychic needs are often different from his natural ones, and that the question of human needs is not to be answered in logical or rational terms:

Gon.   Hear me, my lord,
          What need you five-and-twenty, ten, or five,
          To follow in a house where twice so many
          Have a command to tend you?
Reg.   What need one?
Lear.   O, reason not the need! Our basest beggars
          Are in the poorest things superfluous.
          Allow not nature more than nature needs,
          Man's life is cheap as beast's.

                                                    (263–70)

That is, if human nature is allowed not more than animal
nature needs—sustenance, shelter, copulation—it turns into
something too near to animal nature to be readily distinguishable from it. Man is unique, and his unique needs are those of
the psyche and the imagination. In the middle of the storm,
accompanied by his Fool and confronted by Edgar's Poor Tom,
Lear undergoes another humanist perception. Here he apprehends that unclothed man is not merely naked to the elements:
much worse, he is naked to himself, and, thinking ill of himself,
finds heroic images and action impossible. Lear says to Edgar:

> Why, thou wert better in thy grave than to answer with
> thy uncovered body this extremity of the skies. Is man no
> more than this? Consider him well. Thou ow'st the worm
> no silk, the beast no hide, the sheep no wool, the cat no
> perfume. Ha! Here's three on's are sophisticated! Thou
> art the thing itself; unaccommodated man is no more but
> such a poor, bare, forked animal as thou art. . . .
>
>   (iii, iv, 106–13)

To the Shakespeare of *King Lear* as well as to the Burke of the
Reflections, it is man's nature to be 'accommodated' with
clothing, symbols, institutions, and inheritances so that, in his
own imagination, he shall not approach too near to the beast.
But in the *Reflections*, the Jacobins, re-enacting the betrayals and
the brutalities of the unnatural sisters and the bastard in *King
Lear*, have 'rudely torn off' the 'decent drapery' of life. Once
the drapery is gone, a king to the Jacobins is like a king to
Goneril and Regan: 'a king is but a man', and 'the murder of a
king . . . or a father, are only common homicide'. It is this vast
and terrible vision of the horrors of man unaccommodated,
together with the images of clothing and of shivering nakedness

through which the vision is embodied, that Burke derives from
Lear, although he derives much else too. His Marie Antoinette
becomes a version of the Cordelia of Act v, an emblem of
innocence menaced by brutality. And in the *Letter to a Noble
Lord* he seems to recall this speech of Albany's when he says of
the Jacobins that 'they have tigers to fall upon animated
strength':

> What have you done?
> Tigers, not daughters, what have you perform'd?
> A father, and a gracious, aged man,
> Whose reverence even the head-lugg'd bear would lick,
> Most barbarous, most degenerate, have you madded.

So deeply permeated is Burke's imagination with the materials
of *King Lear* that at times he actually identifies himself with
Lear, as he does when he repeats to the House of Commons
Lear's puzzled lines about even his dogs' apostasy. Burke's
political enemies found it a plausible point of attack to insinuate
that he was actually mad, and Burke himself provided some
grounds for such an insinuation. When Boswell told Johnson
that some were representing Burke as mad, Johnson answered,
'Sir, if A Man will appear extravagant, as he does, and cry, can
he wonder that he is represented as Mad?' (*PJB*, xv, 234). On
another occasion Johnson depicted Burke as 'a lion, who lashes
himself into a fury with his own tail' (*BLJ*, v, 575). Burke's
final fury at the Jacobins rises to such a pitch that the conclusion
of Albany's speech sounds like the Burke of *Letters on a Regicide
Peace*:

> If that the heavens do not their visible spirits
> Send quickly down to tame these vile offences,
> It will come,
> Humanity must perforce prey on itself,
> Like monsters of the deep.
>
> (iv, ii, 39–49)

To Burke, the outrages of the Jacobins have likewise shattered
universal order. 'It has not been', he explains, 'as has been
falsely and insidiously represented, that these miscreants had
only broke with their old government. They made a schism with
the whole universe.'

A comment of Stuart Hampshire's seems to illuminate the

equivalence of Shakespeare's and Burke's attitudes towards man's relation to physical nature:

'Art is man's nature.' This is the centre of Burke's thought. He had to start from the idea of Nature, because every thinker of his century, and particularly his enemies, had started there. The idea of the stripped, natural man, liberated from the draperies of convention and of obedience, had guided the Jacobins and the philosophical radicals. In this ancient and simple picture Nature and Convention, or Manners, are true opposites, contrasted as innocence and corruption, as equality and difference. Nature is something to which you can return for renewal. . . .

Consistently and throughout his life Burke strove to reverse this picture. That which is distinctively human in men, and therefore their nature, flows from the conventions and manners, from the imposed style of life, which over the years have formed their moral sentiments.[3]

'Unaccommodated man' is like the 'wild man' familiar to the British imagination through heraldry: he carries a club. Clothing is the achievement of civilization, but the achievement of a high civilization is the creation of a symbolic clothing of conventions and institutions. Burke's 'decent drapery of life', consisting of the 'superadded ideas, furnished from the wardrobe of a moral imagination', is needed alike by Poor Tom, Lear, Gulliver, and the citizens of France. And as we have seen, just as 'drapery' is the dress of man, style is the dress of thought. The dress may vary from Poor Tom's rags to Johnson's 'laced or embroidered waistcoat', but in expression as well as in action external conventions are indispensable: the 'dresses' which clothe thought come from the same objective 'moral' wardrobe as the conventions and institutions which humanize and dignify man. Styles and institutions are ultimately the same thing, and in either to try to invent one's own is to renounce one's humanity.

---

[3] 'Political Arithmetic', *New Statesman* (9 June 1961), p. 920.

10

'THE VERMIN OF NATURE':
HIERARCHY AND MORAL CONTEMPT

'You can hardly conceive', Pope writes Aaron Hill, 'how little either Pique or Contempt I bear to any Creature' —and up to this point the rhetorical role he assumes is that of the new moral monist. But as he concludes his sentence he reverses direction wittily and recovers the stability of the satirist's posture: 'unless', he adds, 'for immoral or dirty Actions' (*CAP*, iv, 102). Pope's immense poetic readiness at 'Pique or Contempt' seems to be a function less of his character than of his professional literary stance as moralist and satirist, a stance which kept him perpetually on the alert for 'immoral or dirty Actions'. Justifications of Pope's character no longer seem very interesting, for what has come to matter is the poetry, that is, the adequacy with which the satiric rhetoric succeeds in realizing the moral contempt which is the indispensable attribute of the genre. Surrounded by what, as a humanist, he naturally takes to be 'immoral or dirty Actions', Pope is confronted with the problem not of responding to them accurately —his outrage is learned and all but instinctive—but of finding moral images for realizing them. The image most accessible for this purpose, it proves, is that of the nasty or showy or unstable insect.

Pope's *Imitation of the Earl of Dorset*, written before he was twenty-two, already exhibits the habitual humanist mode of serious moral contempt and already reveals the Augustan instinct for realizing this contempt through insect imagery. Satirizing 'Phryne', a lascivious and indiscriminate jade who finally marries for money, the young Pope writes:

> So have I known those Insects fair,
> (Which curious *Germans* hold so rare,)

> Still vary Shapes and Dyes;
> Still gain new Titles with new Forms;
> First Grubs obscene, then wriggling Worms,
> Then painted Butterflies.
>
> (ii, 19–24)

Twenty-one years later he is still at it. In the *Epistle to Burlington* poor vulgar Timon, by devoting himself to quantitative display, has reduced himself to

> A puny insect, shiv'ring at a breeze!
>
> (108)

And near the end of his career the *Epilogue to the Satires* and the final version of *The Dunciad* swarm as ever with contemptible 'tinsel Insects' and 'industrious Bugs'. The Augustan humanist association between moral disgust and the idea of insects is by no means the property of Pope alone: it is pervasive in the tradition, from Swift's nasty, self-satisfied spider to Gibbon's 'swarms' of Christian hermits infesting the deserts and Burke's revolutionary locusts pouring 'from the rotten carcass of their own murdered country'.

There is no doubt that the Augustan conservative imagination delights to image the contemptible by recourse to insects. It is when we essay to interpret this phenomenon that we run risks of oversimplifying, for it is obvious that insects are both an actual and a symbolic constant from the Biblical locust-plagues and Virgil's gnats to 'Grub street' and the actual Caledonian bedbugs encountered by Johnson and Boswell on the Hebridean tour. It is true also that in the eighteenth century insects were simply more apparent nuisances to everyone, whether humanist or progressive, than they appear today. A horse economy—the kind that provides a context for the comedy of the Houyhnhnms —will be troubled by flies and maggots just as a gasoline and diesel economy is vexed by fumes and racket. In the eighteenth century nicotine was just being introduced as a primitive plant insecticide, and the chances were excellent that the nectarine about to be enjoyed by Shenstone's Cloe did actually conceal a nasty surprise in the form of a worm or earwig. The inns—as Johnson and Boswell found—were buggy beyond our power to conceive. Despite a high standard of personal cleanliness among the middle and upper classes, the general attitude towards public sanitation tended to the frivolous: the foetid and notorious Fleet 'River' (actually sewer) was covered over only in the 1730's. No one had anything like windowscreens. Swift's very fondness for the term 'pester' suggests the vigour that will reside in insect images in an age when bugs, both outdoors and in, were a constant annoyance. But in addition to the simple ubiquity of actual bugs and their disconcerting, ironic contrast with the progressivist implications of the new comfort and elegance, there are other reasons for this predominance of insect images in the Augustan humanist tradition.

Writing out of a medieval and Renaissance background, Andrew Marvell could conceive of the glow-worm as a benign and amiable creature devoted to man's service. In *The Mower to the Glo-Worms* Marvell equips this little creature with a 'dear light', an 'officious Flame' which 'courteously' reveals the way to benighted mowers, and whose tender glow is eclipsed only by that of the speaker's beloved arriving in the fields for a tryst. But after the initial British experience with the microscope in the later seventeenth century such tenderness towards insects is rare, for the new microscopy revealed for all to see the presumed savagery, squalor, ugliness, and 'meanness' of the insect kingdom and thus tended to confirm by ocular evidence the moral implications of the insects' disadvantageous station in the Great Chain of Being. It was as if Hobbes's findings about man himself had been confirmed analogically by the behaviour of the littler world of insects, now for the first time fully accessible for scrutiny and interpretation. Once the world of the 'peopled grass' had been opened by the microscope, horror, moral outrage, or breezy contempt are the most common reactions until the time of Blake and Keats. Blake's *The Fly* recovers something of Marvell's affection for insects, and Keats's sonnet *On the Grasshopper and Cricket* dignifies insect life—the 'vermin of nature' to the Augustans—and manages to transform it into 'the poetry of earth'. Again, the decay of the Augustan moral sense of hierarchy, the sense that informs Swift's treatment of his spider, is reflected in Whitman's 'noiseless, patient spider', whose 'filament', spun out of itself, so far from suggesting a hopeless enslavement to subjectivity actually becomes analogous to the 'gossamer thread' thrown out by the human soul as a 'bridge' to 'the spheres'. What to Swift is naturally an evidence of excremental grossness appears to Whitman a link with the transcendent. And the insect that is Gregor Samsa in Kafka's *Metamorphosis* evokes pathos and perhaps even laughter rather than feelings of moral contempt. As a representative bourgeois travelling-salesman he becomes in his metamorphosis an emblem not of self-corruption but of the externally determined absurd.

But the early eighteenth century, as Marjorie Nicolson has shown in *The Microscope and English Imagination*, was dominated by a microscopic vision very different from Blake's or Keats's or Whitman's or Kafka's. The imaginations of Swift and Pope were exercised by books like Henry Power's *Experimental Philosophy* (1664) and, more importantly, Robert Hooke's *Micrographia* (1665). Power and Hooke distinguished themselves by recording and illustrating their observations through the newly perfected microscope, and for the first time Englishmen were privileged to peer with horror at engravings of a sixteen-inch flea and a twenty-one-inch louse. The engraving of the magnified flea in *Micrographia* is especially revolting: looking like some enormous monster, it is clearly capable of disturbing momentarily any assumption that the Deity has designed the elements of the Great Chain with any close attention to beauty or dignity. The fame of this engraving of the magnified flea was such that one favourite type of home magnifier became known as the Flea Microscope, and as the science of practical optics developed, no home was considered complete in which the master could not carry on, in an amateur way, the tradition of Hooke. But even Hooke, for all his assiduity in investigation, is humanist enough to feel apologetic for focusing so minutely on the contemptible bottom of the Chain. He writes: 'It is my *hope*, as well as *belief*, that these my *Labours* will be no more comparable to the *Productions* of many other *Natural Philosophers*, who are now every where busie about *greater* things; then [*sic*] my *little objects* are to be compar'd to the greater and more beautiful *Works of Nature*, A Flea, a Mite, a gnat, to an Horse, an Elephant, or a Lyon.' Thus even the naturalist Hooke feels the orthodox contempt for things so small, mercurial, evanescent, and hideous as insects. Close to the bottom of the moral hierarchy, insects even to the professional entomologist constitute 'mean' objects of contemplation.

Under the stimulus of manufacturers like James Wilson, the microscope became as stylish a novelty as the wind-harp a century later, and soon everyone was scrutinizing bugs. Locke carried a microscope with him on his travels to France and used it to examine silkworms. Writing Caryll about a Mr. Hatton, a new acquaintance, Pope reports—a bit alarmingly, perhaps—that 'he is . . . curious in microscopes and showed my mother some of the *semen masculinum*, with animalcula in it' (*CAP*, i, 465). Swift, of whom Taine said, 'Il a toujours le microscope en main', once thought of buying one for Stella's amusement. And his sport with magnification in the Second Voyage of *Gulliver's Travels* suggests that he was a delighted reader of Hooke, who, in addition to his engravings of the vermin of nature, depicts also the point of a needle, the edge of a razor, magnified fabrics looking like coarse matting—his silk looks like canvas—and the surprising texture of human skin.

The Royal Society ordered one of Hooke's microscopes in the 1660's, and in his *History of the Royal Society* (1667) Thomas Sprat, who believed that 'the meanest and most trivial matters may be so cultivated, as to bear excellent Fruit, when they come under the management of an accurate, and prudent Observer', expressed the standard contemporary sense of wonder at the new worlds opened by optics. He writes: 'there may be an infinit number of *Creatures*, over our heads, round about us, and under our feet, in the large space of the *Air*, in the Caverns of the *Earth*, in the Bowels of *Mountains*, in the bottoms of *Seas*, and in the shades of *Forests*: which have hitherto escap'd all *mortal Senses*.' And he goes on to assert that, although before the development of the microscope man's vision was sadly limited, now 'by the means of that excellent *Instrument*, we have a far greater number of different kinds of things reveal'd to us . . .'. Sprat's wonder and excitement minister to his 'modern' delight in quantity and the idea of progress, and we encounter a similarly 'modern' reaction three-quarters of a century later in Henry Baker's *The Microscope Made Easy* (1743). Baker, called by his contemporaries 'Microscope' Baker the way Johnson was called 'Dictionary' Johnson and the way Boswell burned to be known as 'Corsica' Boswell, is moved by his discoveries in microscopy to complacent rhapsody and praise of the Creator. But the humanists, just as interested as Sprat or Baker in micro-

scopic phenomena, tend to employ the findings of the microscopists in a significantly less optimistic way. They will find in
this tiny new world evidence less of benign plenitude than of
severe moral hierarchy, and they will settle upon the newly
revealed kingdom of mites and maggots as the symbolic region
of the morally contemptible. 'Beëlzebub', as they seem to
recall, means traditionally 'The Lord of the Flies'. Insects, after
all, are not only tiny: they are given to nastiness, and their
stings and fly-specks constitute a standing assault against
human dignity. Indeed, their purpose in the whole scheme of
things is puzzling. But what is worse about them is their
evanescence, their mechanical promiscuity, and their apparent
giddiness and instability, the sort of thing manifested, say, by
the flight pattern of the fly. If we except the ant and the bee—
and the Bible, Virgil, and folklore had already excepted them—
insects, like earthquakes, tidal waves, and volcanoes, constitute
a prime embarrassment to an anthropocentric teleology. In his
Thoughts on Various Subjects Swift finds it worth while to 'answer'
the sceptical objection that 'Storms and Tempests, unfruitful
Seasons, Spiders, Flies, and other noxious or troublesome
Animals . . . discover an Imperfection in Nature . . .'. Swift's
argument in rebuttal is that the purpose of these evils is to stir
man to ingenuity and thus save him from stagnation. We are
hardly convinced, and it is doubtful that Swift was either. So
embarrassing is the presence of insects in a world in which man
is presumed to occupy a special place. No wonder the humanists
hold insects in such contempt and employ them so readily as an
emblem of all the self-destructive moral vices, the 'immoral or
dirty Actions', which it is their business to stigmatize.

For all their amateur delight in inspecting the animalcula in
the *semen masculinum* and in peering at the mites in cheese, the
Augustan conservatives, mindful perhaps of Raphael's warning
to Adam, adopt a moral and hierarchical view of the serious
practice of entomology. While Newtonian speculation was held
to 'enlarge' the mind, Hookeian inquiry was conceived, at least
by the literary, to diminish it. The mechanics of this process of
diminishment are suggested by Goldsmith in Letter 89 of *The
Citizen of the World*. Speaking of the microscopists, Lien Chi
Altangi, Goldsmith's spokesman, finds them 'laborious in
trifles, constant in experiment, without one single abstraction,

by which alone knowledge may be properly said to encrease; till, at last, their ideas, ever employed upon minute things, contract to the size of the diminutive object, and a single mite shall fill their whole mind's capacity'. The process is the exact reverse of that which Reynolds's theory of heroic painting assumes. A stock character encountered everywhere in humanist literature is the mad entomologist who has forgot what is mankind's proper study and whose mind has finally shrunk to 'match' the contemptible object of his pursuits. A representative conservative attitude is that embodied in Thomas Shadwell's comedy *The Virtuoso* (1676), where Sir Nicholas Gimcrack is said by Clarinda to be 'A Sot, that has spent 2000 l. in Microscopes, to find out the Nature of . . . Mites in Cheese . . .'. Miranda adds her findings: he is, she reports, 'One who has broken his brains about the nature of Maggots; who has studi'd these twenty years to find out the several sorts of Spiders, and never cares for understanding Mankind'. Clearly intended by Shadwell to suggest moral enormity is Sir Nicholas's announcement, in the middle of the play, 'I ha' found more curious Phaenomena in these minute Animals, than those of vaster magnitude'. But the perverse Sir Nicholas receives comic retribution for his folly: he is swindled, and by the end of the play he has been brought to belated wisdom: 'I wou'd I had studi'd Mankind', he says, 'instead of Spiders and Insects.' In the same way Mr. Periwinkle, in Susannah Centlivre's *Bold Stroke for a Wife* (1718), is advised by Mistress Lovely: 'study your country's good, . . . and not her insects'. The conservative disgust at insects is one of William Shenstone's frequent gestures. In *The Progress of Taste* we are presented with a foolish virtuoso named Damon, whose folly it is to minister to the health of noxious insects: his crime is in keeping them alive even though they constitute a palpable blemish on man's universe. He is a bug's physician:

> Behold him, at some crise, prescribe,
> And raise with drugs the sick'ning tribe.

(iv, 55–56)

The naturalist Benjamin Wilks is similarly the target of Shenstone's scorn:

> O Wilks! what poet's loftiest lays
> Can match thy labours, and thy praise?

> Immortal sage! by fate decreed
> To guard the moth's illustrious breed;
> 'Till flutt'ring swarms on swarms arise,
> And all our wardrobes teem with flies!

(iv, 67–72)

Shenstone returns to this theme in *To the Virtuosos*, addressed to those

> . . . curious wights, to whom so fair
>   The form of mortal flies is!
> Who deem those grubs beyond compare,
>   Which common sense despises.

Virtuosos like Damon and Benjamin Wilks err by assisting insects in breeding:

> . . . if [nature's] brood of insects dies,
>   You sage assistance lend her;
> Can stoop to pimp for am'rous flies,
>   And help 'em to engender.

> 'Tis you protect their pregnant hour;
>   And when the birth's at hand,
> Exerting your obstetric pow'r,
>   Prevent a mothless land.

Shenstone finally exhorts the entomologists to recover an appropriate object of sexual concern:

> Let FLAVIA's eyes more deeply warm,
>   Nor thus your hearts determine,
> To slight dame Nature's fairest form,
>   And sigh for Nature's vermin.

That the conservative suspicion of entomological studies persisted among conservatives until very late in the century is suggested by George Adams's *Essays on the Microscope* (1787), where the author takes elaborate pains to argue the usefulness and even the grandeur of such minute studies of such contemptible creatures.

The sort of attitude which Adams feels obliged to confront is exemplified in Goldsmith's *History of the Earth, and Animated Nature* (1774), which applies to insects terms like 'hideous', 'odious', 'nauseous', and 'obnoxious'. Goldsmith's assumption is that insects are placed in the lowest class of animated nature quite justly: their very numerousness suggests their trivial value in the order of creation, and their noxiousness to man is a clear indication of their fundamental 'mischievousness'. We find a similarly hierarchical response—although a more ironical one —in a comic print drawn by George Woodward and engraved by Isaac Cruikshank in 1796. Here we see two self-indulgent old men of the middle class, both far gone in gout, who tremble at the approach of the fly which, if it buzzes any nearer, will oblige them to shoo it away and thus bestir their ailing limbs to an agony. The print is titled *Lords of the Creation frightened at a Fly*.

The traditions in collision here in the quarrel between Adams and Goldsmith are essentially those of Ancient and Modern again. To the Augustans, the newly accessible world of bugs, although interesting in a quaint way, is useful primarily as evidence of the 'fallen' and unredeemable squalor of that part of the creation which is sub-human. But to the Moderns, bolstered by the entomological enthusiasms of the Royal Society, the world of insects suggests an optimistic, often Deistic conviction of divine benignity. The satisfaction with which Addison considers the implications of the insect kingdom in *Spectator* 519 is typical of the progressivist position. This essay constitutes a rhapsody on the principle of plenitude. The Creator's goodness is argued from His presumed attention to filling every rank of nature with teeming life, the more, presumably, the better. As Addison says, 'Every part of Matter is peopled: Every green Leaf swarms with Inhabitants. There is scarce a single Humour in the Body of a Man, or of any other Animal, in which our Glasses do not discover Myriads of living Creatures.' The end of Addison's meditation is a high cosmic optimism which anticipates the monistic transcendentalism of the following century. Even Pope occasionally reflects a similar tone of satisfaction, as when, in the *Essay on Man*, he traces the Chain of Being from 'the green myriads in the peopled grass' all the way up to 'Man's imperial race'. But even in this 'official' utterance what seems to interest him is less the similarity of species in being all expressive of the divine delight in sheer plenitude than the fixity of the distinguishing lines which separate them. An 'insuperable line' has been drawn as a boundary between species, and the coherence of the whole Chain depends upon distinctions and subordination—that is, almost upon the divine principle of genre.

The whole tone and method of the eighteenth-century humanist use of insect imagery seems to be established by Dryden, who, like Swift with his spider, is fond of employing the insect figure to realize the kind of pert self-satisfaction and complacency associated with 'crowds unlearn'd', Puritans, experimental scientists, and political projectors. Attacking the Puritan reliance on 'opinion' in scriptural interpretation, Dryden asserts in *Religio Laici*:

> This was the fruit the private spirit brought,
> Occasion'd by great zeal and little thought.
> While crowds unlearn'd, with rude devotion warm,
> About the sacred viands buzz and swarm,
> The fly-blown text creates a crawling brood;
> And turns to maggots what was meant for food.
>
> (415–20)

Dryden's antitheses—*zeal: thought; maggots: food*—help define the kind of dualism which humanist insect images generally seem to reinforce. The vast and all-important distance between man and insect is what the imagery argues.

Swift's moral contempt for the Honorable Richard Tighe, a Dublin privy-councillor who not only beat his wife but also uttered vigorous Whig sentiments, takes the shape of a maggot figure in *Dick, A Maggot*, where Dick's undisguisable maggothood becomes exactly as noisome as a human excrement:

> As when rooting in a Bin,
> All powder'd o'er from Tail to Chin;
> A lively Maggot sallies out,
> You know him by his hazel Snout:
> . . . 'tis beyond the Pow'r of Meal,
> The Gypsey Visage to conceal:
> For, as he shakes his Wainscot Chops,
> Down ev'ry mealy Atom drops
> And leaves the Tartar Phiz, in show
> Like a fresh T—d just dropt on Snow.

In the same way a vigorous part of Swift's campaign against William Wood, the copper-coinage entrepreneur, is conducted by reducing him to the station of vermin. In *Wood, An Insect* Swift manages symbolically the campaign which, in the *Drapier's Letters*, he conducts discursively. The distinctly different audiences of the poem and the dramatistic essays would seem to help dictate the two different modes of rhetoric. In *Wood, An Insect* Swift metamorphoses his victim into both a '*Wood*-Louse' and a '*Wood*-Worm', or Death-watch Beetle. Just as the sovereign remedy against the Death-watch Beetle is the application of scalding water, so

> . . . since the *Drapier* hath heartilly maul'd him,
> I think the best Thing we can do is to scald him.
> For which Operation there's nothing more proper
> Than the Liquor he deals in, his own melted Copper.

(33–36)

The violence of Swift's reaction to Wood is paralleled by the violence of Johnson's response to those who, for commercial advantage, hoped to melt and peddle the lead roof of Lichfield cathedral. Johnson's answer to this architectural and devotional sacrilege is, like Swift's, an image of violent physical torment, and an image so extravagant that Johnson was finally prevailed upon to cancel the page in the *Journey to the Western Islands* on which it first appeared. 'What they shall melt', writes Johnson, 'it were just that they should swallow.' And to Swift, bad poets are thoroughly as contemptible as greedy businessmen. One of the most verminous practices of bad poets is pestering and traducing writers who occupy the next higher rank in the chain of literary being. This is also a nasty practice of insect parasites, Swift has discovered from his reading of the microscopists. As he says in *On Poetry: A Rhapsody*,

> The Vermin only teaze and pinch
> Their Foes superior by an Inch.
> So, Nat'ralists observe, a Flea
> Hath smaller Fleas that on him prey,
> And these have smaller yet to bite 'em,
> And so proceed *ad infinitum*:
> Thus ev'ry Poet in his Kind,
> Is bit by him that comes behind.

(335–42)

The attempt of the Dissenters to attain a measure of equality in the early 1730's sets Swift off again, and again it is to the vermin of nature that he goes for imagery adequate to the moral occasion. His poem *On the Words—Brother Protestants, and Fellow Christians, so familiarly used by the Advocates for the Repeal of the Test Act in Ireland, 1733* operates by denying the affinity with Angli-

R

cans claimed by the Dissenters, and in the process the imagery asserts the distinct boundaries between species and the unbridgeable distance between high and low on the Chain of Being:

> . . . Fanatic Saints, tho' neither in
> Doctrine, or Discipline our Brethren,
> Are *Brother Protestants and Christians,*
> As much as *Hebrews* and *Philistines*:
> But in no other Sense, than Nature
> Has made the Rat our Fellow-Creature.
> Lice from your Body suck their Food;
> But is a Louse your Flesh and Blood?
> Tho' born of human Filth and Sweat, it
> May well be said Man did beget it.
> But Maggots in your Nose and Chin,
> As well may claim you for their Kin.
>
> (29–40)

By arguing that the Dissenters are not Christians, Swift manages to imply through the insect figures that they are not men either. Having abdicated as men, therefore, they deserve to be metamorphosed to the dust from which they spring. In a passage which may recall the wonderful transformations in *The Dunciad*, Swift writes:

> As *Moses*, by divine Advice,
> In *Egypt* turn'd the Dust to Lice;
> And as our Sects, by all Descriptions,
> Have Hearts more harden'd than *Egyptians*;
> As from the trodden Dust they spring,
> And, turn'd to Lice, infest the King:
> For Pity's Sake it would be just,
> A *Rod* should turn them back to *Dust*.
>
> (49–56)

The conclusion of Swift's poem constitutes a final warning against ecumenical fusion which, by obliterating indispensable humanistic distinctions, would end in the kind of universal darkness deplored likewise by the images of the end of *The Dunciad*:

> Let Folks in high, or holy Stations,
> Be proud of owning such Relations;
> Let Courtiers hug them in their Bosom,
> As if they were afraid to lose 'em:

> While I, with humble *Job*, had rather,
> Say to Corruption—*Thou'rt my Father.*
> For he that has so little Wit,
> To nourish Vermin, may be *bit.*
>
> (57–64)

That is, an insect-bite and a human swindle come to much the same thing.

Dissenters are not the only extremists to be transformed into insects by the conservative imagination. Freethinkers receive the same treatment. *Guardian* 70, presumably by Richard Steele, exhibits a happy coalescence of architectural and insect figures which suggests the way image-systems of given polemic associations tend to cluster together or even to generate each other. We find a similar juxtaposition of the architectural and the verminous in Swift's poem *Vanbrug's House* (1703), where details of stones, beams, slates, tiles, and thatch curiously seem to invite into the poem a host of silkworms, maggots, and flies. The speaker in *Guardian* 70 begins by developing a highly self-conscious analogy between a Palladian building and Christian doctrine:

> As I was the other day taking a solitary walk in St. Paul's, I indulged my thoughts in the pursuit of a certain analogy between that fabrick and the Christian Church in the largest sense. The divine order and œconomy of the one seemed to be emblematically set forth by the just, plain, and majestick architecture of the other. And as the one consists of a great variety of parts united in the same regular design, according to the truest art, and most exact proportion; so the other contains a decent subordination of members, various sacred institutions, sublime doctrines, and solid precepts of morality digested into the same design, and with an admirable concurrence tending to one view, the happiness and exaltation of human nature.

His imagination enlarged by this image of permanence and strength, the speaker makes an easy transition to the traditional contrasting figure of the ephemeral and the shrunken:

> In the midst of my contemplation, I beheld a fly upon one of the pillars; and it straightway came into my head, that this same fly was a Free-Thinker: for it required some comprehension in the eye of the spectator, to take in at one view the various parts of the building, in order to observe their symmetry and design. But to the fly, whose

prospect was confined to a little part of one of the stones of a single pillar, the joint beauty of the whole, or the distinct use of its parts, were inconspicuous, and nothing could appear but small inequalities in the surface of the hewn stone, which in the view of that insect seemed so many deformed rocks and precipices.

This is the equivalent of Pope's insistence in the *Essay on Criticism* that the critic of literature as well as of man and his institutions shall

Survey the *Whole*, nor seek slight Faults to find.

(235)

It is also suggestive of Pope's reprehension of the fly's 'microscopic eye' as an instrument fit for human use: man is the only creature whose dignity is a function of his capacity for viewing 'wholes'. He deviates from his humanity as he loses himself in either 'parts' or microscopy. As the writer of *Guardian* 70 finds, 'The mind of man seems to adapt itself to the different nature of its objects; it is contracted and debased by being conversant in little and low things, and feels a proportionable enlargement arising from the contemplation of . . . great and sublime ideas'. It would be hard to contrive a more precise psychological explanation of Joshua Reynolds's theory of history-painting.

Johnson's infrequent recourse to insect imagery seems more whimsical than the practice of most of the conservatives, although we may suspect that a residue of gentle humanist contempt underlies even such benign sallies as the following. Mrs. Thrale once appeared before him in a dark dress, to be told: 'You little creatures should never wear those sort of clothes . . .; they are unsuitable in every way. What! have not all insects gay colours?' (*BLJ*, i, 495). But Johnson occasionally deploys Swift's and Pope's sense of insect malevolence in the service of the more overtly moral and satiric. In *Rambler* 144, indeed, we find that, just as in *Guardian* 70 the image of the fly seems to harbour curiously near the heroic-architecture figure, so here the insect figure emerges from a deep layer of military imagery. Johnson announces his implicitly Augustinian theme in the first paragraph: 'The first appearance of excellence unites multitudes against it.' And before we know it we are involved in the customary Johnsonian combat between merit and wickedness. He continues: 'unexpected opposition rises up on every side: the celebrated and the obscure join the confederacy; subtlety furnishes arms to impudence, and invention leads on credulity'. As he proceeds, we are conducted by means of the imagery to a view of the battlefield where the 'hostilities' of the 'armies of malignity' are played out before us, where the arrows fly, 'volunteers flock to the standard', and 'multitudes follow the camp only for want of employment . . .'. After considering that in the universal warfare of envy against distinction 'every weapon is accounted lawful', Johnson goes on to classify calumniators, and it is here—in the midst of this humanistic figurative framework—that the insect figure makes its appearance: '. . . as the industry of observation has divided the most miscellaneous and confused assemblages into proper classes, and ranged the insects of the summer, that torment us with their drones or stings, by their several tribes; the persecutors of merit, notwithstanding their numbers, may be likewise commodiously distinguished into Roarers, Whisperers, and Moderators.'

With their devotion to the idea of the permanently human, it is to be expected that the humanists will make much of the contrasting attributes of ephemerae. Such is Burke's emphasis in the *Reflections*. After accusing Dr. Price of a want of humanity for 'exulting' over the downfall of the French royal family, Burke proceeds to direct his addressee's attention to the nature of the real—that is, the typical—Englishman, lest he mistake Dr. Price for a representative man: 'I have often been astonished,' he says, 'considering that we are divided from you but by a slender dyke of about twenty-four miles, and that the mutual intercourse between the two countries has lately been very great, to find how little you seem to know of us.' The general silence of Englishmen in the face of provocative Jacobin publications is not to be interpreted as any kind of acquiescence: 'The vanity, restlessness, petulance, and spirit of intrigue of several petty cabals, who attempt to hide their total want of consequence in bustle and noise, and puffing, and mutual quotation of each other, makes you imagine that our contemptuous neglect of their abilities is a mark of general acquiescence in their opinions. No such thing, I assure you.' And he goes on in a mode reminiscent of the Windsor Castle figure, in the sense that, as we are presented with the 'British oak', we are again the willing victims of a humanistically suggestive heroic rhetoric:

'Because half a dozen grasshoppers under a fern make the field ring with their importunate chink, whilst thousands of great cattle, reposed beneath the shadow of the British oak, chew the cud and are silent, pray do not imagine, that those who make the noise are the only inhabitants of the field; that of course, they are many in number; or that, after all, they are other than the little shrivelled, meagre, hopping, though loud and troublesome insects of the hour.' The image operates largely through the startling opposition between the silent, self-composed longevity of both cattle and the 'British oak', on the one hand, and, on the other, the noisy, self-important transcience of the vermin of nature. A similar figure is put to the same moral use some paragraphs later, where Burke is arguing that once the premises of a set of laws are changed, a citizen is forcibly disconnected from past and future, disinherited, and obliged mechanically to turn traitor to his fathers. And this time the insect figure is accompanied by an architectural image suggestive of the contrasting values of magnitude, permanence, and universality:

... one of the first and most leading principles on which the commonwealth and the laws are consecrated [by being connected with a religious establishment], is lest the temporary possessors and life-renters in it, unmindful of what they have received from their ancestors, or of what is due to their posterity, should act as if they were the entire masters: that they should not think it amongst their rights to cut off the entail, or commit waste on the inheritance, by destroying at their pleasure the whole original fabric of their society; hazarding to leave to those who come after them, a ruin instead of an habitation—and teaching these successors as little to respect their contrivances, as they had themselves respected the institutions of their forefathers.

This image of persons who 'commit waste on the inheritance' suggests Burke's interesting situation as a legatee of Swift's figures and motifs: here we are reminded of Swift's three brothers despoiling a similar sort of 'fabric', just as Burke's next image—we have encountered it earlier—carries us back to the world of Swift's spider allegory: 'By this unprincipled facility of changing the state as often, and as much, and in as many ways, as there are floating fancies or fashions, the whole chain and continuity of the commonwealth would be broken. No one generation could link with the other. Men would become little better than the flies of the summer.'

The humanistic pivot on which these words turn is the term 'better'. The flies of *King Lear*, in all their nastiness, are in Burke's passage, and from words like 'chain' and 'link' we derive the impression that his figure has in part come to him ready-made from Pope's and others' visualizations of the Chain of Being. It is as if Burke were disposing the Chain horizontally instead of vertically and thus making it suggestive less of the paradoxical relation between distinct species than of the dependence of the units upon the 'federal' mystique of the whole. Although Pope's spatial chain is translated by Burke into a temporal one, it is as true of his as of Pope's that

> From Nature's chain whatever link you strike,
> Tenth or ten thousandth, breaks the chain alike.
>
> *(Essay on Man*, i, 245–56)

Discontinuity with the past deprives man of essential humanity and precipitates a rapid descent in the scale of being. If a focus on the eternal can make man angel and a focus on the historical can make him human, a focus on the local and the present makes him a fly.

Gibbon's use of the humanist insect figure is less profound, more like the practice of the Pope of the anti-Grub Street satires. As Harold L. Bond has pointed out in *The Literary Art of Edward Gibbon*, 'From Alexander Pope [Gibbon] may have learned the value of reducing his enemies to the size and form of insects and then displaying his own virtuosity in destroying them.'[1] But much more than Gibbon's—or Pope's—virtuosity is at stake in their insect figures. In Chapter XLVII of the *Decline and Fall*, devoted to the internal disputes of the doctrinaire early Christians, Gibbon covers pages with an ironic, melancholy account of theological abuse and violence. Mangled corpses and fired cities are the inevitable product of doctrinal controversy. Gibbon pauses to consider the intolerant theology and polity of the fanatic Christian emperor Justinian, whose mechanical anti-paganism and anti-semitism make him appear a near relative of Swift's Jack, just as his talent for quarrels relates him to the 'little odious vermin' stigmatized by the King

[1] (Oxford, 1960), pp. 128–9.

of Brobdingnag. As Gibbon says, 'he piously laboured to establish with fire and sword the unity of the Christian faith'. Justinian and his kept theologues are finally reduced in Gibbon's hands to noxious insects, destroying whatever they light upon through a sort of mechanical malevolence: of Justinian's attacks on some dead heretics, Gibbon writes: 'If they were already in the fangs of the dæmon, their torments could neither be aggravated nor assuaged by human industry. If in the company of saints and angels they enjoyed the rewards of piety, they must have smiled at the idle fury of the theological insects who still crawled on the surface of the earth. The foremost of these insects, the emperor of the Romans, darted his sting, and distilled his venom . . .'. Gibbon's virtuosity is exhibited here, to be sure; but perhaps more to the point is the appearance of the traditional humanistic image of the sub-human in the customary service of moral satire. In the *Decline and Fall* it is monks and hermits who 'swarm'; Christians who multiply like maggots; religious parasites and 'administrators' who arrive like locusts to devour the land and darken the sky; and doctors of the church who, like Pope's medieval schoolmen and Swift's self-sufficient spider, spin out their sticky cobwebs manufactured from the internal metaphysical obscure.

It can be said in general that the writers of the eighteenth century will appear to exhibit humanistic habits of response to the degree that they exploit the possibilities of moral contempt which reside in images of insects. Perhaps it is not going too far to say that the insect figure can serve as a sort of index or touchstone of eighteenth-century humanism. George Crabbe, who begins as a minor but committed humanist and whose powers are gradually drawn to a pure and self-sufficient narrative irony and symbolism, manifests his humanist devotion largely in his early work, and it is in an early poem like *The Newspaper* (1785) that we encounter images like the following, where the antithesis between literature and journalism is felt to resemble the distinction between man and insects; newspapers, says Crabbe, are both too mechanically predictable and too evanescent:

> In shoals the hours their constant numbers bring,
> Like insects waking to th' advancing spring;
> Which take their rise from grubs obscene that lie
> In shallow pools, or thence ascend the sky:

Such are these base ephemeras, so born
To die before the next revolving morn.

(65–70)

And to Crabbe the effect of newspapers on the mind of the apprehender can be suggested most adequately in insect terms:

Like idle flies, a busy, buzzing train,
They drop their maggots in the trifler's brain;
That genial soil receives the fruitful store,
And there they grow, and breed a thousand more.

(103–6)

It is well to remember here that the advent of newspapers, with all their general implications of the attractions of daily 'newness' and timeliness, is almost precisely coincident with the flowering in the late seventeenth-century of the idea of progress and with the whole optimistic syndrome underlying the modern world. Crabbe's disgust with newspapers becomes equivalent to the sort of rejection of that world expressed in his ministerial career as well as in such later narratives as those in *The Borough*.

A non-humanist like Cowper, on the other hand, usually misses the appropriate tone of contempt even when he apes in other respects the humanistic use of the insect figure. In Book III of *The Task*, for example, while exposing the bulk of mankind as 'wand'rers' devoted to 'Dreams, empty dreams', he invokes the image of the fly, but with what a significant difference:

The million flit as gay
As if created only like the fly,
That spreads his motley wings in th' eye of noon,
To sport their season, and be seen no more.

(133–6)

It is the gaiety and the sport that ring false here and suggest that Cowper has attended closely neither to flies nor to 'the million'. Although still apparently enlisted in the service of general moral satire—albeit benign—the insect figure in Cowper's hands diminishes to cliché, and the image dissolves into visual vagueness and ethical incoherence. Any reader of *King Lear* knows that flies are not 'gay'. Cowper is engaged in bringing to birth Sterne's Uncle Toby, who, ejecting a fly from the dining-room, addresses him thus: 'Go poor devil, get thee gone, why should I hurt thee?—This world surely is wide enough to hold both thee and me.'

To perceive just what has happened in Cowper and in Uncle Toby we must turn back to dwell upon Pope's exquisite manipulation of the insect image as an emblem of humanistic contempt for that which is below man and towards which, alas, man's depraved nature perpetually urges him. We may say of Pope what Walter Raleigh says of Carlyle: 'A certain exercise of contempt was necessary to [his] mind, to keep it in health.'[2] The opposition between the orthodox and the heterodox vision of insects, between, that is, Pope's and Sterne's personal and imaginative worlds, is suggested in a modern treatment—admittedly a slight one—of the theme of insects trapped in amber. A poem by A. Kulik, which appeared in the New York *Times* for 29 April 1956, exhibits the final exhaustion of the Uncle Toby tradition. Addressing a 'Fossil Insect in Amber', Mr. Kulik takes pains to humanize and thus to dignify his insect:

> Your pale wings caught in frozen flight
> Are poised as if you stopped to hear
> Some rhythm in your lambent night,
> Some clock-like cadence in your ear.

Mr. Kulik proceeds to make of his fossilized insect a metaphoric register of the undefined eternal and thus, we are asked to assume, the significant:

> I hope that you may never learn
> Just what it is you listen to.
> For the sound you hear can only be
> The ticking of eternity.

I bring forth this example less to ridicule Mr. Kulik than to suggest how utterly instinctive the a-humanistic attitude towards insects has become since the eighteenth century. Or at least in the special, conventional world of rhetoric and the poem, where the assumptions about insects are remarkably different from those betrayed on the label of the aerosol bomb. After Mr. Kulik, who will not be refreshed to return to the *Epistle to Arbuthnot* and to hear Pope's response to the phenomenon of insects trapped in amber? Satirizing verbal and punc-

---

[2] *Six Essays on Johnson* (Oxford, 1910), p. 140.

tuational critics, 'Each Word-catcher that lives on syllables', Pope equates Milton's and Shakespeare's emenders and commentators with the bugs preserved to all time in blocks of amber. His 'Pretty!' constitutes a totally ironic thrust of contempt which exposes all the more painfully Mr. Kulik's genuine discovery of beauty and high significance in the object of his concern:

> Pretty! in Amber to observe the forms
> Of hairs, or straws, or dirt, or grubs, or worms;
> The things, we know, are neither rich nor rare,
> But wonder how the Devil they got there?
>
> (169–72)

Which is a humanistic way of saying that annotators who focus on parts at the expense of wholes transform themselves into subhuman creatures. In Book IV of *The Dunciad* Bentley is made to utter this ironically wise appraisal of the techniques applied in common by verbal critics, microscopists, and insects:

> The critic Eye, that microscope of Wit,
> Sees hairs and pores, examines bit by bit:
> How parts relate to parts, or they to whole,
> The body's harmony, the beaming soul,
> Are things which Kuster, Burman, Wasse shall see,
> When Man's whole frame is obvious to a *Flea*.
>
> (233–8)

Those who attend to the bug instead of the amber, the mere item instead of the context, are like the 'partial critics' satirized in the *Essay on Criticism*. They

> See Nature in some partial narrow shape,
> And let the Author of the whole escape.
>
> (*Dunciad*, iv, 455–6)

Pope's very first satire, *To the Author of a Poem, intitled Successio* (that is, to Elkanah Settle), shows its fourteen-year-old author to be already an adept at the imagery of contemptible insects as well as at the technique of rhetorical dualism. Offering Settle some mock-consolation, the boy Pope writes:

> What tho' no Bees around your Cradle flew,
> Nor on your Lips distill'd their golden Dew?
> Yet have we oft discover'd in their stead,
> A Swarm of Drones, that buzz'd about your Head.
>
> (5–8)

A quarter of a century later, inspired by *Gulliver's Travels*, Pope contrives a happy humanistic opposition between the idea of insects and his conviction of the urgency of human moral imperatives. The poem is *The Words of the King of Brobdingnag, As he held Captain* GULLIVER *between his Finger and Thumb for the Inspection of the Sages and Learned Men of the Court*. The King's first reaction to Gulliver's person succeeds in transforming him into an insect placed on a glass slide for microscopic scrutiny:

> In Miniature see *Nature's* Power appear;
> Which wings the Sun-born Insects of the Air,
> Which frames the Harvest-bug, too small for Sight,
> And forms the Bones and Muscles of the Mite!
> Here view him stretch'd. The Microscope explains
> That the Blood, circling, flows in human Veins;
> See, in the Tube he pants, and sprawling lies,
> Stretches his little Hands, and rolls his Eyes!
>
> (1–8)

The next verse-paragraph explains why Pope is impelled to image Gulliver as insect: Gulliver even after his travels remains parochial, afflicted with a 'partial view'. The King goes on:

> Smit with his Countrey's Love, I've heard him prate
> Of Laws and Manners in his Pigmy State.
>
> (9–10)

And the ninth line here, by recalling Milton's

> Smit with the love of sacred song . . .
>
> (*PL*, iii, 29)

helps enforce an antithesis between, on the one hand, the love of mere local, temporary customs or modes of humanity and, on the other, the love of literature, which is to say, uniform human nature realized and formalized. As the King has learned through his conversations with Gulliver,

> Fond of his Hillock Isle, his narrow Mind
> Thinks Worth, Wit, Learning, to that Spot confin'd;

So with insects, the poor stupid things:

> Thus Ants, who for a Grain employ their Cares,
> Think all the Business of the Earth is theirs.
> Thus Honey-combs seem Palaces to Bees;
> And Mites imagine all the World a Cheese.
>
> (25–30)

Struck with the Chain-of-Being implications of Gulliver's fatuity, the King concludes his utterance by reminding his noble auditors that, despite their size, they themselves are perhaps only one or two jumps up the hierarchy from insect Gulliver. Since vanity and parochialism are insect attributes, it behoves those who are not bugs by nature to look to themselves:

> When Pride in such contemptuous Beings lies,
> In Beetles, Britons, Bugs, and Butterflies,
> Shall we, like Reptiles, glory in Conceit?
> Humility's the Virtue of the Great.

> (31–34)

Another Popian *jeu d'esprit* which derives its chief strength from the humanistic scorn for the vermin of nature is the poem *To Mr. John Moore, Author of the Celebrated Worm Powder*, written around 1716. The Augustinian proposition which this poem sets itself to demonstrate is that

> All Humankind are Worms,

but Pope's 'All' is designed to be polemic rather than descriptive: his satire exposes only the learned stupid man, the nymphomaniac, the fop, the flatterer, the miser, the corrupt politician, the courtier, and the coffee-house wit, only those, that is, whose actions, disgracing human nature, would persuade any objective observer of the validity of the initial proposition. For example:

> The Learn'd themselves we Book-Worms name;
> The Blockhead is a Slow-worm;
> The Nymph whose Tail is all on Flame
> Is aptly term'd a Glow-worm.

> (13–16)

Marvell's benign glow worm, with its 'dear light', has been transformed by the microscope and by Pope's hierarchical imagination into an undeniably luscious but still contemptible mock-pastoral 'Nymph'. And in *The Dunciad* it is Dulness herself who awards degrees and honours to those who, in Royal Societies, have learned to 'Impale a Glow-worm' (iv, 569). Like lubricious 'Nymphs', fops are vermin too: they are 'painted Butterflies'. The flatterer is, naturally, an earwig; misers become 'Muckworms'; beaus, silkworms;

> And Death-watches, Physicians.

Politicians, worms by calling if not by nature, generate smaller worms—consciences—to bite 'em. We proceed to mock-moralizing in the elegiac vein as Pope turns to address John Moore directly:

> O learned Friend of *Abchurch-Lane*,
> Who sett'est our Entrails free!
> Vain is thy Art, thy Powder vain,
> Since Worms shall eat ev'n thee.

And the final stanza prolongs the air of mock-morality to transform it halfway through into political wit as Pope jibes at the Whig—to Pope, 'Modern'—small politicians and kept journalists who infest Button's coffee-house. Still addressing Moore, Pope says:

> Our Fate thou only can'st adjourn
> Some few short Years, no more!
> Ev'n *Button's* Wits to Worms shall turn,
> Who Maggots were before.

Given the larger background against which this poem takes place, there is much more here than mere waspish abuse or even an attempt at 'virtuosity', of which, actually, there is very little at all. Pope is making a moral point, and he is making one that in his moral context could hardly be made without recourse to insect imagery. The imagery becomes something very like the substance, rather than the décor, of his expression.

Maggots, their every mechanic impulse urging them towards fully developed verminhood, present themselves to Pope as ready emblems of the self-corrupted and the morally uncertain. Thus we are told in the *Essay on Criticism*,

> Some neither can for *Wits* nor *Criticks* pass,
> As heavy Mules are neither *Horse* nor *Ass*.
> Those half-learn'd Witlings, num'rous in our Isle,
> As half-form'd Insects on the Banks of *Nile*;
> Unfinish'd Things, one knows not what to call,
> Their Generation's so *equivocal*.

(38–43)

And in Grub Street, as we might expect, the publisher Jacob Tonson plays the role of sun or even sun-god and broods over the generation of the vile, ambiguous creations—most of them unidentifiable or ambiguous genres—which are modern litera-

ture. In Book I of *The Dunciad*, Dulness, peering down into the
minor chasm of Grub Street,

> beholds the Chaos dark and deep,
> Where nameless Somethings in their Causes sleep,
> 'Till genial Jacob, or a warm Third day,
> Call forth each mass, a Poem, or a Play.

The goddess perceives also

> How hints, like spawn, scarce quick in embryo lie,
> How new-born nonsense first is taught to cry,
> Maggots half-form'd in rhyme exactly meet,
> And learn to crawl upon poetic feet.
>
> (55–62)

Although now and then Pope will pause to find beauty in the
spider, as he does in the first Epistle of the *Essay on Man*:

> The spider's touch, how exquisitely fine!
> Feels at each thread, and lives along the line:
>
> (217–18)

his customary practice is, like Swift, to find in the spider an
emblem of ugliness, self-satisfaction, showy complexity, and
complacent obscurantism. Far from being 'noiseless' and
'patient', Pope's spiders create so much perverse disturbance
that satire is the only weapon left against them. In Dialogue II
of the *Epilogue to the Satires* flattering courtiers who obscure the
light of humanistic truth can be threatened only by satire:

> Ye tinsel Insects! whom a Court maintains,
> That counts your Beauties only by your Stains,
> Spin all your Cobwebs o'er the Eye of Day!
> The Muse's wing shall brush you all away:
> All his Grace preaches, all his Lordship sings,
> All that makes Saints of Queens, and Gods of Kings.
>
> (220–5)

As dangerous to humanity as the flatterers of the Great are bad
modern writers, with their temporary subjects, their unprecedented caddish tone, and their quaint techniques. They are
perhaps less susceptible to satiric correction than their counterparts at court, as we are informed in the *Epistle to Arbuthnot*:

> Who shames a Scribler? break one cobweb thro',
> He spins the slight, self-pleasing thread anew;

Destroy his Fib, or Sophistry; in vain
The Creature's at his dirty work again;
Thron'd in the Centre of his thin designs;
Proud of a vast Extent of flimzy lines.

(89–94)

And the medieval Schoolmen of course become pre-eminent cobweb weavers in Pope's hands. Because they were insufficiently attentive to the permanent and the total in human nature, the medieval Fathers are now relegated to the shabbiest of the second-hand book stores. Pope transforms them into spiders in the *Essay on Criticism*:

> *Scotists* and *Thomists*, now, in Peace remain,
> Amidst their *kindred Cobwebs* in *Duck-Lane*.

(444–5)

In one sense, Pope is merely recovering a Renaissance symbolic orthodoxy in these images of spiders. As Aubrey Williams has pointed out in his *Pope's Dunciad*: 'by the humanist the dialectitian is likely to be described as the spider that spins forth [as Bacon says] "cobwebs of learning, admirable for the fineness of thread and work, but of no substance or profit" . . .'.[3] But traditional as the Renaissance spider image is, it becomes sharpened and focused in the eighteenth century both by the new revelations of microscopy and by such findings in aesthetics as Hogarth's. He discovers in *The Analysis of Beauty* that the spider—like the toad, the hog, and the bear—is ugly because it is 'totally void' of the 'waving-line' which, by uniting variety and uniformity, constitutes the paradigm of the beautiful.

It is true that in *The Rape of the Lock* the pleasant sylphs are often imaged as insects, and as delightful insects. But we miss the delicate irony here if we forget what the sylphs really are: they are the reincarnated souls of 'light Coquettes', whose pleasures, when alive, were bounded by cards, chariots, and changeable flirtations. The Popian contempt for insects and the insect-like is mitigated and softened in *The Rape of the Lock*, but it is still abundantly there. His moral disdain for self-indulgent instability is a constant in his career. The mechanical 'levity' of insect flight, its apparent purposelessness, is the equivalent of the 'unfixed principles' of coquettes and those who admire them.

[3] (London, 1955), p. 107.

The sylphs are undeniably beautiful, but their beauty is to be apprehended in Pope's terms. Like the coquettes they used to be, they are ultimately only another, and a deceptively attractive, species of the vermin of nature. Pope's treatment of 'Rufa' and 'Sappho' in the *Epistle to a Lady* (*Moral Essay* II) shows the association his intelligence usually made between a whimsical changeableness in female character and the evanescence of insect life. What is wanted, as he tells Martha Blount late in the poem, is 'Fix'd Principles' (279): what one sees too often, on the other hand, is an insect-like inconstancy:

> Rufa, whose eye quick-glancing o'er the Park,
> Attracts each light gay meteor of a Spark,
> Agrees as ill with Rufa studying Locke,
> As Sappho's diamonds with her dirty smock,
> Or Sappho at her toilet's greasy task,
> With Sappho fragrant at an evening Mask.

Such changeableness—a mode of personal incoherence, after all—is both physically and morally like that of ephemerae, and contemplating Rufa and Sappho Pope instantly proceeds to thrust forward the most appropriate figure for illustrating his moral argument:

> So morning Insects that in muck begun,
> Shine, buzz, and fly-blow in the setting-sun.
>
> (21–28)

That is, one day is all it takes for flies to change from maggots to full-grown breeders. Quite like the eye and mind of Belinda in *The Rape of the Lock*, they are 'Quick' and 'unfix'd' (ii, 9–10).

Thus through the moral metamorphoses of Pope's imagery, coquettes turn flies; the equivocal Sporus in the *Epistle to Arbuthnot* begins as a quasi-silkworm, alters to a butterfly, and ends as a 'Bug with gilded wings' (309); bad critics are 'like some poor part-lived vermin that die of shooting their own stings' (*CAP*, ii, 353); the impertinent are gnats (*CAP*, ii, 378); Cibber in his role as plagiary is 'an industrious Bug' (*Dunciad*, i, 130); and amateur natural scientists and inhumane collectors become 'Locusts black'ning all the ground' (*Dunciad* iv, 397), just like Burke's similarly 'modern' revolutionaries, whom he images, in the *Letter to a Noble Lord*, as 'innumerable swarms of the lowest, and at once the most destructive, of the classes of

S

animated nature . . .'. These vermin, 'like columns of locusts, have laid waste the fairest part of the world'.

When we find Pope telling Henry Brooke, 'I sincerely worship God, believe in his revelations, . . . [and] love all his creatures' (*CAP*, iv, 207), we will have to recall Johnson on Pope's letters: 'There is . . . no transaction which offers stronger temptations to fallacy and sophistication than epistolary intercourse.' Pope certainly does not love all of God's creatures, and for a good reason: to love insects would be equivalent to loving earthquakes, floods, erupting volcanoes, and other 'trespasses' of nature. We can easily imagine Pope in a less sophistical mood assuming the role of Mercury in Ben Jonson's *Mercury Vindicated from the Alchemists at Court* (1615). Here Mercury taxes Vulcan with the creation of creatures resembling nature's vermin: 'Art thou not ashamed, Vulcan', he says, 'to offer, in defence of thy power and art, against the excellence of the sun and nature, creatures more imperfect than the very flies and insects that are her trespasses and scapes?' It is their conviction of the reality of moral hierarchy that prompts Pope and his humanist successors to oppose the idea of man against the image of these vermin. Moral hierarchy is a principle so indispensable that it operates even within the world of insects. In *Fable* VIII John Gay contrasts the wasp with 'vulgar flies' to the distinct social as well as moral disadvantage of the latter. And to the humanists there is danger in *not* insisting through all the devices of moral contempt on the ugliness, the nastiness, and the viciousness of these 'inferior powers'. Listen to Pope's passionate celebration of the Great Chain of Being, and notice the moral implications of the last line and a half:

> Vast chain of being, which from God began,
> Natures aethereal, human, angel, man,
> Beast, bird, fish, insect! what no eye can see,
> No glass can reach! from Infinite to thee,
> From thee to Nothing!

And here we come to the essential ethical imperative:

> On superior pow'rs
> Were we to press, inferior might on ours.
>
> (*Essay on Man*, i, 237–42)

What lies behind Pope's circumspection here is the traditional humanistic sense of the disaster that beleaguered man invites when he fails to recognize his limits: affecting a god-like self-sufficiency, he leaves his link empty, to be occupied instantly by the brutal nature lying below him. His chief defence against disorder is to study the paradoxical nature of his kind so thoroughly, to become so adept at the knowledge of permanent human nature, that nature which aspires always to the angelic and is tempted always to the brutal, that he will recognize the sub-human for what it is, the proper object of a fully imaginative moral contempt.

THE OPEN—AND IRONIC—ROAD

THE motif of travel, of movement over the open road, is a constant in all literature, from Homer and Dante and Chaucer and Bunyan to such beautiful contemporary diminished things as Frost's 'The Road Not Taken'. Eighteenth-century writers, fully committed as they were to Lockean psychology, produced perhaps slightly more than their share of travel books, travel images, and travel motifs. Indeed, it is easy to forget that the travel book was one of the chief eighteenth-century genres, a genre so appealing in both focus and conventions that almost every writer of consequence—regardless of his moral orientation—chose at some point to work in the form, from Defoe and Addison to Fielding, Smollett, Boswell, Johnson, and Sterne. It hardly needs pointing out that countless works of a more overtly fictional cast tended to ape the travel book: we think of *Gulliver's Travels*, *Joseph Andrews*, and *Rasselas*. In poetry the immense vogue of the 'excursion poem'—Goldsmith titled his exercise in this 'kind' *The Traveller*—reflects the appeal of the prose genre which is its ancestor and analogue. Pope's invitation to Bolingbroke, at the outset of the *Essay on Man*, to 'Expatiate free o'er all this scene of Man' (i, 5) enacts the prime intellectual and psychological invitation of Augustan travel literature. When the twenty-three-year-old Wordsworth wanted to appear in print poetically, it was natural for him to do so under the title *Descriptive Sketches Taken During a Pedestrian Tour Among the Alps* (1793): an audience for 'tours', whether couched in Johnson's prose or in Wordsworth's early heroic couplets, was abundant and prepared to respond with excitement. This audience is largely the same one that sustained the vogue of the picaresque in the novel. Indeed, the eighteenth-century literature we know would hardly be recognizable if we excised from it all its memorable images of a rational and sturdy observer—a combined Spectator and Rambler—wandering about foreign parts, collecting data, patronizing the natives, and reporting his findings for the benefit of stay-at-homes. These images derive not only from our memories of such real personages as Samuel Johnson in the Hebrides and James Boswell on the Grand Tour, but also from a host of fictive counterparts so various—and yet thematically so similar—as the speaker who traverses London in Gay's *Trivia*, Lemuel Gulliver, Lien Chi Altangi of Goldsmith's *Citizen of the World*, and the young Simkin Blunderhead of Christopher Anstey's *New Bath Guide*.

And in one important way the motif of travel, at least travel undertaken as a mode of objective inquiry, appears to be almost a unique property of the eighteenth century. There is something about both the actual experience of travel and the literary experience of the travel report, whether straight, ironic, or 'sentimental', that comes very near the heart of the dominant eighteenth-century idea of knowledge. Knowledge was assumed to result from the sequential accumulation of sense particulars collected from a multifarious but verifiable objective reality. The contemporary plausibility of Lockean psychology thus furnishes the context for the flourishing of the travel book as one of the most vigorous of the contemporary kinds. As Jean H. Hagstrum has said, 'If one is . . . committed to outside reality rather than to introspection, it becomes even more necessary to vary that reality by travel and by the extended observation that it provides.'[1] And in the same way the acceptability of the psychology of Locke helps to generate not merely a multitude of travel books but an even larger number of significant travel images and motifs.

The symbolic journey in the Middle Ages and the Renaissance is likely to be a form of pilgrimage, a journey from Southwark to Canterbury or from this world to the next. The quest is for some supernatural certainty, or at least some supernatural experience. In the nineteenth century the characteristic symbolic journey takes the form of a subjective exploration into the inner recesses of the secret self. The monistic achievements of the unifying, 'esemplastic' imagination are here the goal of the quest. But in the eighteenth century travel is neither an upward

[1] 'Some Opportunities for Research in Eighteenth-Century Literature', *Newberry Library Bulletin*, iii (1954), 180.

nor an inward quest: it is empirical tourism, and when we do sense the presence of elements of the quest, as in Boswell's European jaunts, the quest is for knowledge of actual men and manners, or for knowledge of permanent, common human nature. Outlooks rather than insights are likely to be the goal. Most eighteenth-century writers use the motif of the journey as an occasion for this kind of Lockean discovery. But the Augustan humanists seem to distinguish themselves by a riper, more ironic use of the same motif: they exploit it as an occasion for moral irony and as a device for exposing the frailty of mankind. To juxtapose Defoe's *Tour through England and Wales* with Johnson's *Journey to the Western Islands* is to perceive an important difference between the 'modern' and the humanistic in the travel book. Defoe focuses on the benefits of trade and the progress of industry. To him, the merit of a city or town is a function of its manufactures; the idea of progress lurks behind each of his responses and judgments. But Johnson, betraying the natural turn for elegy with which all humanists are afflicted, focuses on the past, and on the enduring, the permanent, and the unchanging. What emerges from Johnson's travel book is not the sense of kinesis and change that Defoe projects: it is instead the colossal and permanent irony of tiny man attempting to defeat time and the elements by works of stone, the ultimate irony of man's attempt to defeat mortality by works of virtue. On the other hand, the road that Defoe chooses to explore is a precursor of Whitman's in *Song of the Open Road*:

> Afoot and light-hearted I take to the open road,
> Healthy, free, the world before me,
> The long brown path before me leading wherever I choose.

(1–3)

Whiggery, Johnson would respond. Defoe and Whitman are prepared for no complications, and they encounter none. But the road that Johnson explores not merely in his *Journey* but in *Rasselas* and in the numerous smaller figures of travel which animate his prose is a complex, ironic, untrustworthy road. Sometimes it is like Christian's in *The Pilgrim's Progress*, but more often it is like that depicted by Rochester in his *Satyr Against Mankind*, a path, initially rugged enough, from which Reason, that '*Ignis fatuus*, in the *Mind*', seduces the traveller to stumble through

Pathless and dang'rous wandrings ways. . . .,
Through errors, Fenny-*Boggs*, and Thorny *Brakes*;

(14–15)

or the road of the *'weary, wandring* Travellers', who, at the beginning of Dryden's *Religio Laici*, find themselves benighted both by the dimness of moonlight and starlight and by the dim inadequacy of their own unassisted reason. The travel motif is most often exploited by the Augustan humanists to reinforce their conviction of human inadequacy and their apprehension of the liability of man to the disappointment of his hopes.

To a Lockean, the very act of writing is like travelling: one begins at home in the centre of the individual personality and moves outward through systems of objectively meaningful rhetorical symbolism to the destination of the journey, the emotions and will of the anonymous reader. In both travel and expression, the movement is from inside outward, rather than, as it will come to seem a century later, from outside in. And writing is like travelling in the additional sense that an act of composition, when it is what it ought to be, is a planned movement from a starting-point to a known destination. In writing as in travelling the most direct route from beginning to end is the best: digressions, divagations, or detours are equally tiresome in both. This is the import of the elaborate travel image which opens Section XI of *A Tale of a Tub*. In this section the modern speaker has finally returned to his narrative after four sections of 'digressions'; he has detoured once to praise digressions, once to 'reason' over the mysteries of the Aeolists, again to speculate with an ironical mad wisdom about the uses of madness in a commonwealth, and finally to brag after the modern way about the subtlety and complexity of his own book.

Returning at long last to the narrative of Jack, the writer senses that some kind of critical explanation of all the preceding divagations is appropriate. But even in his explanation his erratic course betrays his unstable will:

After so wide a Compass as I have wandred, I do now gladly overtake, and close in with my Subject, and shall henceforth hold on with it at an even Pace to the End of my Journey,

—thus far his purpose holds, but no further:

except some beautiful Prospect appears within sight of my Way; whereof, tho' at present I have neither Warning nor Expectation, yet upon such an Accident, come when it will, I shall beg my Readers Favour and Company, allowing me to conduct him thro' it along with my self.

An overt analogy is now appropriate:

For in *Writing*, it is as in *Travelling*: If a Man is in haste to be at home, (which I acknowledge to be none of my Case, having never so little Business, as when I am there) if his *Horse* be tired with long Riding, and ill Ways, or be naturally a Jade, I advise him clearly to make the straitest and commonest Road, be it ever so dirty. . . .

Perhaps the most illuminating gloss on the speaker's parenthesis is Pope's observation to Hugh Bethel, 'one's chief business is to be really at home' (*CAP*, ii, 386), a remark which implies most of the Augustan attitude towards man's moral duties within the overwhelming, incomprehensible universe in which he finds himself. The 'straitest and commonest Road' implies that contract with the reader which the premise of the uniformity of human nature makes almost a moral imperative. The speaker here, devoted to digressions and surprises, will have none of it: 'On the other side, when a Traveller and his *Horse* are in Heart and Plight, when his Purse is full, and the Day before him; he takes the Road only where it is clean or convenient; entertains his Company there as agreeably he can; but upon the first Occasion, carries them along with him to every delightful Scene in View, whether of Art, or Nature, or of both; and if they chance to refuse out of Stupidity or Weariness; let them jog on by themselves, and be d—n'd . . .'. The self-satisfaction of this tour-guide finds a natural outlet in the final three-word directive, which is entirely worthy of the rhetoric of Swift's Peter engaged in the task of persuading his brothers that a twelve-penny loaf is actually '*excellent good Mutton*'. This is the rhetoric with which Swift's modern writer is obliged to justify his outrageous penchant for detours and confusion. Like a fatuous and self-satisfied traveller, Swift's writer grows more certain of his location and direction the more 'lost' he becomes.

The thing Swift contrives that his self-sufficient speaker shall not recognize is that the road is dangerous, delusive, and supremely difficult. This realization is the one projected by Pope's famous figure in the *Essay on Criticism* of learning as alpine journeying, the figure to which Johnson, in the *Life of Pope*, responded in these extravagant moral as well as literary terms: 'the comparison of a student's progress in the sciences with the journey of a traveller in the Alps is perhaps the best that English poetry can shew'. Pope's image works by exploiting the irony resident in the physical fact that the higher the traveller climbs the more of the road and the landscape is revealed to him. As learners we begin, like Swift's modern writer, with full confidence in the human capacity to complete the journey:

> Fir'd at first Sight with what the *Muse* imparts,
> In *fearless Youth* we tempt the Heights of Arts,
> While from the bounded *Level* of our Mind,
> *Short Views* we take, nor see the *Lengths behind*.

Pope's 'bounded *Level*' is exactly a foreshadowing of Johnson's mountain-enclosed Happy Valley, in which the 'fearless' and naïve youth Rasselas speculates on the ease and delight with which he will accumulate knowledge once he is released from the towering confines of the valley. But an illuminating surprise awaits Pope's youth just as a whole series of surprises and disappointments awaits Johnson's:

> But *more advanc'd*, behold with strange Surprize
> New, distant Scenes of endless *Science* rise!

The journey that has begun with fire and enthusiasm ends with exhaustion, and the eyes that at first were clear and readily fixed on the accessible goal now wander in wonderment:

> Th' *increasing* Prospect *tires* our wandring Eyes,
> Hills peep o'er Hills, and *Alps* on *Alps* arise!
> (219–32)

The road that appears so straight, simple, and benign to a Defoe or a Whitman proves to the humanist to conduct the traveller finally to delusion and disappointment, but not merely to those destinations alone: it conducts him also to the very kind of wisdom which, for example, Thomas Gray would withhold from his young Eton innocents.

But Pope does not always conceive of roads as instruments for complicating experience. Sometimes his argument requires that his roads and paths be clear, open, and well lighted. Such is 'Nature's path' in the *Essay on Man*: to attain earthly happiness we are exhorted to

> Take Nature's path, and mad Opinion's leave,
> All states can reach it, and all heads conceive;
> Obvious her goods, in no extreme they dwell. . . .
>
> (iv, 29–31)

The figure of the clear and open road of permanent human sense as opposed to the cranky trail of temporary, limited personal 'Opinion' is reinforced by the Latin implications of 'Obvious', a word whose etymological sense is preserved by such a rendering as 'standing in the middle of the road'. Johnson's initial definition is 'Meeting any thing'. So clear are the benefits of hewing to the centre of man's experience. Again, in the *Essay on Man*, the Latin sense of 'deviate', which is almost entirely retained in Johnson's definition, 'To wander from the right or common way', intensifies the covert figure of Nature and Will rambling off the open *via* in a mistaken quest for the un-obvious:

> What makes all physical or moral ill?
> There deviates Nature, and here wanders Will.
>
> (iv, 111–12)

Happiness is thus in the power of him who stays on the highway, of the man who is

> Slave to no sect, who takes no private road,

but instead

> . . . looks thro' Nature, up to Nature's God.
>
> (iv, 331–2)

Pope's instructions here—or are they Bolingbroke's?—sound a little too easy. When we turn to Johnson's manipulation of the image of the open road we encounter again the refreshing complications of a high irony. Johnson seems never to forget the shape or the implications of Pope's alpine figure. He is strongly drawn to images of mountain-climbing, as in *The Vision of Theodore*, and such images are frequently used to suggest the difficulties encountered by the will when in the act of 'inventing' literary materials and techniques. In *Rambler* 21, for example, he asserts that 'The garlands gained by the heroes of literature must be gathered from summits equally difficult to climb with those that bear the civick or triumphal wreaths. . . .' Like the road trod by Dryden's all but totally lost wanderers, the symbolic traveller in Johnson moves on roads which are dark, obscure, and untrustworthy: they abound with fogs, snares, pitfalls, and ambuscades, and false fires perpetually lure the traveller into fatal marshes and fens. In *The Vanity of Human Wishes* Johnson announces early that a large part of his theme will be

> how hope and fear, desire and hate,
> O'erspread with snares the clouded maze of fate,
> Where wav'ring man, betray'd by vent'rous pride,
> To tread the dreary paths without a guide,
> As treach'rous phantoms in the mist delude,
> Shuns fancied ills, or chases airy good.
>
> (5–10)

To Johnson, a 'wav'ring man' treading 'the dreary paths without a guide' seems always a type of the husband who has lost his spouse. Such at least would seem to be the import of his repeated use of the same image elsewhere. Writing Mrs. Thrale in 1776, for example, Johnson reveals that he is unable to contemplate the death of his acquaintance V. J. Peyton without recalling the travel imagery of *The Vanity of Human Wishes*: he tells Mrs. Thrale that 'Poor Peyton' is dead after having been tied to a hopelessly ill wife for years, and then he speculates with his usual ironic and pathetic thrust: 'he probably thought often how lightly he should tread the path of life without his burthen' (*LSJ*, ii, 120). Even more poignantly Johnson, in writing Thomas Warton in 1754, recalls his dead Tetty—only two years gone—in the same symbolic terms of the traveller who does not know where he is: 'You know poor Mr. Dodsly has lost his Wife, I believe he is much affected. I hope he will not suffer so much as I yet suffer for the loss of mine. . . . I have ever since seemed to myself broken off from mankind a kind of solitary wanderer in the wild of life, without any certain direction, or fixed point of view. A gloomy gazer on a World to which I have little relation' (*LSJ*, i, 59).

Whether accompanied by guides or not, even the wisest of wayfarers are not proof against delusion in their travels. Shakespeare himself, we are told in Johnson's *Preface*, sometimes deviates while chasing puns: 'A quibble is to Shakespeare, what luminous vapours are to the traveller; he follows it at all adventures: it is sure to lead him out of his way, and sure to engulf him in the mire.' William Collins is another writer who 'deviates' from the open road of Nature. As Johnson explains in the *Life of Collins*, 'His mind [is] not deficient in fire, . . . but somewhat obstructed in its progress by deviation in quest of mistaken beauties.'

Two of Johnson's works of the 1750's, the *Preface to the Dictionary* (1755) and the preface to John Payne's *New Tables of Interest* (1758), conduct their arguments by means of images of foot travel. The travel image generates the most irony in the *Dictionary* preface, where it becomes suggestive of the delusions of hope, the imminence of failure, and the salutary moral comedy of disappointment. Some eight years before, Johnson had already implied that he was going to be fond of envisaging the making of dictionaries in terms of the frustrations and longeurs of foot travel. In *The Plan of an English Dictionary*, addressed to Lord Chesterfield in 1747, he had suggested that to most people lexicography seems to ask for no higher talents than those required for 'beating the track of the alphabet with sluggish resolution'. (In the *Dictionary* Johnson defined *track* as 'A road; a beaten path'.) And when the *Dictionary* with its preface finally appeared, he is still resolutely adhering to the image of travel as the readiest device for suggesting the ironies of lexicography. Mankind, he says, associating his travel figure with his customary military one, have long considered the maker of dictionaries as the mere 'pioneer of literature, doomed only to remove rubbish and clear obstructions from the paths through which Learning and Genius press forward to conquest and glory . . .'. Early philologists are travellers just like their contemporary counterparts. Discussing his use of the etymologies of Junius and Skinner, Johnson chooses to contrast them this way: 'the learning of Junius is often of no other use than to shew him a track by which he may deviate from his purpose, to which Skinner always presses forward by the shortest way'. A lexicographer's searches into other books are 'excursions', but none of these excursions proves as simple as it first appears. Definitions pose their special problems. 'Hapless lexicography' is like a hopelessly lost traveller: 'such is the fate of hapless lexicography, that not only darkness, but light, impedes and distresses it; things may be not only too little, but too much known, to be happily illustrated'. Some English verbs like *come*, *get*, and *take* are so ambiguous that they lead the exhausted definer a merry but not very funny chase over a nightmare or funhouse landscape: 'it is hard', says Johnson, 'to trace them through the maze of variation, to catch them on the brink of utter inanity . . .'. The paths of philology generally wind over mere 'desarts' of boredom, but occasionally the weary traveller comes upon an oasis made of an especially attractive or wise illustrative quotation. Since these oases are few, Johnson has chosen to preserve most of them, even though in general he has had to cut his quotations drastically: 'Some passages I have yet spared, which may relieve the labour of verbal searches, and intersperse with verdure and flowers the dusty desarts of barren philology.'

When he began work on the *Dictionary*, he imagined that he could travel without limit into the various realms of learning in the hope that his book 'might be in place of all other dictionaries whether appellative or technical. But these were the dreams of a poet doomed to wake at last a lexicographer.' Experience finally taught him more of his own limitations than he had known at the outset, and his experience, it proves, has been that of Pope's initially optimistic Alpine traveller: 'I saw that one enquiry only gave occasion to another, that book referred to book, that to search was not always to find, and to find was not always to be informed; and that thus to pursue perfection was, like the first inhabitants of Arcadia, to chace the sun, which, when they had reached the hill where he seemed to rest, was still beheld at the same distance from them.' Indeed, such is the predicament of man that difficulties and ironical complications open before the traveller on all sides. No journey, no posture is safe: 'in things difficult there is danger from ignorance, and in things easy from confidence; the mind, afraid of greatness, and disdainful of littleness, hastily withdraws herself from painful searches, and passes with scornful rapidity over tasks not adequate to her powers. . . . [The mind is] sometimes idle in a plain path, and sometimes distracted in labyrinths. . . .'

If Johnson's meditations on the ironies of lexicography urge him to figures of the perplexities of travel, his speculations about the kind of value at which applied science aims do the same. His anonymous preface to John Payne's *New Tables of Interest*, like the preface to the *Dictionary*, would be a flat, discursive thing without its lively texture of travel figures. Johnson's point in this preface is that, no matter what arguments may arise over the

value of given artistic performances, all agree that practical
books are to be valued according to their accuracy and efficiency. This is the justification for the emission of the admittedly
dull mathematical tables contrived by Payne, one of Johnson's
friends who became Chief Accountant of the Bank of England.
Johnson begins by asserting that such is the uniformity of human
nature—and such, by implication, the force of Lockean
psychology—that fiction can offer no new images. Thus
'Fancy, led by the hand of a skilful guide, treads over again the
flowery path she has often trod before. . . .' But readers of
practical works expect something genuinely new, and this
expectation permits the devotees of the practical arts to travel in
an unecstatic way: 'the Understanding and the Judgment' tour
the regions of science 'in the persuit of Truth, whom they
always expect to find in one simple form, free from the disguises
of dress and ornament'. And Understanding and Judgment
naturally are less enterprising and more stable travellers than
Fancy: 'as they travel with laborious step and a fixed eye, they
are content to stop when the shades of night darken the prospect, and patiently wait the radiance of a new morning, to lead
them forward in the path they have chosen, which, however
thorny or however steep, is severely preferred to the most
pleasing excursions that bring them no nearer to the object of
their search'.

After moving on to posit two kinds of travel—the delightful
and the useful—and after assigning Payne's *Tables* to the second
class, Johnson finds it hard to shake off the foot-travel figure. It
persists as he turns to compare stock-jobbers with a special
breed of cowardly highwaymen. The evil of stock-jobbing,
although some years ago it flourished, has finally been 'subdued
by its own violence; and the reputable Stock-brokers seem now
to have it in their power effectually to prevent its return, by not
suffering the most distant approaches of it to take footing in
their own practice, and by opposing every effort made for its
recovery by the desperate sons of fortune, who, not having the
courage of highwaymen, *take* 'Change-alley rather than the
road . . .'.

The travel imagery conducts Johnson to his final point, a
point necessitated logically and morally by the image of the
highwayman: 'no motive can sanction the accumulation of

wealth, but an ardent desire to make the most honourable and virtuous use of it, by contributing to the support of good government, the increase of arts and industry, the rewards of genius and virtue, and the relief of wretchedness and want'. The prefaces to the *Dictionary* and to Payne's work thus become by virtue of their imagery something like miniature moral travelogues, and in so doing they resemble versions of *Rasselas* and the *Journey to the Western Islands*.

That the humanist open road often leads to spiritual embarrassment or diminishment is suggested by Johnson's performance in the *Journey*. By dropping a very occasional whimsical reference to Ulysses or to lotus-eating, Johnson hints that he and Boswell are playing out a sort of diminished parody of the *Odyssey* or the *Aeneid*. Several happy ironies reverberate in a passage like this: 'At *Dunvegan* I had tasted lotus, and was in danger of forgetting that I was ever to depart, till Mr. Boswell sagely reproached me with my sluggishness and softness.' Boswell in the role of moral tutor is comical enough, but Boswell enacting the part of Ulysses himself is nothing short of triumphant mock-epic: the comedy is like that generated in *The Rape of the Lock* when the wailing females of the Hampton Court tea-party are viewed momentarily as the bereaved women of Troy.

These occasional Johnsonian mock-heroisms in the *Journey to the Western Islands* are more traditional than original. Two years before Johnson brought out his *Journey*, for example, the Scottish traveller Patrick Brydone, in his *Tour through Sicily and Malta*—a book which Johnson admired—had exercised himself in the same mode. The travel disappointments depicted by Brydone often take on a similar colour of mock-heroic, specifically, indeed, of mock-*Odyssey*. Leaving Malta by ship for Agrigento, Brydone passes near the island of Gozzo, which he takes to be the ancient abode of Calypso. Brydone is never more the humanist than when he writes: 'You may believe we expected something very fine; but we were disappointed.' He goes on: 'We looked, as we went along the coast, for the grotto of the goddess, but could see nothing that resembled it. Neither could we observe those verdant banks eternally covered with flowers; nor those lofty trees for ever in blossom, that lost their heads in the clouds, and afforded a shade to the sacred baths of her and her nymphs.' Here the mention of the 'verdant banks eternally covered with flowers', even if it is only their disappearance which is notable, tends to mitigate the harshness of the opening note of disappointment: we end with a tone, frequent likewise in Johnson, which seriously regrets something like the Miltonic lost paradise. The mock-heroic ends, as it often does in Augustan humanist literature, in something close to real elegy. Consider Pope's fond lingering over the motif of Belinda's mortality, for example, or Johnson's transformation of the end of the preface to the *Dictionary* into a covert lament for his lost wife and his dead friends.

To Johnson there is hardly a moral circumstance that cannot be embodied in the imagery of foot travel. Perseverance and fixity of purpose are thus recommended in *Rambler* 63: 'The traveller that resolutely follows a rough and winding path, will sooner reach the end of his journey, than he that is always changing his direction, and wastes the hours of day-light in looking for smoother ground and shorter passages.' Learning tends ironically to isolate the learned from each other, a point we find developed in *Adventurer* 107: 'At our first sally into the intellectual world, we all march together along one straight and open road; but as we proceed further, and wider prospects open to our view, every eye fixes upon a different scene; we divide into various paths, and, as we move forward, we are still at a greater distance from each other.' But it is in learning as in life: the 'straight and open road', superficially so inviting, is actually surrounded by perils: as Johnson puts it in *Rambler* 38, 'the middle path is the road of security, on either side of which are not only the pitfalls of vice, but the precipices of ruin'. Morally significant likewise are the 'gulphs' which open everywhere in Johnson. And even the more trivial moral choices involve the chooser in a vexatious journey. Johnson praises *The Spectator* for its usefulness as a 'guide' to the perplexed moral traveller. Before Addison's contrivance of *The Spectator*, says Johnson in the *Life of Addison*, 'We had many books to teach us our more important duties, and to settle opinions in philosophy or politicks; but an *Arbiter Elegantiarum*, a judge of propriety, was yet wanting, who should survey the track of daily conversation, and free it from thorns and prickles, which teaze the passer, though they do not wound him.'

As we have seen, writing is travelling just as moral action is, and it is both to Addison's credit and discredit that his prose style is 'always equable, and always easy': he 'never deviates from his track to snatch a grace'; the result is that 'His page is always luminous, but'—unfortunately—'never blazes in unexpected splendour'. Dryden's 'deviations', when successful, are perhaps more exciting. As Johnson says in the *Life of Dryden*, discussing *Annus Mirabilis*, Dryden's 'digression to the original and progress of navigation . . . may be considered as an example seldom equalled of seasonable excursion and artful return'. Thus in writing as in conduct more credit attaches to a bold confrontation of the dangers of the journey than to a merely prudent maintenance of the safe middle way down the crown of the road, although there remains the ever-present danger and irony that the slightest 'deviation' invites the risk of total disaster.

So many of these Augustan open roads lead to disappointment and destruction that we must consider here a related traditional motif. When we scrutinize the literature of the eighteenth century with an eye to characteristic recurring actions, both thematic and rhetorical, we begin to perceive a pervasive ironic pattern which we can call the pattern of comic—or ironic—reversal. This motif—a perennial favourite of conservatives—suggests a pitfall concealed at the end of an inviting open road or a sudden, unmarked precipice which opens at the end of a pleasant mountain trail. Whether we encounter it in fiction—Fielding and Smollett delight in it—in memoirs, letters, journals, essays, poems, or travel books, the pattern is the same. It consists of two elements betokening in their way the perpetual dualistic rhythms which introduce a kind of moral order into the continuum of human experience. We have first a protracted but smooth ascent to some height of felicity or optimistic perception; this condition then precipitates a sudden, surprising reversal, a rapid descent into perception or comic disillusion—the two being very much the same thing. One implication of this beloved humanist motif is that, although the human capacity for self-delusion is infinitely varied, it is yet possible for humanity to redeem itself by sudden, last-minute perceptions of its natural limitations. A similar implication of the motif seems to be this: it renders metaphorically the action of the movement towards wisdom. It is as if the eighteenth-

T

century protagonist were condemned to re-enact constantly a
sort of wry, psychological, secular version of the action of losing
a paradise but—*O felix culpa!*—gaining a firmer humanity.

Perhaps the canonical form of this motif is established in
Gulliver's experience with the Struldbrugs, in Chapter X of his
Third Voyage. After rhapsodizing for pages on the sublime
progressivist possibilities for man in the infinite prolongation of
life, Gulliver is finally dropped into enlightenment, whereupon
he finds that his 'keen appetite for perpetuity of life was much
abated'. The sense of shame usually attends the enlightenment
portion of the total comic action, as if humiliation—always
associated with the loss of innocence—were, as Johnson seems
persistently aware, an inseparable concomitant of wisdom. In
the same way, Pope's treatment of man's scientific and metaphysical ambitions takes the form of an ironic descent—and
almost a physical one—into the paradoxical wisdom that
resides in a due awareness of limitations. We recall Pope ironically commanding the 'glory, jest, and riddle of the World' in
Epistle II of the *Essay on Man*:

> Go, wond'rous creature! mount where Science guides,
> Go, measure earth, weigh air, and state the tides;

And after eleven lines of this, ending with

> Go, teach Eternal Wisdom how to rule—

the short, sharp, ironic drop follows with no more warning than
that implied in the sardonic tone of the preceding imperatives:

> Then drop into thyself, and be a fool!
>
> (19–30)

And we find that *Peri Bathous* is a catalogue of analogous 'drops'
from pretension into silliness.

It is the motif of comic reversal that provides Boswell with the
structure of the Louisa episode in the *London Journal*, as well as
with the structure of his account of the Johnson-Wilkes meeting
(*BLJ*, iii, 64 ff.), the meeting from which Boswell expects that
either Johnson or Wilkes will emerge the butt, only to find that
he himself becomes the victim of their sudden surprising
alliance. Boswell's literary delight in shaping these naïve,
illusioned episodes long after he has experienced their actual,
disillusioning denouéments suggests his fine sensitivity to the

pattern of comic disillusion in much of the literature he admired. One work he greatly admired was *Rasselas*, whose structure can be said to constitute one great action of comic reversal generated from the accumulation of many small analogous actions. The motif is clearest, perhaps, in Chapter VI, 'A Dissertation on the Art of Flying', where we find ten paragraphs devoted to the Flying-Machine Projector's plausible, abstract theories of flight, and where only one final paragraph is needed to release both the projector and the observing Rasselas into enlightenment: 'he waved his pinions a while to gather air, then leaped from his stand, and in an instant dropped into the lake'. The ten-to-one proportioning of the two elements here is traditional: Pope's 'Go, wond'rous creature!' passage, which, like the *Rasselas* chapter, ends with a 'drop' into actuality, is similarly proportioned. The proportioning suggests that illusions take days and weeks for their construction, but that enlightenment takes place 'in an instant'. Even William Shenstone catches the trick of manipulating this motif for humanist ends. In *Essays on Men, Manners, and Things* (1764) he indulges this pleasing fantasy:

Had I a fortune of 8 or 10,000 l. a year, I would methinks make myself a neighbourhood. I would first build a village with a church, and people it with inhabitants of some branch of trade that was suitable to the country round. I would then at proper distances erect a number of genteel boxes of about a 1000 l. a piece, and amuse myself with giving them all the advantages they could receive from taste. These would I people with a select number of well-chosen friends, assigning to each annually the sum of 200 l. for life. The salary should be irrevocable, in order to give them independency. The house, of a more precarious tenure, that, in cases of ingratitude, I might introduce another inhabitant.

After soaring thus to a cheerful *O altitudo*, Shenstone suddenly consults his experience and drops the whole vision into reasonableness: 'How plausible soever this may appear in speculation, perhaps a very natural and lively novel might be founded upon the inconvenient consequences of it, when put in execution.' The relation of this final perception of Shenstone's to what has gone before perfectly illustrates the Johnsonian conception of the supremely important humanistic distinction between 'romance' and 'novel' which is projected in *Rambler* 4.

Patrick Brydone is as skilful at exploiting the pattern of comic reversal as he is at enacting the humanist mock-heroic. As Brydone and his travelling companions depart from Naples by ship on a calm evening, we are given six pages of rhapsodic scenic description of the Bay of Naples, description which exploits the full resources of the standard imagery of the Sublime and the Beautiful. After luxuriating in 'this delightful prospect', Brydone observes: 'Our ship is going so smooth, that we are scarce sensible of the motion; and if this wind continue, before to-morrow night we shall be in sight of Sicily. . . . The captain is making a bowl of grog, and promising us a happy voyage.' At this point Brydone has the reader entirely with him, and it is time for the comic reversal. He proceeds: '16th [May, 1770]. All wrong—Sick to death—Execrable sirocc wind, and directly contrary—Vile heaving waves—A plague of all sea voyages.' Again, while pausing on the summit of Mt. Etna, Brydone indulges in two pages of rapt speculation on the excellence of mountain-tops as sites for philosophic meditation. Wrought to an elevation by the delightful prospect before both his outer and his inner eye, he is suddenly dropped back to earth—he sprains his ankle. He comments: 'In the very midst of these meditations, my philosophy was at once overset, and in a moment I found myself relapsed into a poor miserable mortal; . . . and your poor philosopher was obliged to hop on one leg, with two men supporting him, for several miles over the snow.' It is all a little like Aldous Huxley's 'Wordsworth in the Tropics'. We can hardly help recalling the dualistic findings of the speaker in Swift's *Mechanical Operation of the Spirit*: 'Spiritual Intrigues . . . generally conclude like all others; they may branch upwards towards Heaven, but the Root is in the Earth. Too intense a Contemplation is not the Business of Flesh and Blood; it must by the necessary Course of Things, in a little Time, let go its Hold, and *fall* into Matter.' And the illustration from foot travel next invoked by Swift provides the pattern for Brydone's ironic accident on Etna. Swift instances 'that Philosopher, who, while his Thoughts and Eyes were fixed upon the *Constellations*, found himself seduced by his *lower Parts* into a Ditch'.

Gibbon's fondness for debunking the delusive or the euphemistic by a mock-afterthought—one of the palpable earmarks of his style—seems to enact stylistically the general humanist motif of ironic reversal. The pattern is again one of illusions shattered, of the fake-elevated brought to earth, of pitfalls encountered in the flowery path. Speaking in Chapter XV of the *Decline and Fall* of 'a few sages of Greece and Rome' and their disposition for metaphysical speculation on the permanence of the human soul, Gibbon says that these thinkers 'summoned to their aid the science, or rather the language, of Metaphysics'. Again, 'the primitive Christians . . . felt, or they fancied, that on every side they were incessantly assaulted by demons . . .'. In the same way, Gibbon tells us that 'they disdained, or they affected to disdain, every earthly and corporeal delight'. Reporting years later on the clerical reaction to these witticisms, the Gibbon of the *Autobiography* is still at it: 'Had I foreseen', he says, 'that the pious, the timid, and the prudent would feel (or affect to feel) with such exquisite sensibility, I might perhaps have softened the two invidious chapters which would create many enemies and conciliate few friends.' The habit of the mock-afterthought is so deeply ingrained in Gibbon that in the *Autobiography* it urges him sometimes towards rich and happy dualisms and paradoxes. Thus he explains why he felt no disconnexion from the great world when he decided to settle in Lausanne: 'My friends had been kindly apprehensive that I should not be able to exist in a Swiss town at the foot of the Alps after so long conversing with the first men of the first cities of the world. Such lofty connections may attract the curious and gratify the vain. But I am too modest, or too proud, to rate my own value at that of my associates . . . .' In Gibbon's pseudo-afterthought 'or too proud' ironic reversal achieves the dignity of paradox, and the simple rhetorical device is made to imply at once the dualism of Gibbon's own character, the proper relation of Augustan writers to 'the Great', and the contrary poles between which permanent human nature is constantly oscillating.

But it is in Johnson that we find the humanist cast of mind realizing itself most expressively in the motif of ironic reversal. We have already encountered his general conviction that disappointment constitutes a central humanist moral exercise, that it is a perpetually instructive conscious method for disciplining the will and bringing the psyche into a productive—

that is, a redemptive—relation to actuality. The delusions of hope and the useful pathos of disillusion are what Johnson embodies and implies in his repeated returns to the motif of ironic reversal. Just as in the *Lives of the Poets* he shapes many episodes, especially those which touch the topic of mortality, in conformity with this motif, so he tends to conceive of his own experience, both personal and literary, as if it described a similar shape. This is the way he chooses to inform Mrs. Thrale of his stroke on 16 June 1783: 'In the afternoon and evening I felt myself light and easy, and began to plan schemes of life. Thus I went to bed, and in a short time waked and sat up as has long been my custom, when I felt a confusion and indistinctness in my head which lasted, I suppose about half a minute; I was alarmed and prayed God, that however he might afflict my body he would spare my understanding. . . . Soon after I perceived that I had suffered a paralytick stroke . . .' (*LSJ*, iii, 34). The descent from 'schemes of life' to 'paralytick stroke' is the equivalent of Pope's descent from 'wond'rous creature' to 'fool' or of Gulliver's discovery that he has been sadly duped by the plausibility of the Struldbrugs' advance to felicity.

Ironic reversal is one of the thematic staples of the *Idler*. *Idler* 71, which retails the story of Dick Shifter, is typical. Shifter, a Templar, has read Horace and Virgil so injudiciously that he has mistaken their literary praise of pastoral retirement for the enunciation of a principle of life. He finally buys a small estate thirty miles from London and settles down to taste the joys of rural retirement. Fully expecting to be enraptured, he rapidly encounters an unsuspected version of pastoral. His first stroll into the woods brings him into painful contact with furze and briars, and very quickly he discovers high prices, bad food, and sullen rustics; indeed, one of the local boys, 'by pretending to shew him a bird's nest, decoyed him into a ditch' just as if he were Swift's comical philosopher. Another time he is surprised by the ditch while mounted: he buys an expensive horse from a neighbouring farmer 'and, riding out to enjoy the evening, fell with his new horse into a ditch'. When Shifter discovers that the horse had been quite blind all along, he 'began to be tired with rustick simplicity', and after five days he returns to his London lodgings more learned than before in the delusions wrought by hope.

The young Persian philosopher Gelaleddin, in *Idler* 75, is another type of enthusiast who unconsciously invites the rigorous retribution of ironic reversal. Gelaleddin, a student from Tauris in attendance at the provincial university of Bassora, exhibits such distinction in philosophy and letters that he is offered a professorship. He meditates pleasingly on this prospect: 'If I am thus eminent . . . in the regions of literature, I shall be yet more conspicuous in any other place. . . . I will therefore depart to Tauris, where the Persian monarch resides in all the splendour of absolute dominion.' He easily persuades himself that 'my reputation will fly before me, my arrival will be congratulated by my kinsmen and my friends'. In short, 'He could not bear to delay the honours to which he was destined, and therefore hastened away, and in a short time entered the capital of Persia'. The trap drops instantly: 'His father had, in his absence, suffered many losses, and Gelaleddin was considered as an additional burden to a falling family.' Disgusted with his ensuing failure to impress the citizens of Tauris with his philosophic powers—a severe economic depression has struck, and everyone is labouring under poverty—Gelaleddin returns to Bassora 'confident of resuming his former rank, and revelling again in satiety of praise'. But now he discovers that 'he who had been neglected at Tauris, was not much regarded at Bassora', and it is now only natural for his companions to find 'that they had formerly over-rated his abilities . . .'. Johnson concludes: 'he lived long without notice or esteem'.

We have seen that the preface to the *Dictionary* is couched essentially in figures of frustrated travel, and we find there also some of Johnson's most tender and eloquent enactments of the motif of ironic reversal. Perhaps the most conspicuous is his juxtaposing the fond hopes of the aspirant to lexicography with the sad actualities of the experienced lexicographer. When he projected the *Dictionary*, he says, he entertained the pleasing hopes of delightful reading and of researches terminating in triumph. But experience 'dooms' the dreams of the poet to dissipate into sheer drudgery, and the open road which beckons to the traveller initially turns without warning into labyrinths and into Alps which open merely onto further Alps. The humanist deployment of the allied motifs of ironic travel and ironic reversal circumscribes and fleshes out a world in which the lost traveller's goal can be expected to be worse than his point of departure, a world whose dimensions are to be explored only by ironic quests and frustrated wanderings.

If Whitman's excursion on the nineteenth-century open road conducts him to the conviction that

> I am larger, better than I thought,
> I did not know I held so much goodness,
>
> (60–61)

the Augustan humanist journey arrives at quite a different destination. From his discovery that '*Alps* on *Alps* arise' the humanist infers that he is both smaller and worse than he thought: he infers, that is, his obligation of self-distrust, his duty to remark his own frailty and mortality, and his ethical and aesthetic accountability for registering the dangers and ironies that he meets—and, if he is lucky, passes—along the way.

12

ELEGIAC ACTION

'MOURNING', D. A. N. Jones reminds us, 'is a powerful element in conservative feeling.'[1] Under the impact of change, the conservative of all places and times turns backward to identify his moral urgencies with vanished usages, turns to make one last prolonged gesture of contact with the heroes of the past. Burke's apology in *A Letter to a Noble Lord* while invoking the heroic memory of Admiral Keppel could be uttered by any of the Augustan humanists: 'Pardon . . . the feeble garrulity of age, which loves to diffuse itself in discourse of the departed great.' The fixed retrospection of a humanist is not primarily sentimental or passive, self-pitying or self-regarding: his motive is moral and social action, the maintenance of continuity and coherence, the vivification of the present by a linkage to the temporal chain of being that is the past. And among the Augustans elegiac action is seldom undertaken at any great distance from satiric or mock-heroic manoeuvres, for to regret the past is by implication to condemn the present. When we penetrate deeply into the themes of eighteenth-century works, we begin to sense that every serious Augustan writer conceives of his role as that of *laudator temporis acti*, just as in the twentieth century the poet becomes *ipso facto* an ironist. In the eighteenth century, as Thomas Edwards has suggested, 'the celebration of virtue must be an elegy'.[2] To write satire is implicitly to undertake elegiac action, for all satire assumes some identifiable paradigm of virtue which folly has willingly let die. Things were not always so silly and corrupt, *Gulliver's Travels* implies. Noblemen and ladies have not always been so vacuous, *The Rape of the Lock* suggests. Poets like Thomson, Shenstone, Collins, and Gray operate as overt

[1] 'Sense and Sensuality', *New Statesman* (26 July 1963), p. 117.
[2] *This Dark Estate*, p. 94.

elegists, but, among the humanists, elegiac feelings are likely to take a more covert and devious course. The *Life of Savage* effectively opens Johnson's long career as covert elegist, a career finally memorialized by that longest of all elegies, Boswell's *Life of Johnson*. It is instructive how many of Johnson's most memorable phrasings issue from elegiac occasions. Garrick's death, for example, 'has eclipsed the gaiety of nations' (*BLJ*, i, 82). Gibbon sings the sad dissolution of the Roman empire and elegizes Julian the Apostate. Burke remembers Marie Antoinette as well as Admiral Keppel and mourns the death of European chivalry. Reynolds leads the fifteen *Discourses* towards a final 'Roman' tribute to Michelangelo.

The prevailing secular atmosphere seems to furnish eighteenth-century elegiac actions and motifs with a large part of their unique pathos. The absolute certainty with which Milton assures his woeful shepherds that

> . . . *Lycidas* your sorrow is not dead
>
> (166)

is not readily accessible to the Augustans. An element of the elegiac impulse that deepens and complicates *The Rape of the Lock* results from Pope's feeling that when Belinda's eyes, 'those fair Suns',

> . . . shall sett, as sett they must,
>
> (147)

they will set for ever. Not for them nor for the Belinda they signify the resurrection of the sinking day-star which is the lamented poet in *Lycidas*. The only thing resurrected in *The Rape of the Lock* is not Belinda's soul but her lock of hair, a part of her which will resist physical dissolution anyhow: this it is, and this it is only, that is destined to ascend the heavens in the form of a bright comet. In the same way, mock-elegies like *Verses on the Death of Dr. Swift* or Gay's 'The Dirge' in *The Shepherd's Week* can operate as poems only within a secular climate: the thing their wit suggests is that the day for genuine elegies, whether Pagan or Christian, is long past. One of Johnson's objections to *Lycidas* is that the poem dares to take its metaphoric Christianity seriously, that it makes bold to effect an alliance between Pagan literary conventions and Christian principle. Johnson's shock is perhaps a measure of the profundity of his scepticism: his assumption is that real Christian elegy is now impossible. Indeed, the whole contemporary attempt to pump some life into a new Christian poetry, from the theorizing of John Dennis to the practice of Smart and the hymnodists, betrays its impossibility by its self-consciousness. The more Dennis argues and speculates, the more hymns Wesley and Cowper grind out, the more clearly they reveal that the atmosphere in which they find themselves is not favourable to either traditional Christianity or traditional elegy. When traditional elegy becomes impossible—when, that is, it merely furnishes a Shenstone with materials for graceful but witless little poetic exercises, or when a travesty of its spirit is used to supply theatricality to Graveyard poems—the elegiac impulse, obviously one of the constants in human nature, will express itself elsewhere. And just as the dramatic tends to take temporary refuge in Augustan satire and in Augustan polemic prose, so does the elegiac.

We can distinguish two distinct traditions in the eighteenth-century posture towards death both as fact and as literary motif. The 'modern' tradition tends to turn the motif in a dramatistic direction, to play it for thrills and shudders. It is in this tradition that we find the Graveyard Poets and the Gothic Romancers, performers like Edward Young, Robert Blair, and the Walpole of Strawberry Hill and *The Castle of Otranto*. Characteristic of this approach is a deployment of the graveyard materials of *Hamlet* for melodramatic purposes, the use of a blank verse vaguely Shakespearian, and an obsession with the theme embodied in Hamlet's soliloquy on suicide and oblivion. In 'Night I' of *The Complaint, or Night Thoughts on Life, Death, and Immortality*, Edward Young plays at Hamlet thus:

> From short (as usual) and disturbed repose,
> I wake: how happy they who wake no more!
> Yet that were vain, if dreams infest the grave.
>
> (6–8)

Johnson's and Boswell's use of *Hamlet* is as an accessory to moral action; Young's use of it is as an adjunct to titillation. Young does the same thing with the moral images which make of the end of *The Dunciad* a profound pageant of lament for a self-murdered civilization. Young seizes on these images of Pope's, drains them of all wit and resonance, and turns them to the shabby purposes of mere personal pose and self-regard. In 'Night I' these are the descriptive and sentimental terms in which he recalls the final images of Book IV of *The Dunciad*:

> Night, sable goddess! from her ebon throne,
> In rayless majesty now stretches forth
> Her leaden sceptre o'er a slumbering world.
> Silence, how dead! and darkness, how profound!
> Nor eye nor listening ear an object finds;
> Creation sleeps. 'Tis as the general pulse
> Of life stood still, and Nature made a pause;
> An awful pause! prophetic of her end.

These images Young then uses to trigger a melodramatization of his personal bereavements:

> And let her prophecy be soon fulfilled;
> Fate! drop the curtain; I can lose no more.

(18–27)

Against this sort of thing we must set the humanist approach to the motifs of mortality, loss, and regret. Although Pope is capable of committing his own *Night Thoughts*, as he does in *Elegy to the Memory of an Unfortunate Lady*, his more successful exploitation of elegiac themes occurs within satiric or mock-heroic contexts, where the regretful and even the funerary operate less as décor or as self-indulgence than as moral argument urging the reader to redemptive action. By contrast, the elegizing of Young and even of Gray is passive: nothing— except perhaps vague meditation expressed in a genteel sighing —is meant to happen to the reader as a result. The speech of the wise and 'grave' Clarissa in the fifth Canto of *The Rape of the Lock* is a good example of Pope's moral domestication of humanist elegiac materials within the domain of the mock-heroic. Canto IV has ended with Belinda's disproportionate lament over the loss of her lock: her tone has been that of the Trojan women bereft of sons and husbands. At the beginning of Canto V Clarissa, clearly the only humanist at the whole party and probably invited by mistake, steps forward to deliver a speech of advice which begins in 'good sense' and ends in moral elegy. The subtlety of its advance towards the moral elegiac makes it one of the most moving and admirable things in Pope.

Clarissa begins by inquiring into the wisdom of the human devotion to mortal beauty:

> Say, why are Beauties prais'd and honour'd most,
> The wise Man's Passion, and the vain Man's Toast?
> Why deck'd with all that Land and Sea afford,
> Why Angels call'd, and Angel-like ador'd?
> Why round our Coaches crowd the white-glov'd Beaus,
> Why bows the Side-box from its inmost Rows?

She goes on in the vein of Swift praising Stella for refusing to take refuge from the values of general humanity in a merely female posture:

> How vain are all these Glories, all our Pains,
> Unless good Sense preserve what Beauty gains:
> That Men may say, when we the Front-box grace,
> Behold the first in Virtue, as in Face!

After this conventional opening, with its quiet appeals to reasonableness and simple justice, Clarissa turns to collect the materials of mutability to buttress her theme. Her 'Oh!' is a gauge of her own capacity for sensing human life in elegiac terms:

> Oh! if to dance all Night, and dress all Day,
> Charm'd the Small-pox, or chas'd old Age away;
> Who would not scorn what Huswife's Cares produce,
> Or who would learn one earthly Thing of Use?

Pope opens up the delicate mixture of emotions in those four lines by so unmysterious a rhetorical device as the initial trochaic substitution in the first foot of the second line. And the reader is obliged to linger and contemplate by the way that same line is slowed by the extra stressing in the fourth foot: heaviness and slowness are the effect of 'chás'd óld Áge ăwáy'. If the vanities of mortal beauty could redeem disease, time, and death, Clarissa continues,

> To patch, nay ogle, might become a Saint,
> Nor could it sure be such a Sin to paint.

And now Clarissa's moral syllogism—structured like Marvell's in *To His Coy Mistress*, but with what a difference!—works itself out to its elegiac conclusion, and her next three lines assume a tone which only a master can introduce into a mock-epic without a disaster of incoherence:

> But since, alas! frail Beauty must decay,
> Curl'd or uncurl'd, since Locks will turn to grey,
> Since painted or not painted, all shall fade

—and her next line relieves the growing pressure of pathos to return us to the more normal mode of the poem:

> And she who scorns a Man, must die a Maid;

'What then remains', she goes on,

> . . . but well our Pow'r to use,
> And keep good Humour still whate'er we lose?

The thing that has been 'lost' is the lock, but Clarissa's last line here serves to warn Belinda that she will suffer losses infinitely more grievous before she is through, losses which will destroy her unless she can accustom herself to the posture of wisdom which can withstand all that mutability can do. Clarissa concludes her performance in the moving and slow moral elegiac by a rapid recovery of the poem's normal tone of rhetorical briskness:

> And trust me, Dear! good Humour can prevail,
> When Airs, and Flights, and Screams, and Scolding fail.
> Beauties in vain their pretty Eyes may roll;
> Charms strike the Sight, but Merit wins the Soul.

Clarissa's arrival at the standard polemic antithesis of her final line signals that pathos and elegy are over, and that mock-heroic may resume. Such is the condition of man and of society that Clarissa's speech proves to have no effect whatever on the combatants, despite the effect it has had on the tone of the poem. Given the vacuousness of the audience, we are not surprised to find that when Clarissa finishes speaking

> . . . no Applause ensu'd.

> (9–35)

When Belinda's lock becomes a comet as the poem closes, her mortality is blazoned across the heavens by this contrasting emblem of the permanent, indeed, of the Newtonian. The contrast between the permanence of her lock and the impermanence of her person is like that drawn in Swift's *The Progress of Beauty* between the restorative powers of the moon and the unremitting advance towards decay of poor rotting Celia. When he writes of Celia, Swift is mindful of Horace's Ode vii, Book

IV, a poem towards which the naturally elegiac sensibility of Samuel Johnson was also strongly attracted. Johnson's translation of this ode is his last poem in English, and as he translates and composes he manages to imply a fusion of the mortal worlds of Homer's Priam, Horace's Torquatus, Swift's Celia, Pope's Belinda, and Samuel Johnson:

> Her losses soon the Moon supplies,
> But wretched Man, when once he lies
> Where Priam and his sons are laid,
> Is naught but Ashes and a Shade.
>
> (13–16)

Pulvis et umbra sumus: to the humanist the Horatian commonplace constitutes an imperative to redemption rather than a pretext for thrilling shudders, passive self-pity, or a neo-pagan hedonism. If the Young of the *Night Thoughts* appeals to his reader's desire to suffer vicariously, the humanists address his impulse to act. We remember what was inscribed on the dial-plate of Johnson's pocket-watch: 'a short Greek inscription', as Boswell reports, 'taken from the New Testament, . . . being the first words of our SAVIOUR's solemn admonition to the improvement of that time which is allowed us to prepare for eternity: "the night cometh, when no man can work" ' (*BLJ*, ii, 57).

Among the humanists the urge to elegize seems never very far from the surface. The dissolution of the complex of values to which they are committed is monitory of their own impermanence and that of all human things. Surely one of Johnson's most exquisite moments, as a man and as a writer, is that in which at the age of sixty-three he composes a brief letter to Hester Maria Thrale, aged eight. It is entirely characteristic of Johnson to turn a tidbit of domestic intelligence in a moral direction, and it is equally characteristic of him to regard no child as too young to begin to acquire wisdom: to Johnson, 'tis never folly to be wise. He writes the Thrale child: 'Miss Porter has buried her fine black cat. So things come and go. Generations, as Homer says, are but like leaves; and you now see the faded leaves falling about you' (*LSJ*, i, 287). It would be pleasant to know just what effect that utterance had on Hester, just as it would be pleasant to know what the child Margaret's reaction was to the Horatian and Virgilian emblem of the falling leaves in Gerard Manley Hopkins's similar elegiac action, *Spring and Fall: To a Young Child.*

Johnson seems unable to contemplate any event involving children without experiencing intimations of mortality. Thus, writing Bennet Langton in 1772 to congratulate him on the birth of a son, he seems at the same time to glance just fleetingly at the inevitability of the infant's death: 'I congratulate You and Lady Rothes', he says, 'on your little Man, and hope you will all be many years happy together' (*LSJ*, i, 275). What Johnson hints at here becomes clearer when we remind ourselves of the ghastly rate of infant mortality in his time. Every mother could assume that at least half her children would not survive infancy. Mrs. Thrale's experience is typical: five children were all that remained of twelve. The *Annual Register* for 1780 prints this eloquent little Bill of Mortality:

Died under two years of age	6,810
2 and 5	1,713
5 and 10	598
10 and 20	602

It is in this frightful context of perpetually aborted hopes and unrecompensed pains that we must apprehend Johnson's letter to Mrs. Thrale of 25 March, 1776, where, commenting on the death of her nine-year-old son Harry, he widens his observation to embrace his correspondent and himself as well: 'He is gone', he writes, 'and we are going' (*LSJ*, ii, 117). Johnson's occasion here is terrible: it is one of those things 'not to be endured'; but what he makes of it is terrible too, and we will never get wholly inside eighteenth-century humanist literature until we can recover the import of that kind of horror, and shock, and fear. The inevitability of death is a cliché, and Johnson knows that it is a cliché, but at the same time his massive humanity makes it quite impossible for him to leave it alone. Writing Hester Thrale after an accident to her mother, he feels impelled to point out that 'It teaches . . . what though every thing teaches, is yet always forgotten, that we are perpetually within the reach of death' (*LSJ*, iii, 25). In 1779 Henry Thrale is afflicted by a stroke, and Johnson writes Mrs. Thrale: 'How near we all are to extreme danger. We are merry or sad, or busy or idle, and forget that Death is hovering over us' (*LSJ*, ii, 291). Thus even his

attempts to contrive consolation move inevitably in the direction of moral warnings. It is astonishing how much of Johnson's
work can be said to constitute one vast *memento mori*, one immense elegiac action arguing nothing but the urgency of moral
redemption. Johnson's elegiac response to the fact of change
itself is beautifully enacted in a letter to Mrs. Thrale of 1770. He
has been visiting Lichfield—an event that always generates
elegiac sensations in him—and has been leafing through a
hundred-year-old manuscript containing the record of local
taxes. What to most people would be a moderately interesting
antiquarian inquiry becomes to Johnson an emblem of the
whole sad predicament of human beings, ancient as well as
modern. 'Do you not think we study this book hard?' he asks
Mrs. Thrale. And he goes on: '... Many families that paid the
parish rates are now extinct, like the race of Hercules. Pulvis et
umbra sumus. What is nearest us touches us most. The passions
rise higher at domestick than at imperial tragedies. I am not
wholly unaffected by the revolutions of Sadler street, nor can
forbear to mourn a little when old names vanish away, and new
come into their place' (*LSJ*, i, 240). Such is his humanistic
vision of the conditions of life that he can seldom 'forbear to
mourn', wherever his immediate attention is centred. The
mutability of fine black cats, leaves, children, adults, and old
families presents man with the same unbearable spectacle, and
one which, if he is wise, he will employ as a spring to action.

Johnson gives three definitions of *elegy* in the *Dictionary*, and
there is little to surprise us in the first two. An elegy first of all is
'A mournful song', and it is secondly 'A funeral song'. But the
third definition seems to embody Johnson's more or less personal idea of elegy as a genre and to imply the absolutely open,
unblinkable, flat emptiness of the occasion which conventionally causes elegy. An elegy is finally, he says, 'A short poem
without points or affected elegancies'. And a *point* in this sense
means 'A sting of an epigram; a sentence terminated with some
remarkable turn of words or thought'. Thus elegy as genre to
Johnson, we gather, just because it focuses on an experience so
central, so permanent and uniform in human nature, must be
stripped of all literary pretties, must be brought as close as
possible to 'Nature' if it is to be tolerable at all. Of all traditional poetic genres the elegy—and its nearest neighbour, the

U

epitaph—would seem to come the closest to Nature itself, and in this sense elegy and epitaph are *the* literary kinds, the kinds to which—given the nature of man and the conditions of his brief tenure—all the others are ultimately reducible.

We are in a position to appreciate Johnson's reprehension of the elegancies and 'points' of *Lycidas* when we compare his own performance in the elegy, *On the Death of Dr. Robert Levet*. Here all is sombre, all is simple, all is unpretentious as both the occasion and the form, to Johnson, naturally seem to demand. The image-system of the poem aspires only to the simple and the universal: the images are those of dark places underground, the black underworld of mine, cavern, and grave. 'Hope' itself becomes a mine in which we labour incessantly like manacled slaves, to be released only when death severs 'the vital chain' and lets us—ironically—go 'free'. The unpretentiousness of the stanza-form, the imagery, and the rhetoric accord perfectly with the unpretentiousness of Levet himself. All the elements of the poem are enlisted in a quiet, orderly recital of Levet's virtues. We are told that as a physician he exercised 'the power of art without the show'—a happy description of the way this elegy itself works—and that there was no blackened London hovel, no 'darkest cavern', which did not know his quiet solicitude. Johnson's homely elegy—'what is nearest us touches us most'—is unable to perform its task without recourse to something like the traditional humanist image of the ironic road: but here the road is a path which forms a circle, and Levet's numerous virtues constitute a crowded file which treads this closed path endlessly:

> His virtues walk'd their narrow round,
>   Nor made a pause, nor left a void;

And Johnson concludes the stanza by developing his never-failing moral theme, that of the Parable of the Talents:

> And sure th' Eternal Master found
>   The single talent well employ'd.

>   (25–28)

Because he knows that Levet's 'talent' is to his own like one to one hundred, these last two lines imply a degree of moral self-accusation. Levet at least did employ his 'single talent' unremittingly: can the same be said, Johnson seems to be wondering, of his elegist? As usual in the Augustan humanist use of elegy, mourning is put to the service of moral stiffening. As usual, the end of elegy is action. It is the very commonness of the moral issues and the images and the terms of *Levet* that places it at the furthest possible remove from *Lycidas*. The poem has the bravery of its own unpretentiousness, and that bravery has kept it vital to this day. In Johnson's terms, its art is such that it transmits an illusion of pure Nature.

The moral tendency of humanist elegy is reflected in the motif of urban ruins or architectural desolation, a motif which offers the humanists a multitude of ethical images. The constant excavation of classical antiquities during the eighteenth century, not in Rome only but also in such sites as Herculaneum and Pompeii, guaranteed that the ruins of Rome would occupy something like the centre of the imagination. These ruins, suggestive at once of the theory of heroic architecture and the spirit of moral elegy, prove especially attractive to the conservative sensibility, which, rather than approaching them baldly as John Dyer does in *The Ruins of Rome* (1740), prefers oblique allusions as a method of covert elegiac action. But whether depicted covertly or overtly, the ruins of Rome provide the humanists with a powerful image of the kind of desolation inevitably wrought by innovation, novelty, and wilful change. It is this sort of desolation that Swift recoils from in Gulliver's Third Voyage, where we are confronted with a Burkean post-revolutionary landscape peopled by creatures in rags and covered with 'Houses . . . ill contrived and . . . ruinous'. This vision of decay is in significant contrast to the house of the 'Ancient' Lord Munodi, who has 'built according to the best rules of ancient Architecture', and who has discovered somehow the secret of contriving an architecture that shall resist time.

Pope is seldom forgetful of the moral meaning of the ruins of Rome, whether he is drawing or writing. The sepia drawing which he made presumably as a model for the frontispiece of the *Essay on Man* depicts the Roman ruins with an irony whose moral obviousness we should perhaps ascribe to Pope's relish of unambiguously elegiac effects. The shattered Colosseum exhibits the ironic legend *'Roma Aeterna'*; a statue commemorating a *'Viro Immortali'*—apparently a writer, to judge from the scroll in his hand—has been broken at the waist, and in falling to the ground has lost its head; a tomb, as if its point were not sufficiently enforced already, advertises *'Sic Transit Gloria Mundi'*; and a broken column babbles on its base of the *'capitoli immobile saxum'*—the immovable stones of the Capitoline Hill—and thus both recalls Virgil and foretells Burke. For all the obviousness of the ironic reversals here, this drawing does exhibit Pope's delight in yoking together the imagery of classical ruins and the idea of elegiac retrospection as moral exercise. In another version of this drawing,[3] Pope places a contemporary figure, and one that looks curiously like a physically idealized Pope, in the foreground, where his emaciated but vital frame contrasts with the broken statue on the ground. It is Pope's own wry version of a medieval *memento mori*.

It is the ironic totality of the desolation of Rome that seems to stir Pope's imagination. In *To Mr. Addison, Occasioned by his Dialogues on Medals*, he invites Addison to

> See the wild Waste of all-devouring years!
> How Rome her own sad Sepulchre appears,
> With nodding arches, broken temples spread!
> The very Tombs now vanish'd like their dead!
>
> (1–4)

In the same way, in the third book of *The Dunciad* Elkanah Settle images for Cibber, his successor, the state of past and future human dulness:

> See, the Cirque falls, th' unpillar'd Temple nods,
> Streets pav'd with Heroes, Tyber choak'd with Gods.
>
> (107–8)

And yet even the ruins of Rome, fallen to an ironic decay, can be redeemed by the historical imagination, just as fallen man himself can be recovered by similar means. In his *Epistle to Mr. Jervas*, Pope recounts his friendship with the painter Charles Jervas and rehearses their hours of painterly and literary conversation, which, we are asked to believe, was largely funerary, architectural, and elegiac:

> Together o'er the *Alps* methinks we fly,
> Fir'd with ideas of fair *Italy*.

[3] For both, see *The Poems of Alexander Pope*, ed. John Butt (London and New Haven, 1939–61, 6 vols.), III-i.

With thee, on *Raphael's* Monument I mourn,
Or wait inspiring dreams at *Maro's* Urn:
With thee repose, where *Tully* once was laid,
Or seek some ruin's formidable shade;
While fancy brings the vanish'd piles to view,
And builds imaginary *Rome* a-new.
Here thy well-study'd Marbles fix our eye;
A fading Fresco here demands a sigh:

(23–34)

'And builds imaginary *Rome* a-new': such is the reconstructive power of the elegiac imagination that even the ruins of Rome can be turned to redemptive moral uses. Pope's and Jervas's search for 'some ruin's formidable shade' is more than an attempt to escape the imaginary midday heat: it is an active attempt at recovery of the very spirit—or the 'shade'—of vanished heroic Rome.

The architectural desolation which greeted Johnson in the Hebrides drew from him numerous elegiac-moral utterances which seem to derive their shape from the Ruins-of-Rome tradition in his time. Rome had been sacked by the Goths; Scottish religious establishments had been sacked by a set of Swiftian innovators: the results are remarkably the same. As Johnson writes in the *Journey to the Western Islands*, 'It was not without some mournful emotion that we contemplated the ruins of religious structures, and the monuments of the dead.' The skeletons of the old flourishing Scottish city of life stand everywhere as ironic memorials, as 'faithful witnesses of the triumph of Reformation'. Wilful, violent change is the enemy, and from the pathetic symbolism of change a humanist derives the materials for his elegiac actions. 'It was among the ruins of the Capitol', says Gibbon in the very last sentence of the *Decline and Fall*, 'that I first conceived the idea of a work which has amused and exercised near twenty years of my life, and which, however inadequate to my own wishes, I finally deliver to the curiosity and candour of the public.' Even Thomas Gray's conception of what might have happened had Lord Bute remained in government takes the shape of a vision of the collapse of Rome and its English parallel:

Purg'd by the sword and beautifyed by fire,
Then had we seen proud London's hated walls,

Owls might have hooted in St. Peters Quire,
And foxes stunk and litter'd in St. Pauls.

(On L—d H—d's Seat near M—e, K—t, 21–24)

In exploiting the same motif of desolation, Burke seems to glance at the profoundly moral imagery with which *The Dunciad* concludes. The new age of Gothic barbarism arrives upon the expiration of light, in England as in Rome; Augustus is 'replaced' by a line of tyrants and incompetents, and in France a simple-minded political monism lays waste a land once vitalized by the complex 'natural' principle of the competing balance of estates. Looking back on his polemic career, Burke writes in *A Letter to a Noble Lord*: 'It was my endeavour . . . to preserve, while they can be preserved, pure and untainted, the ancient, inbred integrity, piety, good nature, and good humour of the people of England, from the dreadful pestilence, which, beginning in France, threatens to lay waste the whole moral, and in a great degree the whole physical world, having done both in the focus of its most intense malignity.' What is happening in France is very like what has happened earlier in India, where that brute Warren Hastings has managed to transform a whole country into a wasteland, 'the country itself', as Burke says in his *Speech in General Reply: Ninth Day*, 'all its beauty and glory, ending in a jungle for wild beasts'. And the Burke who reprehends 'ecclesiastical pillage' in *A Letter to a Noble Lord* is a version of the Johnson who gazes with dismay upon the Catholic ruins which strew the Hebrides. During his whole career, Burke argues, his merit 'was in defending the whole of the national Church of my own time and my own country, and the whole of the national Churches of all countries, from the principles and the examples which lead to ecclesiastical pillage, thence to a contempt of *all* prescriptive titles, thence to the pillage of *all* property, and thence to universal desolation.' Thus this last important elegiac action undertaken by an Augustan humanist assumes the form of a polemic warning against the sort of social and political changes which are to be justified only by abandoning the sacred principle of the historical uniformity of human nature. The spirit of formal elegy has been subsumed into an infinitely larger moral purpose: in humanistic hands, that spirit becomes one of the chief weapons in the moral warfare the humanists wage against the idea of progress.

The moral force of the contemporary invitation to the elegiac we can measure in Johnson's *Essay on Epitaphs*, published in the *Gentleman's Magazine* in 1740. The constant archaeological recovery of classical inscriptions during the century made it difficult for anyone to forget that epitaph was an honourable genre, and one dignified especially by its almost inevitable associations with classical architecture and with the great classical sites of heroic moral action. In his essay Johnson sets forth his own significantly un-classical theory of 'sepulchral inscriptions', a literary genre which the uniformity of human nature has suffered no people to neglect. It will not surprise us to find that Johnson, always ready to turn elegiac instincts to moral uses, holds that 'Those EPITAPHS are . . . the most perfect, which set virtue in the strongest light, and are best adapted to exalt the reader's ideas and rouse his emulation'. Because the British beholder encounters epitaphs inevitably within sacred surroundings—either in churches or in consecrated cemeteries—the epitaph in English must differ from its Roman counterpart in always urging the reader towards an appropriate self-distrust, a redemptive awareness of frailty:

The custom of burying our dead either in or near our churches . . . makes it proper to exclude from our EPITAPHS all such allusions as are contrary to the doctrines for the propagation of which the churches are erected, and to the end for which those who peruse the monuments must be supposed to come thither. Nothing is, therefore, more ridiculous than to copy the Roman inscriptions, which were engraven on stones by the high-way, and composed by those who generally reflected on mortality only to excite in themselves and others a quickened relish of pleasure, and a more luxurious enjoyment of life, and whose regard for the dead extended no farther than a wish that *the earth might be light upon them.*

The end of elegy is not a quickened hedonism but a deepened awareness of human failure. 'We profess to reverence the dead', Johnson explains, 'not for their sake, but for our own.' Thus 'The best subject for EPITAPHS is private [i.e. domestic] virtue; virtue exerted in the same circumstances in which the bulk of mankind are placed, and which, therefore, may admit of many imitators.' Johnson concludes his essay by praising two Greek inscriptions. Both commemorate virtuous slaves, and it is impossible to hear Johnson's moral commendations without thinking again of his own praise of Levet. Of the first Greek epitaph, which Johnson translates, 'ZOSIMA, who in her life could only have her body enslaved, now finds her body likewise set at liberty', he observes: 'It is impossible to read this EPITAPH without being animated to bear the evils of life with constancy, and to support the dignity of human nature under the most pressing afflictions . . .'. The second epitaph, on Epictetus, slave and Stoic philosopher, Johnson translates: 'EPICTETUS, who lies here, was a slave and a cripple, poor as the beggar in the proverb, and the favourite of Heaven'. From this example, Johnson continues, 'we may learn . . . that virtue is impracticable in no condition . . .'. Thus those epitaphs are to be valued which, like Johnson's *Levet*, 'animate' the beholder 'to support the dignity of human nature'. The sanction of epitaph, just like the sanction of history-painting according to Reynolds, is an entirely moral one, which is to say, an entirely humanistic one. This is why, to Johnson, 'An Epitaph is no easy thing' (*LSJ*, i, 273), and this is also why it takes Reynolds fifteen discourses and twenty-one years to outline the rudiments of humanistic painting.

Yeats has written of John Locke:

> Locke sank into a swoon;
> The Garden died;
> God took the spinning-jenny
> Out of his side.

(Fragments, i)

And God took much more than the machines of the new industrialism out of Locke's side: even before He did that, He brought forth the whole Augustan account of mind and memory which sanctions humanistic imagery. Explaining for the eighteenth century the operation of the human memory, Locke chooses to do so by means of an elegiac action which is intensely humanistic in its dual focus—at once pathetic and ironic—on the impermanence of memory and the delusions of hope. The image which is Locke's elegiac action conducts us both backwards to childhood and forwards to age and oblivion. In Book II of the *Essay Concerning Human Understanding*, he speaks of human ideas as frail, living things, just as frail as the children whose multitudinous early deaths sometimes give to the Augustan city the

appearance of a collection of charnel-houses. It is an attribute of
the human understanding, says Locke, that its memories fade
irrecoverably away: 'Thus the ideas, as well as children, of our
youth, often die before us: and our minds represent to us those
tombs to which we are approaching; where, though the brass
and marble remain, yet the inscriptions are effaced by time, and
the imagery moulders away.' Much of the humanist sense of
elegy is captured in that single superb sentence: the frailty of the
mind, the vulnerability of hopes, the mutability of that which is
loved, the ironic impermanence even of the memorial stones
erected with such a touching and flattering hope. Minds themselves, says Locke, are like the cool tombs; and like the fading
epitaphs engraved on those tombs, they have much to mourn
for. The mind itself is a thing made precisely of lost images and
ironic hopes. When we discover thus the chief contemporary
account of the psychology of memory couched in these elegiac
terms, we begin to suspect that of all the Augustan humanist
images and motifs, it is elegiac action which conducts us into the
closest recesses of the humanist experience. 'What is nearest us
touches us most': the primary human attribute, the fear of
death and the horror of nothingness, proves at last to sustain the
primary humanist motif.

*   *   *

In his preface to *The Preceptor* (1748) Samuel Johnson recommends the study of geography in these terms: 'no studies afford
more extensive, more wonderful, or more pleasing scenes; and
therefore there can be no ideas impressed upon the soul, which
can more conduce to its future entertainment'. Humanist
imagery in the eighteenth century limns a kind of moral
geography, and it is now time to contemplate the geography of
this Augustan humanist rhetorical world, to mark its limits and
extent, to inspect its terrain-features, and to tour its constructions and monuments. In arriving at this curious country built
entirely of polemic imagery, the first thing we notice is the
rigour of the boundaries which delimit this domain from the
unknowable universe outside. Just as the early-eighteenth-
century title-page customarily contains itself within a double
ruled line,[4] as if to exclude firmly an irrelevant and possibly

[4] See Bertrand H. Bronson, *Printing as an Index of Taste in Eighteenth
Century England* (New York, 1958), p. 22.

x

dangerous otherness, so the imaginative world embodied by
Augustan humanism protects itself by strict boundaries that cut
it off from the maddening universe, a universe that extends
infinitely out from the Lockean empirically knowable. As
Geoffrey Scott has said, 'A sharply-defined circle formed the
limit of eighteenth-century vision; within it, all was precisely
seen, brilliantly illumined; beyond it, outer darkness.'[5] The
Reynolds of the *Fifth Discourse*, recommending the conventions
of art, asserts the value of known, permanent immovable frontiers when he says, 'Art has its boundaries, though Imagination
has none.' It is only a Shakespeare, Johnson tells us in the *Drury
Lane Prologue*, who can venture with safety outside the boundaries enforced by experience:

> Existence saw him spurn her bounded Reign.
>
> (5)

Others than Shakespeare will be well advised to remain within
the frontiers of the ironical Happy Valley. Pope projects his own
boundaries in 'The Design' of the *Essay on Man*. 'The science of
Human Nature', he says, 'is, like all other sciences, reduced to a
few clear points: There are not *many certain truths* in this world.'
Like the Happy Valley or the world of Pope's 'Man', the
closely circumscribed country of the humanist imagination is
not a large one: it has more in common with Gibbon's tight
little Switzerland, say, than with Tolstoy's Russia, Whitman's
America, or Conrad's Africa.

Like Switzerland, this is a land-locked country: it has no
beaches, no seaports, indeed no access at all to the open sea,
which is to say that it experiences no need for a symbolism of
infinitude. For the same reason the sky seems no part of the
physical setting. One looks not upward but straight ahead or
downward. One wanders lonely not as a cloud but as a traveller
bemired. There is little vegetation, and that little is vaguely
seen, blurred to a conventionalized indistinctness. Mountains
very like the Alps abound, but they have this peculiarity: whenever one climbs them, one is able to see only more of the same.
The terrain is laced by a road network which seems to promise
easy travelling, but when one is actually on the roads they prove
ill marked and really almost impossible to use. They seem to

[5] *Architecture of Humanism*, p. 167.

lead everywhere but where the traveller expects. Their edges
are bordered by concealed bogs and fens; many run right along
shockingly dangerous precipices, and the footing in those places
is very likely to be untrustworthy.

But the fortunate traveller who manages to persevere will
arrive finally at the Augustan city, which appears to be strongly
fortified. Here he will see a host of buildings, ranging from
Palladian palaces and cathedrals to hovels and stables, with the
public buildings greatly outnumbering the domestic. The public
buildings are likely to be splendid, or at least to strive for splendour; the domestic, although modest, are not inelegant.
Although there are remarkably few theatres, there are numerous
cathedrals and churches, all abundantly furnished with tomb-
stones and memorials, epitaphs and moral inscriptions: the
tourist is constantly encountering exhortations to pause and
reflect. Some of the buildings are covered with scaffolding;
others are in a very shaky condition, of which their occupants
seem curiously unaware. If we enter a building, we are struck
immediately not merely by the number of scales and balances
hanging everywhere but by the vast amount of clothing stored
inside. Wardrobes are everywhere, and when we inspect the
clothes we find them singular in this: they seem always to cover
the whole body. There is clearly no nudism here, and of course
nothing like sunbathing. The inhabitants seem to need their
clothing not only for the purposes of modesty and symbolic
identity; they appear to have found that the more of the body is
covered, the less likely it is to be stung and otherwise harassed
by the hordes of noxious insects with which this commonwealth
is afflicted.

As the elaborate clothing of the inhabitants provides them
with a fence against insects, so the fortified works which the
visitor sees everywhere protect them—usually—from their very
numerous and cunning enemies. The walker even in the city
must guard himself perpetually against ambushes, and he is
almost sure to suffer assault if he ventures far from a fortified
post. The terrain outside the cities offers a terrifying spectacle of
trenches, mine craters, guarded passes, fortified frontier posts,
and sentinels. These last are visited and inspected very frequently by their commanders, who bear a curious resemblance
to authors and artists. This country is clearly one in a state of

constant siege. The enemy presses not only against the militarized frontier, but everywhere else as well. Indeed, civil war seems to rage inside, and nowhere does one feel entirely safe.

If the physical geography of this country strikes us as odd, the behaviour of those who live here impresses us as odder still. For all their physical gusto—they are fond of food, more fond of drink—the natives are mournful, perpetually searching for objects and occasions over which to elegize. And when they are not elegizing they are satirizing something. Mourning and moral ridicule are their two favourite actions: they would rather mourn than anticipate or celebrate; they would rather ridicule than rhapsodize. They are a profoundly 'protestant' people: and it is the very conditions of their circumscribed existence which receive the sharpest points of their protests. But even in their laments, their ridicule, and their protests, there is always irony. This is the rhetorical mode which colours their every utterance. It is likely that the visitor will feel slightly uncomfortable in this atmosphere of constant irony, until he gradually learns to practise the mode himself.

This is the world, then, which harbours just below the literal surface of Augustan humanist literature. Its founders and architects are Cicero and Locke. Its scripture is *De Officiis*; its Baedeker, *An Essay Concerning Human Understanding*. It is an imaginative world created by a passionate revivification of traditional received metaphors from antiquity, the Middle Ages, and the Renaissance. This world is breathed upon and vitalized by a rhetorical vigour—born perhaps of shock and a measure of fear—which animates and finally glorifies what begins as the mere inert platitudes of 'self-improvement'. The passion which has the power to redeem the commonplace is generated in large part by the natural anger and frustration of the hard-pressed and ultimately the defeated, by the cold fury which everywhere attaches to small armies outnumbered and forced into retreat.

It is the humanists' consciousness of defeat or at least of a dangerous diminishing of allies which seems to prompt their recourse to the method of irony at every possible point. Irony always assumes an in-group at war with an out-group. Irony is a device for consolidating the small homogeneous group, for strengthening its consciousness of solidarity against the assaults of the obvious, the literal, or the one-dimensional. Images which earlier had been employed in the service of sensual delight or of supernatural celebration are turned by Augustan humanist irony to the ends of a severely defensive conduct and action. It is polity which is the end of Augustan humanist imagery, but it is a polity less of the state than of the person and the psyche.

The hypertrophying enemy against whom the humanists conduct their unremitting combat of irony is conceived of as a collection of apostates from the human condition, and these apostates constitute a mighty ragged platoon when we see them lined up for inspection. Their progenitors are Rosencrantz and Guildenstern, Dryden's Puritans, Rochester's vain, stumbling, 'misguided' wanderers, and the permanent residents of Milton's Paradise of Fools. The enemy apostates consist of Swift's spider in *The Battle of the Books*; the utterer of the digressions in *A Tale of a Tub*, as well as Jack in the narrative; the Laputians and the members of The Grand Academy of Lagado in Gulliver's Third Voyage; the Gulliver of the end of the Fourth Voyage; and the Modest Proposer of the simple plan to ease Ireland's miseries. Perhaps Pope's chief apostates are the figure of Theobald-Cibber in *The Dunciad* and the Timon of *Moral Essay* IV. Johnson's are both benign and malignant: benign like Dick Minim of the *Idler* or the mad astronomer of *Rasselas*, malignant like Jenyns or Charles XII—a couple of innovating proselyters of the sort pronounced mad by Section IX of *A Tale of a Tub*—or, for that matter, the Scottish reformers in their role as ruiners of ecclesiastical architecture. Reynolds's apostate is the speaker of the *Ironical Discourse*, whose certainties about original genius reflect those of Reynolds's own brash young art students. Gibbon's is the collective personality of the early Roman Christians, who, in their turn, find their counterpart in Burke's conception of the collective personality of the clods, pedants, and fools who constitute the French National Assembly, or in the figure of Dr. Richard Price or of his willing tool, the Duke of Bedford. Despite their differences of mien, posture, and costume, all these are versions of the same character, a man—at once naïve and sinister—who has ceded his complex humanity to systems which propose either an expedient accommodation with a fallen world or else a facile and spurious mechanical redemption. It is their instinct for happy promises, for a ready optimism, for quantitative rather than qualitative judgments, that unites these apostates into one great type, a type incarnating all the psychological and moral implications of the idea of progress.

And just as the enemy apostate is finally one person, so the Augustan humanists themselves merge, at least within the world of their shared rhetoric, until they come to resemble one person too. To see Johnson discovering his own kind of moral relevance in Pope's figure of the unending Alps, to hear Burke in the *Annual Register* saying of *Rasselas* that 'perhaps no book ever inculcated a purer and sounder morality', is to appreciate the power and vigour of the living links which bind the humanists to each other. It is their common horror of the mechanical operation of the spirit that animates them all; it is their insistence, largely by means of the passionate non-literal, on the redemptive imperative that finally makes them appear as one. And the horror of the end of *The Dunciad* is that exactly an inverse redemption has somehow been enacted:

> Lo! thy dread Empire, CHAOS, is *restor'd*.
>
> (iv, 653)

The plea for individual, personal reconstruction is always there, from *Windsor Forest* or *Messiah* or *An Essay on Criticism* to Johnson's *Drury Lane Prologue*:

> Then prompt no more the Follies you decry.
>
> (55)

Satire finds its function in unveiling depravity and thus urging redemption. As Reynolds tells the art students in the *Fifth Discourse*, calling for a redemption of serious painting, '[Painting] has long been much on the decline, and . . . our only hope of its revival will consist in your being thoroughly sensible of its depravation and decay.' The chief humanist theme is the sacred Virgilian one of restoration and renewal, of restoring a sacred institution in a new country of the imagination.

Insisting as always on the freedom of the will as the sole condition for redemption, Johnson writes in *Idler* 84: 'As gold which he cannot spend will make no man rich, so knowledge which he cannot apply will make no man wise.' Johnson would not have thought an injustice done his career had he known that the early-nineteenth-century editions of his writings in twelve volumes would conclude with his sermon for the funeral service of his wife. His elegiac moral imperative here is expressive both of the thematic concerns of the Augustan humanists and of the kinds of actions which animate their rhetorical world: 'Let it . . . be our care, when we retire from this solemnity', Johnson writes, 'that we immediately turn from our wickedness, and do that which is lawful and right; that, whenever disease or violence shall dissolve our bodies, our souls may be saved alive, and received into everlasting habitations. . . .'

INDEX